Think Tanks, Public Policy, and the Politics of Expertise

While the number of think tanks active in American politics has more than quadrupled since the 1970s, their influence has not expanded proportionally. Instead, the known ideological proclivities of many, especially newer think tanks, and their aggressive efforts to obtain high profiles have come to undermine the credibility with which experts and expertise are generally viewed by public officials. In many cases, think tanks have become more marketing than research organizations, with styles of behavior that mimic interest groups more than universities. Rather than organizations committed to objective analysis of policy problems, think tanks have become organizations that turn experts into advocates and policy information into ammunition. The once-real boundaries between experts and advocates in American policy making have become blurred. This book explains this paradox and elaborates on its significant implications both for the practice of policy making and for scholarly debates about agenda setting, interest groups, and lawmaking. The analysis is based on 135 in-depth interviews with officials at think tanks and those in the policymaking and funding organizations that draw upon and support their work. The book reports on results from an original survey of congressional staff and journalists and detailed case studies of the role of experts in health care and telecommunications reform debates in the 1990s and tax reduction in 2001.

Andrew Rich is an assistant professor of political science at City College of New York. He received his Ph.D. in political science from Yale University. Professor Rich taught at Wake Forest University from 1999 to 2003.

Think Tanks, Public Policy, and the Politics of Expertise

ANDREW RICH

City College of New York

CAMBRIDGE UNIVERSITY PRESS

PUBLISHED BY THE PRESS SYNDICATE OF THE UNIVERSITY OF CAMBRIDGE
The Pitt Building, Trumpington Street, Cambridge, United Kingdom

CAMBRIDGE UNIVERSITY PRESS
The Edinburgh Building, Cambridge CB2 2RU, UK
40 West 20th Street, New York, NY 10011-4211, USA
477 Williamstown Road, Port Melbourne, VIC 3207, Australia
Ruiz de Alarcón 13, 28014 Madrid, Spain
Dock House, The Waterfront, Cape Town 8001, South Africa

http://www.cambridge.org

First published 2004

Printed in the United States of America

Typeface Sabon 10/13 pt.   *System* LATEX 2$_\varepsilon$ [TB]

A catalog record for this book is available from the British Library.

Library of Congress Cataloging in Publication Data

Rich, Andrew.
Think tanks, public policy, and the politics of expertise / Andrew Rich.
    p. cm.
Includes bibliographical references and index.
ISBN 0-521-83029-X
1. Policy sciences – Research – United States.   2. Policy scientists – United States.
3. Research institutes – United States.   4. Nonprofit organizations – United States.
5. Expertise – political aspects – United States.   6. Political planning – United States.
7. Legislative hearings – United States.   I. Title.
H97.R53 2004
320.06′0973 – dc22   2003065392

ISBN 0 521 83029 X hardback

To my parents, Daniel and Nancy Rich

Contents

List of Tables   *page* viii
List of Figures   x
Acknowledgments   xi

1   The Political Demography of Think Tanks   1
2   The Evolution of Think Tanks   29
3   Political Credibility   74
4   The Policy Roles of Experts   104
5   Policy Influence: Making Research Matter   152
6   Think Tanks, Experts, and American Politics   204

Appendix A   Details on the Characteristics, Perceptions, and
Visibility of Think Tanks   221
Appendix B   List of In-Depth Interviews   233
Works Cited   239
Index   253

Tables

1-1a: Nationally Focused Think Tanks by Budget and
Research Scope   *page* 17
1-1b: State and Regionally Focused Think Tanks by Budget
and Research Scope   18
1-2: Think Tanks by Ideology, Research Focus, and
Resources   23
1-3: Think Tanks by Ideology and Breadth of Research
Interests   24
3-1: Brookings and Heritage Influence by Respondent
Group   82
3-2: Rank Ordering of Think Tanks by Ratings of Credibility
in 1997   84
3-3: Characteristics of Think Tank Sample   90
3-4: Regression Results   93
3-5: Think Tank Congressional Testimony, Organizational
Forms by Affiliations of Others Testifying   98
3-6: Think Tank Congressional Testimony, Ideological
Clusters by Affiliations of Others Testifying   99
3-7: Think Tank Media Citations, Organizational Forms by
Type of Mention   100
3-8: Think Tank Media Citations, Ideological Clusters by
Type of Mention   102
5-1: Agenda-setting Research in Health Care Reform   158
5-2: Congressional Testimony in Telecommunications
Reform   182

5-3: References to Experts in Floor Debate on
Telecommunications Reform 190

5-4: References in *Washington Post* to Telecommunications
Reform 191

5-5: References to Experts in Floor Debate on the Tax Cut 197

A-1: State and Nationally Focused Think Tanks by
Budget Size 224

A-2: Fifteen Largest Think Tanks Grouped by Ideological
Cluster 224

A-3: Ten Largest Think Tanks in Each Ideological Cluster 226

A-4: Think Tank Influence Scores in 1997 230

A-5: Top Four Think Tanks Rated for Influence in 1997 by
Respondent Group 231

Figures

1-1: Pattern by which think tanks existing in the 1990s
formed   *page* 15

1-2a: Proliferation pattern of nationally focused think tanks
existing in 1990s, by ideology   21

1-2b: Proliferation pattern of state and regionally focused
think tanks existing in 1990s, by ideology   21

3-1: Most effective think tank at being influential by
respondent group   78

3-2a: Think tanks assessed as most influential in 1997   81

3-2b: Think tanks assessed as most influential in 1993   81

3-3: 1997 ideology scores for think tanks from
congressional staff and journalists   85

5-1: Forms of expertise in policy making   154

A-1: Proliferation pattern of think tanks existing
in 1990s   223

Acknowledgments

I have benefited from great guidance and support in writing this book. David Mayhew has been a generous source of ideas and insights on the project since its inception. He helped me design the project when it was a dissertation, and he held me to high standards during all stages of its execution. He encouraged me to be rigorous and thorough in every aspect of the research. I am grateful for his high standards and for his continuing influence on how I think as a political scientist. Kent Weaver was a superb source of good ideas, useful information, and – more often than I like to remember – helpful criticisms as I worked on this book. He encouraged me to persist at points when dead-ends seemed to be looming, and he rescued me more than once from wasting time on avenues that would not have been worthwhile. He is a wonderful colleague and collaborator.

Stephen Skowronek, Rogers Smith, Peter Dobkin Hall, Charles Perrow, and Don Green each provided additional helpful advice when the manuscript was a dissertation. I am grateful, as well, to Josef Braml, Corey Robin, Eric Schickler, James Smith, Diane Stone, Peter Siavelis, and Fiona Wright for reading all or portions of earlier versions of the manuscript. Jacob Hacker kindly shared transcripts from some of his interviews about the Clinton health care reform effort when I was working on that case. I am grateful to him for those transcripts and for his advice on that case. My colleagues at Wake Forest University and City College provided collegial and supportive environments while I rewrote the manuscript (almost completely), transforming it from a dissertation into a book. Heath Bumgardner, Kevin Greer, Jeff Saltzman, Scott Savage, and

Patrice Yang provided valuable research assistance. Robyn Washington designed the dust jacket.

Financial support for the project was provided by the Aspen Institute's Nonprofit Sector Research Fund, Yale University's Program on Nonprofit Organizations, the Rockefeller Archive Center, and Wake Forest University's Archie Fund. My thanks to each for its support. As I began the project, I also benefited from support from the Harry S. Truman Scholarship Foundation. I am grateful to Louis Blair, the executive secretary of the Foundation, for inviting me to participate in the Foundation's Summer Institute in 1996, thus enabling me to begin project interviews in Washington, D.C. In the final stages of my dissertation work, I was a research Fellow at the Brookings Institution. Whatever concerns I had about studying think tanks while at a think tank were quickly allayed when I arrived at Brookings. I enjoyed full independence in my work there as well as frequent fruitful discussions and debates with colleagues that improved the final product. I am grateful to Sarah Binder, Steve Hess, Paul Light, Tom Mann, Jennifer Steen, and Kent Weaver for advice and encouragement during that year. Lew Bateman at Cambridge University Press was a wonderful source of advice and encouragement during my revisions to the project. His suggestions, along with those of two anonymous reviewers, have improved the final book. Eric Newman has my thanks for his careful copyediting of the manuscript.

Last, my thanks to Joel Allen and to my parents, Daniel and Nancy Rich, for their unending support and enthusiasm for the work that went into this book – and for their tolerance of my preoccupations and frustrations along the way.

I

The Political Demography of Think Tanks

The men of [the] Brookings [Institution] did it by analysis, by painstaking research, by objective writing, by an imagination that questioned the "going" way of doing things, and then they proposed alternatives. . . . After 50 years of telling the Government what to do, you are more than a private institution. . . . You are a national institution, so important . . . that if you did not exist we would have to ask someone to create you.

President Lyndon B. Johnson
September 29, 1966[1]

[The Heritage Foundation] is without question the most far-reaching conservative organization in the country in the war of ideas, and one which has had a tremendous impact not just in Washington, but literally across the planet.

Speaker of the House Newt Gingrich
November 15, 1994[2]

These tributes by a president and a speaker of the House more than twenty-eight years apart are high praise for two organizations that are both commonly known as think tanks. Yet, in their praise, Johnson and Gingrich characterize the accomplishments of these organizations in notably different terms: Brookings for its "painstaking research" and "objective writing," Heritage for its "far-reaching" efforts in the "war of ideas." These characterizations evoke two quite different images and suggest quite different understandings of the role of think tanks in American

---

[1] *Public Papers of the Presidents of the United States: Lyndon B. Johnson, 1966, Book II* (Washington, D.C.: Government Printing Office, 1967), p. 1096–7.
[2] *The Heritage Foundation 1994 Annual Report* (Washington, D.C.: The Heritage Foundation, 1995), p. 2.

politics. The first emphasizes their role as producers of credible expertise; the second highlights their contributions to polemical debates over ideas.

The differences signaled by these tributes provoke the central questions for this book: Have think tanks generally evolved from producing painstaking research and objective writing to pursuing ideological agendas with far-reaching impact in the war of ideas? If so, what accounts for these transformations, and what are their consequences for the role and influence of their products – expertise and ideas – in American policy making?

Experts have typically been thought of as neutral, credible, and above the fray of the rough and tumble of policy making. Progressive reformers early in the twentieth century turned to the burgeoning social sciences for salvation. Reformers believed that the new ranks of policy experts trained at universities would be capable of usurping patronage politics; experts would develop *real* solutions to the social and economic instabilities that stemmed from the Industrial Revolution. American politics and American society would be better informed and much improved thanks to their efforts.

While full confidence in expertise waned in the decades that followed, the training of new policy experts became an obsession of reformers through much of the first two-thirds of the twentieth century. The obsession was reflected in the formation and expansion of social science departments and policy schools at universities across the country. It was reflected as well in the founding of scores of independent think tanks, organizations intended to produce policy-relevant research for Washington decision makers.

These developments were observed by twentieth-century scholars of the policymaking process and contribute to what remains the prevailing understanding of experts in American policy making, as important background voices that bring rational, reasoned analysis to long-term policy discourse based on the best evidence available. From Charles Merriam to Harold Lasswell to John Kingdon, political scientists have portrayed research as principally affecting a "general climate of ideas which, in turn, affects policymakers' thinking in the long run."[3] Technical research can inform particular policy provisions; consistent findings from many

---

[3] John W. Kingdon, *Agendas, Alternatives, and Public Policies, Second Edition* (New York: HarperCollins College Publishers, 1995), p. 59. See also Charles E. Merriam, *New Aspects of Politics* (Chicago: University of Chicago Press, 1970); Harold D. Lasswell, "The Policy Orientation," *The Policy Sciences*, ed. by Daniel Lerner and Harold D. Lasswell (Stanford, Calif.: Stanford University Press, 1951).

studies over time can effectively transform ways of thinking about policy issues.[4] Scholars quarrel over whether policy research is most helpful in offering specific prescriptions for public problems or, as is more commonly suggested, as general enlightenment on public issues.[5] But by most all appraisals, more experts are good for policy making. For much of the twentieth century, this judgment was accurate; experts fulfilled these mandates. Even if their work was sometimes used by others for quite political purposes, experts remained ostensibly neutral and detached. Experts offered ideas and policy prescriptions that were rigorously crafted, rational, and, in the long run, helpful to the work of decision makers.

Contrary to these earlier experiences and scholarly understandings, however, by the end of the twentieth century, the ranks of real-life policy experts scarcely conformed to the promise of making policy choices clearer and more rigorous and decisions necessarily more rational. In 2002, as members of Congress considered reauthorization of the welfare reforms first enacted in 1996, there was little agreement among the experts outside of government recommending changes to the 1996 law. Experts produced studies advocating everything from expansions in child care subsidies and low-income housing vouchers to provisions that promote marriage and sexual abstinence.[6]

Along with little agreement among them on how to revise the law, there was also little restraint among experts in expressing their views. Far from reservedly offering detached analysis to affect policy decisions in the long

[4] See Carol Weiss, "Research for Policy's Sake: The Enlightenment Function of Social Research," *Policy Analysis* 3 (1977): 531–45; Charles E. Lindblom and David Cohen, *Usable Knowledge* (New Haven, Conn.: Yale University Press, 1979); and David A. Rochefort and Roger W. Cobb, *The Politics of Problem Definition: Shaping the Policy Agenda* (Lawrence: University Press of Kansas, 1994).

[5] For the first view, see James S. Coleman, *Policy Research in the Social Sciences* (Morristown, N.J.: General Learning Press, 1972). For the latter view, see Carol Weiss, "Research for Policy's Sake: The Enlightenment Function of Social Research"; and Charles E. Lindblom and David Cohen, *Usable Knowledge.*

[6] See, respectively, Gina Adams, Kathleen Snyder, and Jodi R. Sandfort, "Navigating the Child Care Subsidy System: Policies and Practices that Affect Access and Retention," Project Report, Urban Institute's Assessing the New Federalism Project, April 2002; Barbara Sard and Margy Waller, "Housing Strategies to Strengthen Welfare Policy and Support Working Families," Policy Brief, The Brookings Institution Center on Urban and Metropolitan Policy and the Center on Budget and Policy Priorities, April 2002; Patrick Fagan, "Marriage: Next Step for Welfare Reform," press release, The Heritage Foundation, 11 April 2002; Robert Rector, The Effectiveness of Abstinence Education Programs in Reducing Sexual Activity Among Youth," Heritage Backgrounder, The Heritage Foundation, 8 April 2002.

run, many of those who fashioned themselves experts were clamoring to make frequent, loud, aggressive contributions to the immediate public debates over welfare reform. They held press conferences and forums, offered congressional testimony, and sponsored dueling policy briefs. Much of this work emanated from experts and analysts based at think tanks, the numbers of which quadrupled from fewer than 70 to more than 300 between 1970 and the turn of the century.

One typical exchange during this debate was over the effects of welfare on marriage rates. Analysts at the Heritage Foundation, Brookings Institution, Progressive Policy Institute, and Center on Budget and Policy Priorities each produced studies on the subject.[7] In fact, between fall 2001 and spring 2002, each promoted an assortment of reports, policy briefs, and press releases on the topic, followed by public briefings, conferences, and press events, all in anticipation of Congress's reauthorization of the legislation, due by fall 2002. And this think tank work was noted; scholars from the Heritage Foundation, Brookings Institution, Progressive Policy Institute, and Center on Budget and Policy Priorities obtained media visibility for this work that greatly exceeded that for the work of counterparts on the issue based at universities.[8]

The presence of these conflicting, highly visible expert voices illustrates the great distance between historical and scholarly understandings of experts and the ways in which they are most visible and active today. The example points as well to the central role of think tanks in producing research in contemporary policy debates. Many of the most visible expert voices today emanate from public policy think tanks. These think tanks have contributed to a transformation in the role of experts in American policy making. Many experts now behave like advocates. They are not just visible but highly contentious as well. They more actively market their work than conventional views of experts would suggest; their work, in

---

[7] See, for example, Robert Rector, "Using Welfare Reform to Strengthen Marriage," *American Experiment Quarterly*, Summer 2001; Isabel Sawhill, "What Can Be Done to Reduce Teen Pregnancy and Out-of-Wedlock Births?," *Brookings Policy Brief*, October 2001; Daniel T. Lichter, "Marriage as Public Policy," *PPI Policy Report*, 10 September 2001; Shawn Fremstad and Wendell Primus, "Strengthening Families: Ideas for TANF Reauthorization," Center on Budget and Policy Priorities, 22 January 2002.

[8] As one crude indication of the substantial activity among think tanks, these four think tanks received six times more references in relation to welfare reform (twelve) in the *Washington Post* than Harvard, Princeton, Berkeley, and the University of Wisconsin (two), all universities with well-known welfare policy scholars, combined between January 1 and April 30, 2002.

turn, often represents pre-formed points of view rather than even attempts at neutral, rational analysis.

This book examines these developments and their consequences for American policy making. In his analysis of the attributes and roles of experts, Kingdon clearly differentiates the "policy community" from the "political people." Policy experts are part of the former. In his revised edition of *Agendas, Alternatives, and Public Policy*, he remains committed to the view that politicians and experts operate in mutually exclusive spheres. He observes:

As to the policy and political streams, I still find it useful to portray them as independent of one another, but then sometimes joined. . . . The policy community concentrates on matters like technical detail, cost-benefit analyses, gathering data, conducting studies, and honing proposals. The political people, by contrast, paint with a broad brush, are involved in many more issue areas than the policy people are, and concentrate on winning elections, promoting parties, and mobilizing support in the larger polity.[9]

Kingdon maintains that researchers and research organizations are generally peripheral to the hard-fought endgames of policy making. Their research is brought to bear by others, including elected officials, interest group leaders, and journalists, who are among the "political people."

Like Kingdon, scholars in the first half of the twentieth century believed that social scientists were equipped to improve the quality of political debate by providing methodologically rigorous, defensible (if not irrefutable) prescriptions for solving policy problems and that they could and should do so while remaining detached, without becoming mired in the messy and divisive political process.[10] A similar basic view persisted after World War II. In a volume about the *Policy Sciences*, published in 1951, Easton Rothwell predicted:

The policy sciences can serve the need for clarification. They offer rapidly developing techniques for making assumptions explicit and for testing their validity in terms of both the basic values which policy seeks to realize and the actualities of human relations to which policy must be applied. By the method of converting general principles into specific indices of action, the policy sciences provide

---

[9] Kingdon, *Agendas, Alternatives, and Public Policies, Second Edition*, p. 228.

[10] Charles Merriam was one of the leaders of this movement as organizer of the Social Science Research Council in the 1920s. He saw his effort as aimed at suggesting "certain possibilities of approach to a method, in the hope that others may take up the task and through reflection and experiment eventually introduce more intelligent and scientific technique into the study and practices of government, and into popular attitudes toward the governing process." Merriam, *New Aspects of Politics*, p. xiii.

criteria by which to test the applicability of general principles in specific situations. They also equip the policy-maker with a sufficiently sharp image of the full implications of given postulates to enable him to avoid conflicts of principle within the program of action.[11]

Such optimism was echoed by Harold Lasswell, who added the caveat that "the policy approach is not to be confounded with the superficial idea that social scientists ought to desert science and engage full time in practical politics. Nor should it be confused with the suggestion that social scientists ought to spend most of their time advising policy-makers on immediate questions."[12] Through much of the twentieth century, it was viewed as neither desirable that experts should be nor realistic that they could be influential by engaging directly with policy makers in active political debates.

Yet it is a central determination of this book that many contemporary policy experts do seek an active and direct role in ongoing political debates. Far from maintaining a detached neutrality, policy experts are frequently aggressive advocates for ideas and ideologies; they even become brokers of political compromise. Many of these most aggressive experts are based at think tanks; think tanks have become an infrastructure and an engine for their efforts.

The Study of Think Tanks

I attribute substantial importance to a type of organization that has received little scholarly attention. Fewer than a dozen books published since 1970 focus on American think tanks.[13] No articles specifically about think tanks have appeared in the *American Political Science Review*, the *American Journal of Political Science*, or the *Journal of Politics* in the past thirty years, nor in the major policy or sociology journals. By contrast, scores of books

---

[11] C. Easton Rothwell, "Foreword," *The Policy Sciences*, ed. by Daniel Lerner and Harold D. Lasswell (Stanford, Calif.: Stanford University Press, 1951), p. ix.

[12] Lasswell, "The Policy Orientation," *The Policy Sciences*, p. 7.

[13] Only five of these are written by political scientists. David M. Ricci, *The Transformation of American Politics: The New Washington and the Rise of Think Tanks* (New Haven, Conn.: Yale University Press, 1993); James G. McGann, *The Competition for Dollars, Scholars, and Influence in the Public Policy Research Industry* (New York: University Press of America, 1995); Donald E. Abelson, *American Think Tanks and their Role in U.S. Foreign Policy* (New York: St. Martin's Press, 1996); Diane Stone, *Capturing the Political Imagination: Think Tanks and the Policy Process* (Portland, Ore.: Frank Cass, 1996); Donald E. Abelson, *Do Think Tanks Matter? Assessing the Impact of Public Policy Institutes* (Montreal: McGill–Queen's University Press, 2002).

and articles have been published about other types of nongovernmental organizations, particularly interest groups.[14]

One reason why think tanks historically have been granted little attention by social scientists relates to the traditional characteristics of think tanks; another relates to the biases of social scientists, especially political scientists. On the one hand, until the 1960s, American think tanks were generally low-profile actors in the policymaking process. Think tank scholars developed important and frequently used research and ideas for policy makers to assimilate, but these scholars rarely debated them publicly or in highly visible ways either with one another or with other influential actors in the political process.[15] As Kent Weaver recalls, Brookings scholars had a running joke that their "books [we]re written for policymakers and read by college students."[16] Think tank research was generally not intended to grab headlines but rather to become infused into the political lexicon over time. This low profile has contributed to their attracting little scholarly attention.

The lack of attention to think tanks also reflects the outlook of the scholars who might be most likely to study them. Political scientists have

---

[14] Beginning with Bentley, Truman, and Dahl (and confounded by the work of Olson), an extensive interest group literature has evolved through the past half century and continues among rational choice and behavioral scholars in political science and sociology. Think tanks rarely, if ever, receive even a mention in this work, and the force of ideas and expertise receives inadequate attention. For a careful review of the interest group literature, see Frank R. Baumgartner and Beth L. Leech, *Basic Interests: The Importance of Groups in Politics and in Political Science* (Princeton, N.J.: Princeton University Press, 1998).

[15] This is not to say that they did not play important advisory roles in policy making and for policy makers. See, for example, James A. Smith, *The Idea Brokers* (New York: The Free Press, 1991), Chapters 4–6, for a discussion of the role of institutions like the Brookings Institution, the RAND Corporation, and the Committee for Economic Development with presidents, executive branch agencies, and business lobbyists, respectively, through the 1940s, 1950s, and 1960s. And, to be sure, in earlier decades, think tanks were at times visibly credited for important outcomes. A prominent example in the not-too-distant past is the Brookings Institution's influence in the establishment of the Congressional Budget Office (CBO) in 1973. After designing and shepherding the new government agency into existence, one of Brookings' principal economists, Alice Rivlin, became the CBO's first director. See James A. Smith, *Brookings at Seventy-Five* (Washington, D.C.: The Brookings Institution, 1991), pp. 82–6.

[16] As quoted in R. Kent Weaver, "The Changing World of Think Tanks," *PS: Political Science and Politics* 22 (1989): 563–78. Weaver talks about this quality in relation to what he labels "university without student" think tanks, which include most of the oldest institutions like Brookings and the American Enterprise Institute, and, writing in 1989, Weaver talks of this quality in the present tense. I discuss Weaver's categories in more detail in Chapter 2.

long had difficulty accounting for the role of ideas and expertise in American politics, the principal products of think tanks. As Peter Hall observes:

> Ideas are generally acknowledged to have an influence over policymaking. . . . But that role is not easily described. Any attempt to specify the conditions under which ideas acquire political influence inevitably teeters on the brink of reductionism, while the failure to make such an attempt leaves a large lacuna at the center of our understanding of public policy.[17]

A generation of political science scholarship has largely neglected this "lacuna," treating interests, often tied to economically rational calculations, as the principal and overriding source of power in American policy making. In these characterizations, ideas and expertise represent strategic currency in the defense of interests but not substantively important and independent forces.[18]

This limited view of the role of expertise may have been more justifiable in an era when the underlying "rules of the game" were basically agreed by scholars to consist of a "consensus" in support of expanding social welfare commitments on the domestic front. Through the 1960s and 1970s, competing interests may have been legitimately more central to

---

[17] Peter A. Hall, *The Political Power of Economic Ideas: Keynesianism across Nations* (Princeton, N.J.: Princeton University Press, 1989), p. 4. Commenting in a similar vein on this problem, Peter Schuck points out,

> There are pitfalls in emphasizing the causal role of ideas in politics. Compared with votes, institutions, interests, events, and other palpable phenomena that political analysts can observe and even measure, ideas are elusive and their effects on outcomes are hard to gauge. Ideas may simultaneously alter what political actors perceive and what they pursue. At the same time, actors may deploy ideas rhetorically and instrumentally. Thus, ideas' independent causal force in politics must be revealed through inference and the testimony of those most intimately involved. We are wise to be skeptical of such evidence, but we would be foolish to ignore it simply because it is less tangible and quantifiable.

Peter H. Schuck, "The Politics of Rapid Legal Change: Immigration Policy in the 1980s," *The New Politics of Public Policy*, ed. by Marc K. Landy and Martin A. Levin (Baltimore: The Johns Hopkins University Press, 1995), p. 51.

[18] See Aaron Wildavsky and Ellen Tenenbaum, *The Politics of Mistrust* (Beverly Hills, Calif.: Sage, 1981), and Peter Schuck, "The Politics of Rapid Legal Change," pp. 50–1. In relation to the scholarship of positive political theorists, for example, Schuck observes,

> The political role of ideas has not gone unnoticed by positive political theorists. Their theories, however, tend to view ideas as epiphenomenal rather than causal, instrumental rather than normative. These theories note that innovative politicians use agendas, voting, and issues strategically and that these resources may include new ideas. But ideas in this view are little more than additional tools in the politician's kit bag. From the theorist's perspective, ideas may be even *less* than this – if they obscure the "real" interests that lie beneath them.

the policymaking process than contending ideas of the appropriate role and scope of government.[19] When the underlying tenets of Keynesian economics were basically shared by Republicans and Democrats alike, for example, visible battles were often restricted to competing interests' claims to public privileges and resources.[20]

Through this period a diverse literature emerged about the attributes and influence of visible and aggressive interest-based organizations.[21] Many scholars illuminated the efforts and underlying biases associated with interest group politics and the people who participate in the organization of these groups.[22] This empirical scholarship, however, pays little attention to ideas, expertise, or ideological cleavages, and it virtually ignores the efforts of think tanks and experts generally in the political and policymaking processes.

---

[19] Lowi characterizes this period as one of "interest group liberalism." This predicament led him to complain, "The decline of a meaningful dialogue between a liberalism and a conservatism has meant the decline of a meaningful adversary political proceedings in favor of administrative, technical, and logrolling politics.... The emerging public philosophy, interest-group liberalism, has sought to solve the problems of public authority in a large modern state by defining them away.... Interest-group liberalism seeks to justify power by avoiding law and by parceling out to private parties the power to make public policy." Theodore J. Lowi, *The End of Liberalism* (New York: W. W. Norton, 1979), pp. 43–4.

[20] These battles were often intense; for if there was an underlying "expansionist consensus," there was also great controversy over the substance of this expansion, especially on non-economic issues like civil rights and foreign policy.

[21] At least since Truman's *The Governmental Process*, interests and interest groups have guided pluralist inquires and understandings of the political process. David B. Truman, *The Governmental Process* (New York: Knopf, 1951). Olson complicated understandings of the role of economic self-interest and rationality in group politics in *The Logic of Collective Action* (Cambridge, Mass.: Harvard University Press, 1965). The result has been an enhanced and enlarged debate over the role of interests and interest groups in the political and policymaking process. For all of the contention that has surrounded these scholarly debates, few have sought to raise the profile or importance of ideas and expertise. Rather, debates have revolved around the precise role of interests and interest groups in politics and the factors that account for their foundation and growth in the face of counter-incentives to act self-interestedly.

[22] See, for example, Terry M. Moe, *The Organization of Interests* (Chicago: University of Chicago Press, 1980); Robert H. Salisbury, "Interest Representation: The Dominance of Institutions," *American Political Science Review*, 78 (1984): 64–76; Jack L. Walker, Jr., *Mobilizing Interest Groups in America* (Ann Arbor: University of Michigan Press, 1991); Kay Lehman Schlozman and John T. Tierney, *Organized Interests and American Democracy* (New York: Harper & Row, 1986). These four are exemplars of a broader literature. Rational choice scholars have also taken to writing about interest groups, particularly the factors that account for interest group membership and participation. This work also generally does not account for think tanks. See, for example, Dennis Chong, *Collective Action and the Civil Rights Movement* (Chicago: University of Chicago Press, 1991).

Interestingly, while the political environment by many accounts began to favor the preferences of conservatives in the 1970s and 1980s, interest group scholars focused particular energy on understanding the proliferation of mostly liberal public interest and citizen groups. Since Berry's assessment of the proliferation and influence of mostly liberal-minded public interest groups, scholars have followed his example with extensive analysis of the origins, membership, and influence of these organizations.[23] While an important area of study, public interest group scholarship and the interest group literature more generally are of little help in coming to terms with the relationship of organizational politics with the ascendance of conservative principles and ideologies in American politics. By contrast, a focus on think tanks helps to draw links between organized group efforts and developments in the broader political environment.[24]

As the number of think tanks has grown in recent decades, well more than half of those that have emerged have represented identifiable ideological proclivities in their missions and research. The overwhelming majority of these ideological think tanks have been broadly conservative, producing work that favors limited government, free enterprise, and personal freedom. So as contending ideas and ideologies have risen in profile as the principal fodder of political and policy debates, and as think tanks have themselves become more often ideological – frequently conservative – and aggressively promotional, think tanks and their products have come to warrant greater attention. An appreciation of think tanks is helpful not just for understanding the political role of expertise and ideas in American policy making but for accounting for how ideology informs policy making.[25]

---

[23] See Jeffrey M. Berry, *Lobbying for the People* (Princeton, N.J.: Princeton University Press, 1977). More recent work includes Anthony J. Nownes and Grant Neeley, "Public Interest Group Entrepreneurship and Theories of Group Mobilization," *Political Research Quarterly* 49 (1996): 119–46; Anthony J. Nownes, "Public Interest Groups and the Road to Survival," *Polity* 27 (1995): 379–404. For a review of this work and the interest group literature generally, see Frank R. Baumgartner and Beth L. Leech, *Basic Interests: The Importance of Groups in Politics and in Political Science* (Princeton, N.J.: Princeton University Press, 1998).

[24] For a different view on these developments that points out the areas of progress and potential for liberals, see Jeffrey M. Berry, *The New Liberalism: The Rising Power of Citizen Groups* (Washington, D.C.: The Brookings Institution Press, 1999).

[25] Perhaps reflecting their warrant for more attention, think tanks have recently begun to appear in scholarly accounts of interest group politics. For example, think tanks make their first substantial appearance in Berry's work in his third edition of *The Interest Group Society*. Jeffrey M. Berry, *The Interest Group Society, Third Edition* (New York: Longman, 1997), pp. 126–8. See also Andrew Rich and R. Kent Weaver, "Advocates and Analysts:

What Defines Think Tanks?

Considerable disagreement exists over the organizations to which the label "think tank" refers. In some accounts, they are undifferentiated from government research organizations such as the General Accounting Office and the Congressional Research Service.[26] They are occasionally equated with university-affiliated research centers and institutes.[27] In some instances, research organizations based at interest groups, such as the AARP's Policy Institute, are referred to as think tanks.[28] I view none of the aforementioned as think tanks.

I define think tanks as *independent, non–interest-based, nonprofit organizations that produce and principally rely on expertise and ideas to obtain support and to influence the policymaking process.* Operationally, think tanks are 501(c)3 nonprofit organizations that conduct and disseminate research and ideas on public policy issues. Politically, think tanks are aggressive institutions that actively seek to maximize public credibility and political access to make their expertise and ideas influential in policy making.

In truth, drawing irrefutable distinctions between think tanks and other types of organizations is neither entirely possible nor desirable; rather, institutional boundaries are frequently amorphous and overlapping. Nonetheless, the products and objectives of think tanks are central to any clarification of how think tanks might be differentiated from other actors in their operations and influence.

Think Tanks and the Politicization of Expertise," *Interest Group Politics, Fifth Edition*, ed. by Allan J. Cigler and Burdett A. Loomis (Washington, D.C.: CQ Press, 1998); Mark A. Smith, *American Business and Political Power* (Chicago: University of Chicago Press, 2000), pp. 167–96. For a discussion of the policy role of think tanks in the 1970s and 1980s, see also Martha Derthick and Paul J. Quirk, *The Politics of Deregulation* (Washington, D.C.: The Brookings Institution Press, 1985).

[26] William H. Robinson, "The Congressional Research Service: Policy Consultant, Think Tank, and Information Factory," *Organizations for Policy Analysis: Helping Government Think*, ed. by Carol H. Weiss (Beverly Hills, Calif.: Sage Publications, 1992).

[27] Nelson Polsby, "Tanks but No Tanks," *Public Opinion*, April/May 1983, pp. 14–16.

[28] Eleanor Evans Kitfield, *The Capitol Source* (Washington, D.C.: National Journal, 1995); Diane Stone, *Capturing the Political Imagination*. In characterizations of their functions, the principal role of think tanks in American politics has been variously described as producing policy alternatives (Kingdon, *Agendas, Alternatives, and Public Policy*), supporting party politics (Winard Gellner, "The Politics of Policy 'Political Think Tanks' and Their Markets in the U.S. Institutional Environment," *Presidential Studies Quarterly*, Summer 1995), defining "the boundaries of our policy debates" (Smith, *The Idea Brokers*, p. xiii), and appearing at too many different points in the political and policy processes to highlight any one (Polsby, "Tanks but No Tanks").

Think tanks care about maximizing their credibility because, compared with interest groups, think tanks rarely have an explicit and specifically identifiable constituency whom they represent in the eyes of policy makers. Think tanks cannot rely on the size or strength of a voting constituency to carry weight and influence with policy makers. While the AARP might produce research in efforts to affect policymaking decisions, millions of older Americans provide their central and strongest organizational leverage for influencing policy. By contrast, think tanks, even ones that seek to speak for and that benefit from the support of those who share an underlying ideology, are ultimately and fundamentally subject to the credibility and believability of their research products – and vulnerable to attacks on them.

In order to achieve credibility, think tanks seek to maximize their independence. The seriousness with which think tank research is taken depends on its being viewed as independent of specific financial interests. As subsequent chapters illustrate, many think tanks, even those that actively promote research aligned with particular ideologies or points of view, seek to portray an independence from narrow groups of supporters.

Think tanks also pursue political access. Think tanks may aim to inform and affect quite different audiences by their research; but, particularly in recent years, think tanks rarely issue reports and passively move on to their next study. Think tanks seek to gain notice for their research among relevant decision makers and seek access to them in order to influence political outcomes. Whether writing op-eds about the importance of marriage in relation to welfare reauthorization or attracting opportunities to testify before Congress on environmental regulation, most think tanks make establishing access an explicit part of their missions.[29] Their efforts to develop access have consequences for their influence; and, in recent years, these efforts have affected perceptions of the role and effectiveness of experts in policy making generally.

---

[29] The political access of think tanks tends to far surpass that of university-based research institutes, and the incentives to pursue political access are far greater for think tank researchers than university faculty. University-based social scientists often have professional, if not personal, incentives to move quickly from one study to the next and to conduct research relevant to scholarly and theoretically based debates rather than that which confronts the most current and pressing policy questions of the day. Academic journals and university presses, the traditional publication outlets for academics seeking professional rewards, are typically more concerned with advancing disciplinary debates than addressing debates on Capitol Hill.

Think Tanks in a Period of Growth

The origins of the term "think tank" are ambiguous, with most reports suggesting that the label arose during World War II in reference to military research and development organizations.[30] With little consensus in recent decades about what organizations can or should claim the label "think tank," some think tank leaders are actually reluctant to have their organizations categorized as think tanks and nervous, once classified, about what other organizations might be considered among their ranks.[31] Offsetting the apprehensions of some organizations are the eager efforts of some interest groups to win the label "think tank," for whatever added credibility and stature it might bring their efforts.

A result of this jockeying to win or avoid the label is that determining the number of think tanks operating in American politics at any particular moment is difficult. While other types of organizations, like universities and trade associations, may undergo processes of accreditation or may have clear and consistent prestige or survival incentives associated with self-identification as particular types of organizations, think tanks, as I have defined them, may be as apt to reject the label "think tank" as to accept it.

My estimate of the number of think tanks operating in American politics is based on an examination of references from directories, books, and scholarly articles about think tanks as well as newspaper and magazine clippings. The single most comprehensive source of think tank listings, and the one upon which I depend most, is Hellebust's *Think Tank Directory*.[32] The 1996 directory records entries for 1,212 independent and university-affiliated "think tank–like organizations," organizations that were assessed to be "nonprofit public policy research organization[s],

---

[30] See James A. Smith, *The Idea Brokers* (New York: The Free Press, 1991), pp. xiii–xiv. See also Paul Dickson, *Think Tanks* (New York: Atheneum, 1971), pp. 21–34, for a slightly different but not inconsistent explanation of the origins of the term.

[31] As Dickson put it as long ago as 1971, "[M]ost groups that are think tanks don't like the term, while, in contrast, pretentious little research groups often invoke the term to look important." Dickson, *Think Tanks*, 1971, p. 27. Diane Stone points out that some think tanks explicitly reject the label "think tank" while others create alternative labels for themselves. "The Aspen Institute denies in all its promotional material that it is a think tank, while Will Marshall of the Democrat-affiliated Progressive Policy Institute refers to his [organization as an] 'analytic guerrilla group.'" Diane Stone, *Capturing the Political Imagination: Think Tanks and the Policy Process* (Portland, Ore.: Frank Cass, 1996), p. 9.

[32] Lynn Hellebust, ed., *Think Tank Directory: A Guide to Nonprofit Public Policy Research Organizations* (Topeka, Kans.: Government Research Service, 1996).

either independent or associated with a college or university, and located in the United States."[33]

In sorting through Hellebust's entries, I excluded from my count organizations that are not independent or not oriented toward affecting public policy debates, and I added to my count several organizations referenced elsewhere.[34] References from all of the sources consulted combine to create a record of 306 independent, public policy–oriented think tanks operating in American politics in 1996. While *The Think Tank Directory* is now somewhat dated, the status, existence, and qualifications of these think

[33] Hellebust points out, "Not included in the directory are research-oriented government agencies, profit-making research entities, institutes for the development of new technology, and short-term research projects." Hellebust, *The Think Tank Directory*, p. 1.

[34] I left out all 625 university-affiliated research organizations listed by Hellebust. In addition, I excluded another 253 organizations with characteristics similar to those of the Academy for State and Local Government, which functions as a "policy and research center for its Trustee organizations," and the American Family Foundation, which is a "secular nonprofit tax-exempt research center and educational organization" whose purpose is "to study psychological manipulation and high-control and cultic groups." The former organization is closely tied to and run by government officials and thus not sufficiently independent for my purposes. The latter organization, while performing independent research, is oriented toward public education and counseling rather than toward effecting public policy change.

I am left with 302 institutions that qualify as think tanks according to my definition. An additional four think tanks were added to the count based on references made in a variety of other sources. The four organizations added were Campaign for America's Future, a liberal/progressive think tank founded in 1996; Institute for Energy Research, a conservative, Texas-based think tank founded in 1989; Institute for Gay and Lesbian Strategic Studies, a scholarly, liberal-oriented research organization started in 1994; and the German Marshall Fund, a research and grantmaking institution founded in 1972. The first three may have been overlooked by Hellebust because they are new and relatively small. The German Marshall Fund may have been considered a foundation rather than a think tank by Hellebust. Whatever the case, the German Marshall Fund qualifies as a think tank by my definition.

The fact that I added only four additional organizations is actually a testament to the comprehensiveness of Hellebust's directory. The other sources consulted include Robert L. Hollings, *Nonprofit Public Policy Research Organizations: A Sourcebook on Think Tanks in Government* (New York: Garland Publishers, 1993); Eleanor Evans Kitfield, *The Capitol Source* (Washington, D.C.: National Journal, 1995); James G. McGann, *The Competition for Dollars, Scholars and Influence in the Public Policy Research Industry* (New York: University Press of America, 1995); Joseph G. Peschek, *Policy-Planning Organizations: Elite Agendas and America's Rightward Turn* (Philadelphia: Temple University Press, 1987); Smith, *The Idea Brokers*, 1991; Stone, *Capturing the Political Imagination: Think Tanks and the Policy Process*, 1996; Donald E. Abelson, "From Policy Research to Political Advocacy: The Changing Role of Think Tanks in American Politics," *Canadian Review of American Studies*. 25 (1996): 93–126; and Laura Brown Chisolm, "Sinking the Think Tanks Upstream: The Use and Misuse of Tax Exemption Law to Address the Use and Misuse of Tax-exempt Organizations by Politicians," *University of Pittsburgh Law Review*, 1990.

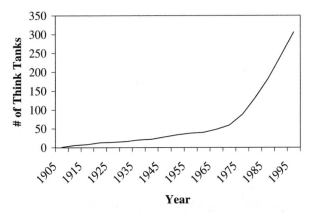

Year

FIGURE 1-1. Pattern by which think tanks existing in the 1990s formed

tanks have been confirmed by cross-checking mission statements and/or annual reports collected for each organization. Appendix A includes more information about my method for counting think tanks.

I identified additional features and patterns among think tanks as well. Figure 1-1 illustrates the pattern by which these 306 think tanks emerged throughout the twentieth century. More than three-quarters of think tanks in existence by 1996 were formed after 1970 (80.7 percent). Only 59 of the think tanks operating in 1996 were more than 25 years old.[35]

Among the many new and old think tanks, there are substantial differences with regard to location, size, and research focus. A full one-third of the think tanks operating in 1996 were principally concerned with state and regional issues, as opposed to national matters. Organizations like the Public Policy Institute of California (formed in 1994 with a $75 million endowment grant from William Hewlett to improve "public policy in California through independent, objective, nonpartisan research"), the Delaware Public Policy Institute (a think tank founded by former Republican Governor Pierre S. DuPont in 1990), and the James Madison Institute

---

[35] There is good reason to believe that this growth in organizational numbers is real and not simply an artifact of organizational replacement over time. In a 1971 book about think tanks, Dickson refers to there being only "a handful of truly independent, nonprofit, self-determining think tanks." Paul Dickson, *Think Tanks* (New York: Atheneum, 1971), p. 30. Herzog, also, in a *New York Times Magazine* article about the Hudson Institute refers to Hudson as one of only "dozens" of points of view and policy analysis for government. Arthur Herzog, "Report on a 'Think Factory,'" *New York Times Magazine*, 10 November 1963, p. 30. This growth in organizational numbers is roughly similar to that among trade associations and many sectors of interest groups. Frank R. Baumgartner and Bryan D. Jones, *Agendas and Instability in American Politics* (Chicago: University of Chicago Press, 1993), pp. 175–92.

(a Florida-based conservative think tank "engaged in the battle of ideas" in that state since 1987) were among the 106 state-focused organizations operating in 1996.[36]

Almost two-thirds (65 percent) of these organizations focused on state policy making were founded just since 1980, with new state think tanks founded at a rate of 5.7 per year between 1985 and 1995. Not surprisingly given their more limited geographic constituencies, state-focused think tanks tend to be smaller than national think tanks. In 1996, almost three quarters of the state-focused think tanks (72.6 percent) were operating with budgets of less than $500,000.[37] None was spending more than $10 million annually.

By contrast, more than two-thirds of the 200 think tanks focused primarily on national policy making (67.5 percent) had budgets of *more than* $500,000 by 1996, with almost half (47.5 percent) sustaining budgets of more than $1 million annually. Twenty of the 200 nationally focused think tanks had budgets in excess of $10 million. Some were operating with resources far in excess of $10 million, most notably the RAND Corporation with a 1996 budget of $120 million. The majority of these large institutions – including the Brookings Institution, Heritage Foundation, and Urban Institute – each had annual budgets ranging from $15–$30 million.[38] All 20 of these organizations had budgets far larger than the biggest state-focused think tank. Appendix A provides additional detailed information and tables about the distribution of think tanks by budget size.

Scope and Diversity of Research Missions

Besides focusing on different policymaking venues, think tanks vary in the scope of their research missions – whether they seek to produce

---

[36] Organizations were coded as state or regionally focused based on references in their mission statements. In the few cases where organizations appeared to devote effort to both state and regional issues and national matters, think tanks were coded for research focus based on where the preponderance of their effort seemed to be devoted. These determinations were made with reference to mission statements in most cases. In several ambiguous cases, publication lists and research products were also consulted.

[37] Think tank budget information was compiled from examination of the IRS forms 990 for think tanks and from classifications made in Hellebust's *Think Tank Directory*.

[38] It is particularly notable that among these largest institutions, 15 of the 20 were founded before 1970, with 9 existing since before 1947. By contrast, of the more than 158 nationally focused think tanks founded since 1970, 62 percent had 1996 budgets of less than $1 million.

research on one, several, or scores of issues. While some think tanks, like the Hudson Institute and the Manhattan Institute, spend between $7 and $10 million a year to influence broad-ranging policy debates in multiple-issue domains, others spend similar amounts but have far narrower focuses. Organizations like the Joint Center for Political and Economic Studies and Resources for the Future, for example, are of similar size but concerned only with issues affecting African-Americans and the environment, respectively.

Nationally focused think tanks fall into three categories with regard to the breadth of their research interests. "Full-service" think tanks produce research and studies that span the broadest array of issue domains, including both foreign and domestic policy topics. "Multi-issue" think tanks have an identifiable interest in a variety of subjects concerning more than one policy domain (e.g., health care and the environment) but not including all (or most) subject areas. Finally, "single-issue" organizations, as the label implies, limit their focus to only one category of issues (e.g., women's rights or low-income housing). At the state level, think tanks fall into only two categories: those that are "full-service" and those that focus on a single or several issues.

Tables 1-1a and 1-1b record the distribution of think tanks with regard to the scope of their research missions, broken down by organizational size. Far more organizations are single-issue (120) than full-service (25), and more than three-quarters of the single-issue, nationally focused think tanks (80.8 percent) were founded after 1970. By contrast, only 12 of the full-service, nationally focused think tanks (48.0 percent) were founded after 1970. And not surprisingly, research scope is positively correlated with budget size. Among nationally focused think tanks (Table 1-1a), close to two-thirds of single-issue think tanks (61.7 percent) have budgets of less than $1 million. By contrast, more than half of the full-service think tanks (52.0 percent) have budgets in excess of $5 million.

TABLE 1-1a. *Nationally focused think tanks by budget and research scope*

	Single-issue	Multi-issue	Full-service
Less than $500,000	38.4% (46)	34.5% (19)	0.0% (0)
$500,001–$1,000,000	23.3% (28)	14.5% (8)	16.0% (4)
$1,000,001–$5,000,000	28.4% (34)	38.2% (21)	32.0% (8)
More than $5,000,000	10.0% (12)	12.7% (7)	52.0% (13)
Total # of organizations:	120	55	25

TABLE 1-1b. *State and regionally focused think tanks by budget and research scope*

	Single- or multi-issue	Full-service
Less than $250,000	51.9% (14)	38.0% (30)
$250,001–$500,000	25.9% (7)	32.9% (26)
$500,001–$1,000,000	3.7% (1)	17.7% (14)
More than $1,000,000	18.5% (5)	11.4% (9)
Total # of organizations:	27	79

Among state and regionally focused think tanks (Table 1-1b), there are no substantial differences in the budget sizes of full-service versus single- or multi-issue think tanks. State-focused think tanks are on average much smaller than nationally focused organizations, as noted earlier. And one additional point of contrast with nationally focused think tanks: Three-quarters of state-focused think tanks (74.5 percent) are full-service as opposed to single- or multi-issue organizations, compared with nearly reversed proportions among nationally focused organizations.

Identifiable Ideologies

Amid the growing number of think tanks, no change has been more re-markable at both the state and national levels than the association of many new think tanks with identifiable ideologies. The emergence of avowedly ideological think tanks, particularly conservative think tanks, has been much remarked upon by journalists and researchers. Yet it is difficult to make clear judgments about the presence and nature of organizational ideologies. If for no other reason than to avoid the risk of jeopardizing their tax-exempt status, most think tanks are less than forthright about the guiding political ideologies in their research and publications. As tax-exempt 501(c)3 nonprofit organizations, they can produce ideologically consistent work, but they are prohibited from devoting "more than an insubstantial part of [their] activities to attempting to influence legislation" or from "directly or indirectly participat[ing] in, or interven[ing] in (including the publishing or distributing of statements), any political campaign on behalf of or in opposition to any candidate for public office."[39]

---

[39] Reg. Section 1.501(c)(3)-1(b)(1)(v). In the past decisions, courts have defined "an insubstantial part" of the activity of 501(c)3 nonprofits as activity that consumes 5 percent or less of their budgets. 501(c)3 nonprofits cannot take part in any partisan

Without explicit acknowledgment of guiding political ideologies, I have classified think tanks as broadly conservative or liberal, or as organizations with "centrist or no identifiable ideology," based on key words and phrases in their mission statements and/or annual reports associated with the general, if not always consistent, concerns of conservative and liberal ideologies. In classifying conservative organizations, I looked for references to promoting the free market system, limited government, individual liberties, religious expression, and traditional family values, or to eliminating racial or ethnic preferences in government policy. I classified organizations as liberal when they expressed interest in using government policies and programs to overcome economic, social, or gender inequalities, poverty, or wage stagnation. I also classified calls for progressive social justice, a sustainable environment, or lower defense spending as signals of liberal organizations. Finally, I classified a think tank as liberal or conservative if its mission was defined as aimed at rebuking a counterideology (e.g., overcoming right-wing hate mongering or dispelling radical efforts at socialist dominance). Those organizations whose published statements either did not readily place them in either broad ideological category or qualified them in both categories make up the third group of think tanks with centrist or no identifiable ideologies.[40]

This method of classifying think tanks relies on information supplied by the think tanks rather than assessments of their ideological proclivities by those who might use their research. Given the risks for think tanks of revealing avowed ideologies or guiding principles, it is reasonable to expect that my method of classification may overestimate the number of think tanks with centrist or no identifiable ideologies and underestimate those that belong in the two broad ideological categories. Yet a comparison of my classifications of portrayed ideology for a sample of twenty-nine think tanks correlates at a remarkably high 0.81 with a scaling of these same organizations by journalists and congressional staff with regard to *perceived* ideologies. And my classifications correlate at an even higher

political campaign activity, although they can take part in voter, candidate, and public education.

[40] One organization, the Progressive Policy Institute (PPI), qualified for both ideological categories, not surprisingly because it consciously seeks to occupy the middle of the road. PPI, which is connected organizationally with the "centrist" Democratic Leadership Council, describes itself as "founded to promote ideas that spring from the progressive tradition of American politics. . . . Believing that a strong ethic of mutual responsibility is fundamental to effective self governance, the Institute advocates creative ways to harness private energies and resources for public purposes – to strengthen the civic infrastructure and to cultivate the civic virtues characteristic of the American experience. . . ."

0.93 with the ideological labeling of a sample of forty-three of the think tanks cited in newspaper stories between 1991 and 1995.[41]

Based on my classifications, the largest single category of think tanks in 1996 was organizations of centrist or no identifiable ideology (45.4 percent). Given a long history of think tanks as balanced or non-ideological institutions in the United States, as well as the propensity for my classification process to overestimate this category of institution, this is not surprising. What is remarkable, however, is that a majority of think tanks in 1996 were avowedly ideological in character, either conservative or liberal. In 1996, 165 of the 306 think tanks – 54 percent – were avowedly conservative or liberal, broadly defined. By contrast, only 14 of the 59 think tanks that existed in 1970 and that were still in existence in 1996 were identifiably conservative or liberal; three-quarters of these 59 organizations (76.3 percent) were coded as centrist or of no identifiable ideology.

Particularly noteworthy among the greatly expanded ranks of avow-edly ideological think tanks, conservative think tanks substantially out-numbered liberal organizations. Of the 165 ideological think tanks, roughly two-thirds (65 percent) were avowedly conservative; only one-third (35 percent) were identifiably liberal. Figures 1-2a and 1-2b illustrate think tanks classified by ideology as they emerged throughout the twenti-eth century, differentiated by those that are nationally versus state focused. As the ranks of think tanks generally exploded during the 1980s and '90s, the rate of formation of conservative think tanks (2.6 per year) was twice that of liberal ones (1.3 each year).[42] Nationally focused think tanks of centrist or no identifiable ideology emerged at a rate of 2.7 each year throughout this period.

The preponderance of conservative over liberal think tanks is even more pronounced among state and regionally focused think tanks. Between 1985 and 1995, new state-focused conservative think tanks emerged at an overall rate of 3.5 each year. By comparison, state-focused think tanks of no identifiable ideology emerged at a rate of 1.3 each year,

---

[41] These high correlations increase confidence in the coding of information according to mission statements and annual reports. The variable used in the correlation with jour-nalists and congressional staff comes from a survey that I conducted jointly with Burson Marsteller of the perceptions of think tanks, which I report on in Chapter 3. The variable representing the coding of ideological labels in newspaper stories comes from a study of the portrayal of think tanks in the *New York Times*, *Washington Post*, and *Wall Street Journal* in the early and mid-1990s. I report on that analysis in Chapter 3 as well.

[42] This was the rate of growth of new think tanks between 1985 and 1995.

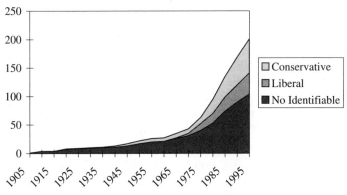

FIGURE 1-2a. Proliferation pattern of nationally focused think tanks existing in the 1990s, by ideology

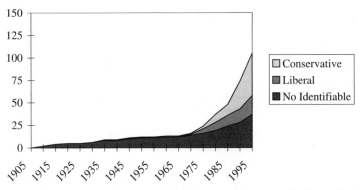

FIGURE 1-2b. Proliferation pattern of state and regionally focused think tanks existing in the 1990s, by ideology

and liberal organizations at a rate of only 0.9 each year through the ten-year period (Figure 1-2b). By 1996, avowedly conservative state-focused think tanks outnumbered liberal organizations by a margin of 2 to 1. Forty-seven avowedly conservative think tanks were operating in thirty-four of the fifty states; by contrast, only twenty-two liberal organizations were visible in just fifteen states.[43]

---

[43] Throughout the book, I consider the ideological differences among think tanks in relation to only the three categories: conservative, liberal, and centrist or no identifiable ideology. There are admittedly important additional distinctions that could be drawn within these categories. One considerable difference is between organizations that might reflect libertarian or conservative economic ideas and those representing the ideals of social and cultural conservatives. By my coding scheme, this distinction might be thought of as

Table 1-2 records the differences in the number and proportion of state-versus nationally focused think tanks in relation to the three ideological clusters. Almost half of the state-focused think tanks (44 percent) operating in the 1990s were avowedly conservative, compared with a bit fewer than one-third of the nationally focused organizations. At both levels of focus – state and national – identifiably liberal think tanks made up only about one-fifth of all organizations. Table 1-2 also reports estimates of the cumulative resources of think tanks grouped by ideology and research focus. Whereas conservative state-focused think tanks *outnumber* liberal organizations by roughly 2 to 1, conservative think tanks *outspend* liberal organizations by more than 3 to 1. Total resources of conservative state-focused think tanks, based on the method of aggregation used, are $28.4 million, compared with $8.8 million for liberal organizations at the state level.[44] Among nationally focused think tanks, the difference

between the fifty-eight organizations coded as conservative because of expressed interest in limited government and/or concerns for promoting free markets and the twelve think tanks coded as conservative because of stated desires to promote religious or "traditional" family values. By this standard, economically conservative and libertarian think tanks outnumber socially conservative think tanks by a ratio of three to one. But another thirty-nine think tanks coded as conservative state concern for matters that match coding criteria for both economic and social conservatives. In the end, distinctions within the broad ideological clusters are difficult to make with a high degree of certainty, so I keep my analysis at the level of only the three broad categories. These categories, by themselves, illustrate a strikingly unequal distribution of think tanks by ideology.

One additional note: Foreign policy think tanks are a group of organizations that are particularly difficult to classify in relation to ideology based on my coding criteria. By many accounts, for example, the Center for Strategic and International Studies (CSIS) is a conservative-oriented foreign policy think tank. It is not classified as such using my coding scheme, however. In 1998, CSIS stated its mission as "to inform and shape selected policy decisions in government and the private sector to meet the increasingly complex and difficult challenges that leaders will confront in the next century." While perhaps it may be more difficult to classify, it might also be the case that foreign policy think tanks truly do not fit conventional ideological categories as easily as domestic policy think tanks. Retired Democratic Senator Sam Nunn, of Georgia (admittedly a person viewed as a conservative) assumed the chairmanship of CSIS's Board of Trustees on January 1, 1999.

[44] The resource amounts and totals come from only a rough approximation of each organization's annual budget, calculated in a way that probably underestimates the extent of true aggregate resources. Resource amounts are based on a combination of values from the budget categories already elaborated. For the purposes of calculating aggregate resources, I assigned each organization a budget that was the mean value of its category (e.g., $1,500,000 for the $1,000,000–$2,000,000 category). For organizations in the "less than $50,000 category," this value was $25,000; for organizations in the "over $10,000,000" category, this value was $12,000,000. The resulting budget values were then summed for each group by ideology and research focus. This system for totaling budget resources inevitably results in estimation error. It should create random error

TABLE 1-2. *Think tanks by ideology, research focus, and resources*

	# of orgs.	1995–6 resources of orgs. (in $ millions)
Nationally focused		
Conservative	62 (31%)	156.4 (n = 59)
Liberal	39 (19%)	47.8 (n = 38)
Centrist or No Identifiable	99 (50%)	319.2 (n = 96)
Contract researchers	*11 (6%)*	*77.9 (n = 11)*
State/regionally focused		
Conservative	47 (44%)	28.4 (n = 47)
Liberal	22 (21%)	8.8 (n = 22)
Centrist or No Identifiable	37 (35%)	33.2 (n = 34)

between conservative and liberal think tank budgets is also more than 3 to 1, a greater differential than between the number of conservative versus liberal organizations, which is only roughly 1.7 to 1.

Table 1-2 also illustrates the substantial resources overall of think tanks with centrist or no identifiable ideologies, at both the state and national level. Think tanks with centrist or no identifiable ideology, in fact, have greater resources than both conservative and liberal think tanks combined. Their advantage is especially pronounced at the national level. This abundance of resources is partly accounted for by the eleven organizations in this category that receive their principal support through government contracts. These "contract research" think tanks make up only 6 percent of the nationally focused think tanks, but they account for nearly 25 percent of the resources of nationally focused think tanks in the centrist or no identifiable ideology cluster.[45] I reserve my discussion of contract research think tanks for the next chapter, but suffice it to say at this point that contract researchers are typically well-financed organizations but ones that compete mainly with one another rather than with the broader ranks of think tanks.

Table 1-3 records percentages of both national and state think tanks according to the scope of their research and their ideology. In combination

across categories, however, thus leaving proportional comparisons between groups valid even if the absolute values are not correct.

[45] These contract research organizations actually had 1995 budgets that combined to more than $216 million, an amount much greater than $78 million. Five of the eleven organizations have budgets that are more than $10,000,000 and so, for the purposes of my categorization scheme, were coded as having $12,000,000 budgets, well below what most of their budgets actually were.

TABLE 1-3. *Think tanks by ideology and breadth of research interests*

	Conservative	Liberal	Centrist or No Identifiable
Nationally focused			
Full-service	21% (13)	8% (3)	9% (9)
Multiple issues	45% (28)	23% (9)	18% (18)
Single-issue	34% (21)	69% (27)	73% (72)
Foreign policy	*8% (5)*	*19% (7)*	*36% (36)*
State/regionally focused			
Full-service	85% (40)	59% (13)	70% (26)
Single or several issues	15% (7)	41% (9)	30% (11)

with the high numbers of conservative think tanks, what is remarkable in these results, at both the national and state levels, is the high proportion of "full-service" think tanks that are conservative. At the national level, 21 percent of conservative think tanks are full service – seeking to justify and advance conservative principles of some kind across numerous policy domains. By comparison, only 8 percent of liberal think tanks at the national level – just three organizations – have such a breadth of concerns. Instead, the overwhelming majority of liberal think tanks at the national level (69 percent) are single issue. Many are concerned exclusively with topics like the environment, women's rights, or conditions of domestic poverty. Single-issue organizations make up the bulk of think tanks with no identifiable ideology as well, half of which are foreign policy–focused.

Turning to state and regionally focused think tanks, an overwhelming 85 percent of the avowedly conservative state-focused think tanks are "full service," resulting in forty full-service conservative think tanks in thirty-two of the fifty states by 1996. By contrast, only 41 percent of liberal think tanks are "full service," resulting in just thirteen identifiably liberal think tanks in nine states. Almost two-thirds of the state-focused think tanks with no identifiable ideology are "full service," many of which are among the oldest state-focused think tanks, founded to advance principles of "good government." Many also sustain themselves with contract work for state governments.

Appendix A includes additional information about some specific think tanks that fit into the different categories, adding "faces" to the numbers. In particular, it includes information about the fifteen largest think tanks overall and the ten largest think tanks in each ideological cluster. The tables and figures there and here combine to suggest both the volume and diverse range of think tanks active in American policy making.

The Influence of Experts

The number of think tanks has exploded. In their expanded numbers, ideological think tanks have come to outnumber think tanks with no identifiable ideology; conservative think tanks have come to outnumber liberal think tanks. All of this is clear. Less clear is what difference these changes make for American politics. How are think tanks, in their expanded numbers and more diverse forms, affecting the policy process?

My interest in presenting an empirical portrait of think tanks is in elevating their standing in understandings of the policy process. But that interest ultimately stems from my concern for how think tanks affect the collective policy influence of experts. Think tanks are unquestionably a major purveyor of policy research in the United States. Their work often finds an attentive audience. It sometimes informs policy decisions. But as the number of think tanks has grown and their efforts have become more ideological and aggressively marketing-oriented, their influence has not expanded in proportion to their numbers. In fact, the collective credibility of their research products has eroded.

My research suggests that the intentional marketing efforts of experts, most notably by ideological think tanks, do increase the size of the audience for their work. Experts who do not market their work often fail to receive the attention of policy makers. After the Heritage Foundation holds a series of public forums about the importance of promoting marriage in the welfare law's reauthorization, for example, the Center on Budget and Policy Priorities cannot modestly release a study on the same subject and expect it to be noticed without matching the promotional efforts of Heritage. The research, whatever the merits of its evidence, will likely be overlooked among the myriad studies being produced. Many think tanks have mastered the process of producing and promoting research in ways that find ready audiences; their mastery goes beyond that of universities and many other sources of research.

At the same time, as more think tanks have emerged whose missions include advancing clear ideologies rather than neutral research, the substantive value of their work – and of the work of think tanks generally – has been called into greater question. Thanks to its marketing, research reaches policy makers. But research is increasingly viewed with a skeptical eye by policy makers who are overwhelmed by scores of studies on similar topics, all with different evidence and conclusions. That which is better promoted might get more of their attention. But the frequent ideological predilections apparent in research leads many who receive it to assess think tank products on the basis of whether it is agreeable rather than on whether it is thorough. Moreover, policy makers increasingly have difficulty distinguishing the work of think tanks from that of advocacy organizations. And with that difficulty, the substantive weight of think tank work is diminished.

And there is another concern. At the same time that the credibility of think tank work has increasingly been called into question, the potential for think tank work to affect substantive policy decisions has been impaired by another development. Much of the work of the newer, more ideological, often more marketing-oriented think tanks – the ones that are self-conscious and aggressive about establishing their standing among policy makers – is directed at the final moments of policy making; these are points in the policy process when sides have already been established and minds have largely been made up. Even if think tank work is perceived as credible and of substantive merit by policy makers, by this point in the policy process their work serves, perhaps all too often, as facile support and ammunition with already reticent policy makers. The welfare reform studies about marriage are a case in point. As Congress moved in the spring and summer of 2002 to broker a compromise on welfare reauthorization, the work of think tanks and experts on marriage and other issues became fodder in already highly politicized debates in which issues were clear and differences in view were well established. The work of think tanks was visible but by no means substantively decisive. This is all too often becoming par for the course. When successful, many of the most aggressive, marketing-oriented think tanks are consequential at precisely the point in the policy process when substantive influence is least possible. More substantive success might accrue from research directed at efforts that occur while problems are being defined and issues are germinating.

The greater substantive potential for policy research early on as opposed to during final deliberation and enactment is recognized by scholars.[46] But this insight does not seem to have guided the behavior of many think tanks, at least not in the past quarter-century. In the chapters that follow, I examine what accounts for these peculiar developments. I consider the paradox of why, at precisely the moment when experts and those who support them are realizing their own power in policy making, those among them that are the most conscious of their own potential devote effort where it can achieve the least substantive effect. This development in combination with the harm to their collective reputation done by some

[46] See Weiss, "Research for Policy's Sake: The Enlightenment Function of Social Research." See also Rochefort and Cobb, *The Politics of Problem Definition.*

ideological think tanks results in little evidence that, amid the proliferation of think tanks active in American policy making, these think tanks
and experts generally are especially – or proportionally – influential. Quite
the opposite, in fact: Their actual standing may be eroding just as their
numbers and scholarly recognition increase.

My analysis proceeds in Chapter 2 to account for the growth and
increased variation among think tanks since the 1960s. I examine why
think tanks became such a popular organizational form and, even more,
why newer think tanks have so frequently adopted identifiable ideologies
and aggressive marketing strategies, as well as behaviors that seem coun-
terproductive to their being influential. The analysis begins to explain
why contemporary think tanks have become more focused on final deliberations and policy enactment rather than agenda setting, where their
substantive contributions might be more important. I examine changes in
funding, staffing patterns, sizes, and areas of specialization for think tanks
and illustrate links between developments among think tanks and changes
in the institutional, funding, and ideological environments in which they
operate.

In Chapter 3, I turn to the image of think tanks in the nation's capital.
I begin with the perceptions of congressional staff and journalists toward
think tanks, with results from a survey assessing their views. I then analyze
the volume and content of political visibility obtained by nationally focused think tanks. I assess the portrayal of think tanks in the news media
and in congressional hearings during the 1990s. The analysis illustrates
that, while ideological and marketing-oriented think tanks make achieving visibility in final policy debates a core activity, they actually receive
little more attention than think tanks that are more restrained and focused
on earlier moments in the policy process. But the nature of their visibility
is different in ways both useful and not for their goals.

The analysis in Chapter 3 lays a foundation for Chapters 4 and 5,
which are the core of my assessment of the policy influence of think
tanks. In Chapter 4, I examine how well different types of issues accommodate think tanks and policy experts generally. This macro analysis
takes a step beyond the core focus of the book, but different issues create
widely varying opportunities for experts. In Chapter 4, I examine how
these differences affect the cumulative opportunities for think tanks and
policy experts generally in three major issue debates: those over health
care and telecommunications reform in the 1990s and tax reduction in
2001. I find that at least four features of issue debates can affect the opportunities for experts to play meaningful roles: the nature of cumulative

knowledge among experts as an issue debate begins, the features of the debate's origins, the speed with which the debate is resolved, and the level of concern and mobilization by vested interests.

In Chapter 5, I examine differences in how successful think tanks and other experts are *within* issue debates in obtaining policy influence. Policy views may vary by the opportunities they present experts, but here my question is how effectively do think tanks and other experts perform against one another, whatever the cumulative opportunities for their work. I continue to draw on the three case studies for evidence: health care, telecommunications, and the tax cut. The analysis identifies a range of criteria relevant to how think tanks and experts generally make their work influential. The results suggest that the intentional efforts of experts matter greatly for how, when, and why their contributions are influential in policy making. It also supports the general conclusion that, while efforts to achieve visibility during policy deliberation and enactment have come to dominate the efforts of many think tanks, it is during agenda setting that think tanks and experts generally can often have their greatest substantive influence.

Millions of dollars have supported the proliferation of hundreds of new think tanks since 1970. But the cumulative substantive impact of think tanks has been impaired by the limits these organizations place on their own potential influence. By emphasizing visibility during the final rather than the early stages of the policy process and by the efforts of some organizations to put advancing ideology ahead of rigorous analysis, the substantive policy guidance of think tanks is often diminished. In Chapter 6, I conclude that the result is to render whatever influence think tanks and experts have as often more diffuse than direct. Their work may affect the general climate on issues but frequently cancels out as competing ammunition in final policy debates. The last chapter reconceptualizes the role of think tanks and policy experts in the policy process. I conclude by considering whether, by their own behaviors, think tanks have in many respects neutralized the power of expertise in American policy making.

2

The Evolution of Think Tanks

The only difference between you and me which may be of some significance is with regard to the proper function of a bureau of municipal research. It seems to me that in the long run the influence of such a bureau is enormously enhanced if it confines its function to investigation, study and recommendation, including such advice and help as may be necessary in securing the initial installation of improved methods adopted on its recommendation. You evidently, and quite logically, consider that the Bureau has an additional function, namely that of promotion, persuasion and agitation (another word that I use here without the slightest prejudice). Now these last named functions are all not only innocent but also highly desirable. My only point is that they interfere with that scientific detachment from partisan strife which would seem to be absolutely necessary if the Bureau's services are to be availed of to the best advantage by the particular administration that happens to be in power.[1]

> Correspondence from Jerome D. Greene, Executive Secretary of the Rockefeller Foundation, to Dr. William H. Allen, Director of the Bureau of Municipal Research, New York City, October 9, 1913

Navigating a course between distanced investigation and active promotion is not a new challenge for think tanks. As the excerpt above illustrates, leaders of think tanks have long been faced with trying to strike a suitable balance between careful "study and recommendation" and aggressive "persuasion and agitation." The debate – and disagreement – that existed about the appropriate role of the Bureau of Municipal Research in 1913 is quite similar to those that surround many think tanks at the beginning of the twenty-first century.

[1] Jerome Greene to William H. Allen, 9 October 1913, RG 1.1, Series 200, Box 14, Folder 147, Rockefeller Foundation Archives, North Tarrytown, New York.

The differences between the debates, however, are in how views are presented and with what consequences for the strategies and behavior of think tanks. Both the process of these debates and their outcomes have changed substantially over the century. As the number of think tanks has grown, they have become notably more diverse with regard to their size, scope of research, and intended policymaking audiences. These are noteworthy developments, but they have occurred within the context of two more striking and consequential changes: the establishment and growth of identifiable ideologies among think tanks, described in Chapter 1, and an increased emphasis in the strategies of think tanks on the marketing and promotion of research. In the next three chapters, I examine how these latter developments have had significant consequences for how expertise is used and becomes influential among policy makers. In this chapter, my focus is on how these two developments evolved. Both have taken shape since the 1960s, and they have reflected – and further contributed to – tensions for think tanks between achieving policy influence and maintaining credible reputations. Moreover, the developments have reinforced why it is critical to notice the intentional efforts of experts – separate from their expertise – in accounts of policy making.

I examine the origins of twelve think tanks, in greater and lesser detail, that formed during the twentieth century, and I explore features of the political environment as they affected opportunities for think tanks at two particular points: in the first decades of the twentieth century, when the first think tanks were forming, and in the last decades of the century, the period of substantial change among think tanks. All of the organizations examined in the chapter exemplify trends among think tanks generally at various points in the century. They are among the best-known organizations from each era and organizations that set the standard for other think tanks that emerged in each of the same periods. My evidence in the chapter is drawn from original archival records, news reports, and in-depth interviews with leaders and researchers at think tanks and those who fund them.[2]

The analysis suggests that think tanks more easily sustained a balance of influence and credibility through the 1960s because the policymaking environment valued "objective expertise" and because the funding environment for think tanks accommodated, even encouraged, their combined pursuit of credibility and low-profile influence with decision makers.

---

[2] These interviews constitute 45 of the 135 in-depth interviews conducted for the project as a whole. The names and affiliations of all of those interviewed are listed in Appendix B.

Beginning in the 1960s, American politics became more ideologically divisive. The number of politically committed and active conservatives grew substantially after Senator Barry Goldwater's 1964 presidential campaign, and over the same period, the business community recommitted itself to engaging the policymaking process. These developments were among those that combined to give rise to a proliferation of more ideological, particularly conservative, think tanks. They also created an environment in which the aggressive marketing of research became a more regular feature of think tank strategies. And while the aggressive marketing of think tank expertise is a development with roots largely similar to those of the emergence of identifiably ideological think tanks, the two developments have evolved separately in the past decade. Marketing has become a feature of the efforts of many think tanks, ideological and not.

Existing Views on Developments among Think Tanks

A growing literature in political science outlines how institutional design affects the ways in which ideas and expertise are useful in the policymaking process. Weir and Skocpol, for example, demonstrate how variations in the state structures of Sweden, Great Britain, and the United States help explain differences in how Keynesianism was adopted and employed in each country.[3] Peter Hall enumerates how intra-state institutional arrangements structured Britain's transition from Keynesian to monetarist economic policies in the 1970s and 1980s.[4] These studies consider how different national institutional configurations affect the ways in which specific research and ideas gain appeal among policy makers at different particular historical moments.

In this chapter, I examine how institutional configurations have important implications as well for the supply and production of ideas and expertise available to policy makers. I consider, in particular, how changes in specific features of American politics have affected the production and availability of expertise and ideas to policy makers from think tanks.

---

[3] Margaret Weir and Theda Skocpol, "State Structures and the Possibilities for 'Keynesian' Responses to the Great Depression in Sweden, Britain, and the United States," *Bringing the State Back In*, ed. by Peter B. Evans, Dietrich Rueschemeyer, and Theda Skocpol (New York: Cambridge University Press, 1985).

[4] Peter A. Hall, "The Movement from Keynesianism to Monetarism: Institutional Analysis and British Economic Policy in the 1970s," *Structuring Politics: Historical Institutionalism in Comparative Analysis*, ed. by Sven Steinmo, et al. (New York: Cambridge University Press, 1992).

In previous work about think tanks, David Ricci explains the proliferation of ideological think tanks by reference to the more accommodating political environment. He argues that the number of think tanks
has grown and become more ideological since the 1960s to accommodate
greater general uncertainty in the conduct of American politics and to
meet a demand by more and more diverse actors for active debate over
policy ideas and directions.[5] Ricci comments, "[T]hink tanks grew as
Washington responded to expertise and professionalism, the new class [of
a more secular and rational educated elite], more governmental roles and
agencies, the rise of minorities, and confusion over national purposes."[6]
He views think tanks as a logical outgrowth of a reorientation in American
politics that began in the 1960s and made ideas and competing ideologies
more central to and more contentious in the political process generally.

James Smith attributes the growth of ideological think tanks in recent decades to both change in the political environment and to the more
active efforts of political elites.[7] He describes how conservative intellectuals, in particular, propagated an anti-statist philosophy in the 1950s and
1960s that contributed to the ideological conflict that began to envelope
Washington in the 1970s. These developments, in turn, paved the way for
a proliferation of more ideological, particularly conservative, think tanks.
Conservatives built an intellectual infrastructure to expand political debates in ways that reevaluated the underlying premises used for decision
making in American politics. "Avowing that ideas were the only weapons
able to overturn the establishment and working diligently to build an establishment of their own, conservatives founded and strengthened scores
of institutions."[8]

Conditions may have been ripe, but the proliferation of financial patrons perhaps mattered even more. For scholars of modern conservatism,
the emergence of conservative think tanks, in particular, is attributable to
the efforts of conservative intellectuals along with corporate and ideological patrons, who formed think tanks and other organizations in order to
disrupt the political status quo.[9] My analysis considers these competing
claims and examines new evidence of the importance of organizational

[5] David M. Ricci, *The Transformation of American Politics: The New Washington and the Rise of Think Tanks* (New Haven, Conn.: Yale University Press, 1993).
[6] Ricci, *The Transformation of American Politics*, p. 208.
[7] James A. Smith, *The Idea Brokers* (New York: The Free Press, 1991).
[8] Smith, *The Idea Brokers*, p. 182.
[9] See, for example, Sidney Blumenthal, *The Rise of the Counter Establishment* (New York: Harper & Row, 1986).

and ideological developments for explaining the growth of ideological think tanks.[10]

In work about think tanks, relatively less attention is paid to the evolution of a more aggressive, marketing-oriented strategy among think tanks.[11] Some, like Smith, imply that a marketing orientation is a feature common to the more ideological think tanks of recent decades. Without disputing that point, my analysis indicates that marketing is not only a quite central feature of the efforts of many of the more ideological think tanks but increasingly a feature of think tanks that are not identifiably ideological as well. While the origins of the more marketing-oriented think tanks are the same ideological and organizational factors that spawned the emergence and growth of ideological think tanks, additional factors have become associated with the sustenance and strength of marketing-oriented strategies that suggest it may grow as a feature – indeed even

[10] These previous explanations of think tank formation have links to well-developed corollaries in interest group theory, which points in three directions relevant to understanding think tank origins. David Truman portrays organizational formation as a two-stage process that begins with greater specialization in specific sectors of society followed by mobilizing "disturbances" in the more complex political environment that trigger organization. A cogent critique of disturbance theory comes from Robert Salisbury, who observes that organizations often do not form even when disturbances occur and, furthermore, that there are many instances in which organizations have successfully formed without any evidence of disturbances at all. Salisbury argues "that interest group origins, growth, death, and associated lobbying activity may all be better explained if we regard them as exchange relationships between entrepreneurs/organizers, who invest capital in a set of benefits, which they offer to prospective members at a price – membership." Since the 1970s, there has been relatively little additional empirical study of the origins of interest groups. Organizational scholars have turned their attention instead to matters of group membership and maintenance in the wake of Mancur Olson's rational choice dictum that group membership – not to mention group formation – is basically irrational behavior. An exception, which offers the third possible direction of inquiry in relation to interest group origins, comes in the work of Jack Walker. In his study of interest group origins since 1960, Walker concludes that scholarly, mostly rational choice concerns about the reasons for – and lack of rationality of – group membership are essentially misdirected because financial patrons, far more than members, are the truly necessary feature in organizational formation as well as in long-term interest group maintenance. Entrepreneurs cannot begin an organization without financial backing, no matter what disturbances may make their cause important and group mobilization desirable. See David B. Truman, *The Governmental Process* (New York: Knopf, 1951), pp. 66-108; Robert H. Salisbury, "An Exchange Theory of Interest Groups," *Midwest Journal of Political Science*, 13 (1969): 1–32; Mancur Olsen, *The Logic of Collective Action* (Cambridge, Mass.: Harvard University Press, 1965); Jack L. Walker, Jr., *Mobilizing Interest Groups in America: Patrons, Professions, and Social Movements* (Ann Arbor: University of Michigan Press, 1991).

[11] For a partial exception, see David Ricci, *The Transformation of American Politics* (New Haven, Conn.: Yale University Press, 1993), Chapter 9.

become a central priority – of think tanks. Marketing may continue to evolve as a strategy of think tanks of all varieties.

The First Think Tanks: Reflections of a Progressive Ideal

The first national think tanks emerged just after the turn of the twentieth century with missions reflecting a Progressive Era confidence that expertise from the burgeoning social sciences could solve public problems and inform government decision making. Progressive reformers looked to experts to generate the "scientific knowledge" that would move policy making beyond rancorous log rolling and partisan patronage.[12] They aimed to make government reflect more efficient and professional standards. The Russell Sage Foundation and the Bureau of Municipal Research were the first think tanks to form in the twentieth century, and both were firmly established to reflect these ideals.

The Russell Sage Foundation was founded in 1907 by Margaret Olivia Sage, who endowed the new institution with a portion of her late husband's substantial fortune. It began with a mission to promote "the improvement of social and living conditions in the United States of America." The Foundation was intended to contribute to the turn-of-the-century charity movement, as an institution that could both define standards for the social work occupation and find systemic solutions for the broader social problems to which the movement was addressed.[13] Knowledge and efficiency were watchwords for the evolving movement and were at the core of Russell Sage's original mission. Early on, the Foundation "played a central role in a national movement to alleviate poverty through the professionalization of social work, the study of social problems, the shaping of legislation, and the creation of private agencies designed to meet specific social needs."[14]

The Bureau of Municipal Research, also incorporated in 1907, took as its mission the efficient reform of government, rather than the solution of social ills. The Bureau evolved from efforts by New York businessmen and intellectuals, who placed high value on the establishment of defensible – and enforceable – budget and accounting standards in the city of

---

[12] On this transition, see Stephen Skowronek, *Building a New American State: The Expansion of National Administrative Capacities, 1877–1920* (New York: Cambridge University Press, 1982).

[13] David C. Hammack and Stanton Wheeler, *Social Science in the Making: Essays on the Russell Sage Foundation, 1907–1972* (New York: Russell Sage Foundation, 1994), p. 3.

[14] Hammack and Wheeler, *Social Science in the Making*, p. 12.

New York. The formation of the Bureau followed publicity about city patronage scandals. Its mission was to meet the "'supreme need' for an 'agency dependent neither upon politics nor upon an average public intelligence.'"[15] Its leaders brought academic credentials from top universities, in both finance and law, and a zeal for making government a more efficient provider of public goods and services.

In their formation at the beginning of the previous century, both Russell Sage and the Bureau of Municipal Research reflected the broader Progressive movement ideology of depoliticizing public decision making. As Critchlow remarks of the wider group of reformers at the time:

These "scientific" reformers, as social scientists and businessmen saw themselves, hoped to restore political order and representative government to American society. All of the measures proposed by the reformers – [which included] the elimination of party labels in municipal elections, the shortening of the ballot, the reduction of the number of elected officials, the weakening of the legislative branch of government, the enacting of an executive budget system, and the shifting of decision making as far as possible from elected bodies – were intended to accomplish a single goal: the *depoliticization of the political process*. In response to machine politics and other perceived excesses, reformers sought to take power away from the partisan politicians who dominated government in the post–Civil War period and to place government administration in the hands of non-partisan experts.[16]

The reformist ideology that dominated the Progressive Era placed a premium on the promise of objective social science and the contributions of experts in devising solutions to public problems.

Money made in the Industrial Revolution formed the core endowment for the Russell Sage Foundation, and industrial-era businessmen made up the early nucleus of support for the Bureau of Municipal Research. Fulton Cutting, a New York banker–turned-philanthropist, led the way in establishing the Bureau, donating $10,000 to its formation.[17] Cutting had been active in the "scientific reform" movement for decades, having served as president of the Association for Improving the Condition of the Poor (AICP) since 1883. The AICP was a merchant association formed in 1843 to aid the destitute. By the turn of the twentieth

---

[15] William H. Allen, *Efficient Democracy* (New York: Macmillan, 1907), 284–5, as quoted in Jonathan Kahn, *Budgeting Democracy: State Building and Citizenship in America, 1890–1928* (Ithaca, N.Y.: Cornell University Press, 1997), 42.

[16] Donald T. Critchlow, *The Brookings Institution, 1916–1952: Expertise and the Public Interest in a Democratic Society* (DeKalb: Northern Illinois University Press, 1985), 17.

[17] Cutting's contribution actually came in the year preceding the Bureau's incorporation, when it operated under the name Bureau of City Betterment.

century, its members had turned their attention to root causes and solutions to problems of poverty and inequality. Cutting was part of a
group that believed making city government more efficient could help
solve broader social problems. He became caught up in the movement to
produce scientific knowledge in order to solve root inefficiencies in city
government.[18]

Within seven years, the Bureau had spent nearly $1 million and had
secured financial contributions from more than 500 different sources,
mostly businessmen. The list of the largest contributors reads like a "who's
who" among giants of industry. John D. Rockefeller Sr. led the group,
providing more than $150,000 in personal support to the Bureau between
1907 and 1914.[19] Fulton Cutting, Andrew Carnegie, E. H. Harriman, and
J. P. Morgan rounded out the group of largest contributors. They, together
with Rockefeller, supplied almost half of the Bureau's support in its first
seven years.[20]

The commitment of the business sector to expertise and scientific management of government came on the heels of massive industrial growth
in the country, when, by many accounts, the very success of industry
leaders helped give rise to new forms of social and economic instability.
Businessmen had selfish reasons for supporting the professionalization of
government administration. Bringing clear and objective standards – akin
to business standards – to government might create an environment that
would enhance their success and ameliorate the social problems caused
by industrialization. Business leaders had a clear interest in promoting the
development of social reforms that would prevent disaffected industrial
workers from mobilizing against them. If, along the way, such reforms
limited the extent of patronage and partisan squabbling in government,
all the better.[21]

However selfish their motives may have been – in fact, perhaps because
of them – the missions of the first think tanks were not identifiably ideological, and their strategies were not visibly promotional. The new think
tanks had missions consistent with the scientific, knowledge-based movement toward efficient government. As Jonathan Kahn observes, despite

---

[18] Donald T. Critchlow, *The Brookings Institution, 1916–1952*, p. 19.

[19] Statement on the Origins of the Bureau of Municipal Research, 1915, RG1.1, Series 200,
Box 14, Folder 148, Rockefeller Foundation Archives, North Tarrytown, New York.

[20] Statement on the Origins of the Bureau of Municipal Research, Rockefeller Foundation
Archives.

[21] Neil J. Mitchell, *The Generous Corporation* (New Haven, Conn.: Yale University Press,
1989).

tensions in how the aims of the Bureau of Municipal Research should be pursued, it

maintained a remarkably low profile in light of the wide-ranging goals it hoped to achieve. Rather than overly dominate public debate on government administration, the bureau sought to define and control the terms of the debate by supplying the information and the vocabulary needed to assess and discuss the city's needs. The bureau thus established its authority indirectly by urging people to defer to and act on the information it provided while presenting itself simply as a neutral conduit of information.[22]

The business leaders and individuals who provided the financial support to the early think tanks were the strongest advocates for their pursuing reform through objective, scientific research and low-profile efforts in policy making. The excerpt at the beginning of the chapter represents, after all, an appeal from funder to think tank (Rockefeller Foundation to the Bureau of Municipal Research) to maintain a distance from political debates and an exclusive focus instead on careful investigation.

The Bureau of Municipal Research became a model for scores of similar municipal agencies that formed around the country in the early 1900s, and the core set of BMR founders became active in discussions to create a bureau to pursue reform of the national budgeting process. These discussions began in the wake of mounting federal debt, when President William Howard Taft in 1910 created a commission to study government administration and budgeting. Frederick Cleveland, one of the founders of the Bureau of Municipal Research, was appointed its director. The Taft Commission, as it was called, proposed to Congress in 1912 a unified, national, executive-controlled budget process. Unpopular among members of Congress for the increased executive authority that it would have created, the Commission was disbanded and its report shelved. The recommendations had been entirely abandoned by the time Woodrow Wilson became president in 1913.

Despite the dissolution of the commission, the idea for a federal budget process remained popular among Cleveland and his staff, which included Frank Goodnow, a professor of law at Columbia University, and William Willoughby, a statistician with the U.S. Labor Department. The men decided that an independent organization should become the advocate for a professionalized budget process. Goodnow and Willoughby were to become chairman and director, respectively, of what was to become the

[22] Jonathan Kahn, *Budgeting Democracy*, p. 64.

Institute for Government Research, the first domestically focused, national, Washington-based think tank.

In 1914, when the Taft Commission was a distant memory, Frederick Cleveland began conferring with Jerome Greene, executive secretary of the fledgling Rockefeller Foundation, about an independent institution that could continue to work on a centralized national budget process as well as find ways to increase efficiency in the national administration of government. The Institute for Government Research (IGR) was incorporated in 1916, with a mission to pursue a nonpartisan, efficient administrative state. Greene, Cleveland, Goodnow, Willoughby, and the others were among the small group that started the organization with principles enumerated in a 1915 charter that began:

> The government of the United States is one of the largest and technically one of the most complicated business undertakings in the world. . . . No question before the people of the United States is of more urgent practical importance than this: How can the citizens exercise intelligent and effective control over the joint public business? . . . Differences of opinion are bound to arise as to the methods by which public moneys shall be raised, and the purposes for which public moneys shall be spent, but there can be no difference of opinion among good citizens as to the urgent necessity for efficiency and intelligent economy of administration.[23]

The leaders of the first think tanks were not without concern for the organizations' political strategies and how best they might become visible among decision makers. The IGR's founders intentionally selected a board of trustees composed of men of high academic rank and with diverse partisan affiliations to provide balance and to promote the appearance of nonpartisanship. Jerome Greene reflected years later, "The college presidents, business men and others in the list were invited to serve with the frank statement that their chief function was to vouch before the public for the integrity of the enterprise and its freedom from the slightest political bias."[24] In their selection of the IGR's first president, trustees and supporters were acutely aware of the challenges facing a nongovernmental research institute trying to influence government decision making. Greene

---

[23] *Institute for Government Research Prospectus*, 1 May 1915, Administration – Formal and Informal Histories, Box 2, Folder 11, Brookings Institution Archive, Washington, D.C. Sounding a similar note on the day of its founding, the *New York Times* reported, "An Institute for Government Research was incorporated here today, the fundamental purpose of which, according to its incorporators, is to apply the test of efficient business methods to administrative and governmental activities and to cooperate with public officers in promoting efficiency" ("For Efficient Government" 1916: 6).

[24] Jerome D. Greene to Robert D. Calkins, 29 April 1954, Administration – Formal and Informal Histories, Box 1, Folder 1, Brookings Institution Archive, Washington, D.C.

preferred William Willoughby, who was ultimately chosen as first president, over Cleveland, the early front runner for the post, because he felt the latter did not possess the "capacity for concise and lucid expression so necessary in obtaining congressional and public support."[25]

Despite such concerns, these leaders recognized that independence from government, specific interests, and business was essential for gaining credibility in the political process. And the dominant ideology of the Progressive movement was one that favored objective, scientific knowledge and the selection of an independent and credible board of directors. With this, the early think tanks were able to nurture credibility and access simultaneously – in an environment where they complemented one another and were jointly appreciated by policy makers and potential funders alike.

The simultaneous nurturing of credibility and subtle access reflected the preferences of those supporting the early think tanks. The Institute for Government Research benefited from many of the same initial funders as the Bureau of Municipal Research. John D. Rockefeller and Fulton Cutting each supplied $10,000 in the first five years. Other large contributors at the outset were Cleveland Dodge, J. P. Morgan, and Robert S. Brookings. The IGR received no support from foundations in its first five years. But through the same period during which the Institute for Government Research established itself, private philanthropy was emerging as a new force in American society.

The Rockefeller Foundation was chartered in 1913 with an endowment, after five years, of $180 million. A novelty at the time, the foundation was intended "to promote the well-being and to advance civilization . . . in the acquisition and dissemination of knowledge, in the prevention and relief of suffering, and in the promotion of any and all of the elements of human progress."[26] Such broadly focused, well-endowed philanthropies were a new product of the industrial era, and supporting the fledgling social sciences was but one of the many early commitments of Rockefeller and other new foundations. For the social science organizations that received it, foundation support became irreplaceable.

At the beginning of the century, Rockefeller and the Rockefeller Foundation became the single greatest contributors to the Institute for Government Research and several other think tanks. Robert Brookings, taking on a fundraising role for the new IGR soon after its formation, helped

[25] Jerome D. Greene to Robert D. Calkins, 29 April 1954.
[26] Raymond B. Fosdick, *The Story of the Rockefeller Foundation* (New York: Harper and Brothers Publishers, 1952), p. 15.

secure a seven-year $525,000 grant from Rockefeller.[27] The Foundation provided similar core support in the early days for the National Bureau of Economic Research (NBER), formed in 1919.[28]

The Carnegie Foundation (today the Carnegie Corporation) began a grantmaking program similar to, if more narrow than, that of the Rockefeller Foundation early in the century. It too provided substantial support to NBER in its early days. Additionally, the Carnegie Foundation was a principal funder of the Institute of Economics in its first years. The Institute combined in 1927 with the Institute for Government Research and another unit to become the Brookings Institution.[29] Finally, among the industrial-era philanthropists, Andrew Carnegie provided an endowment to form the free-standing Carnegie Endowment for International Peace in 1910, a think tank to provide research and education in the areas of international affairs and U.S. foreign policy. Each of these new think tanks and several others that formed in the early decades of the twentieth century reflected the Progressive ideals of their founding supporters.[30]

The industrial magnates who were first interested in supporting social research saw it as wholly desirable for think tanks to form and become credible voices in policymaking circles without becoming promotional or marketing-oriented. Those who supported the first think tanks, in fact, actively discouraged the organizations from including high-profile marketing among their efforts. John Rockefeller was creating his private foundation at the same time that the federal government was filing suit to demand dissolution of his Standard Oil Company.[31] In this environment, many in Congress were openly critical of Rockefeller's attempts to commit part of his fortune to a philanthropic trust by which, they feared, he might extend his reach and power. In making contributions to the new think tanks, Rockefeller and his associates had an interest in establishing the organizations' unassailable credibility and perceived independence and in their avoiding activities that might make them appear at all political as opposed to scholarly. Reflecting on what should be the initial mission of

---

[27] Dr. Harold G. Moulton to Mr. Jerome D. Greene, 3 April 1952, Administration Records and Research Materials, Formal and Informal Histories, Box 2, Folder 12, Brookings Institution Archive, Washington, D.C.

[28] National Bureau of Economic Research, Docket of Laura Spellman Rockefeller Memorial Fund, RG2F, Box 18, Folder 143, Rockefeller Archive Center, Tarrytown, New York.

[29] Memo from B. Ruml to the Rockefeller Foundation, LSRM, Record Group 5II–6, Series B–49, Folder 517, Rockefeller Archive Center, Tarrytown, New York.

[30] James Smith provides a lengthy, careful, and colorful history of these early years. James A. Smith, *The Idea Brokers* (New York: The Free Press, 1991), Chapters 2 and 3.

[31] See Fosdick, *The Story of the Rockefeller Foundation*.

the Institute of Economics in the years before its formation, its soon-to-be founders concluded:

Although it is recognized that there is great need of popular education in economics, it is inadvisable that such work of propaganda be undertaken as the first or main task of an institution for scientific research. . . . It is essential for the permanent standing of an institute of economic research that it should early establish its reputation as scientific, impartial, and unprejudiced in its finding and presenting of the facts as to economic and social conditions. It should not only gain the confidence of the scientific world, but it should also be careful to avoid, as far as is consistent with its objects, the popular prejudice which might conceivably attend an enterprise generously supported by a great capitalist.[32]

Founders of the National Bureau of Economic Research shared similar concerns. Out of concern that support from the Rockefeller Foundation might compromise perceptions of its credibility, the NBER sought the written approval of labor organizations before accepting Rockefeller support.[33]

The Middle of the Century

With the onset of the Great Depression, faith in purely scientific analysis and detached administrative solutions to social problems diminished. However, direct expert intervention in political decision making became more common. Brookings, the National Bureau for Economic Research, and other think tanks continued their policy work, but their scholars became more and more drawn into making political judgments as well. Think tanks had become effectively established in American politics, but intellectual and ideological currents were changing. The almost undisputed confidence in expertly devised administrative solutions to public problems was threatened. Reflecting on this period, Smith writes:

Instead of disinterested knowledge that fostered a consensus on policy solutions, [the work of experts] was now a knowledge that served political actors, justifying policies and rationalizing political convictions. No doubt, experts and intellectuals in power had always been tempted by power. But with modern demands for

---

[32] Statement of Institute of Economic Research, RF1.1, Series 200, Box 26, Folder 290, Rockefeller Archive Center, Tarrytown, New York.

[33] The president of NBER wrote labor organizations a letter asking "whether or not you would approve our approaching Mr. Rockefeller for the purposes of the Economic Foundation, and stating to him that such approach had your approval." NBER President to Mr. George Soule, 17 October 1922, RFA2F, Box 18, Folder 143, Rockefeller Archive Center, Tarrytown, New York.

expertise so great – especially after a decade of crisis – the distance between knowledge and power was being bridged routinely. And as the gap between experts and the political leaders was closed and the experts were drawn into roles as administrators and policy planners, knowledge began to look less like a form of higher intellectual counsel than simply another instrument of political power.[34]

With the national government more active in domestic and, ultimately with World War II, in international affairs than ever before, demands for policy research and technical analysis intensified. The uses of this knowledge were changing. Public officials began hiring social scientists directly. President Franklin D. Roosevelt formed his "brains trust." With the onset of American participation in World War II, many nonprofit policy advisory organizations were formed to provide technical research to the military, including studies of weapons' uses, combat techniques, and an array of tactical and strategic topics.[35]

The RAND Corporation emerged as the largest and most broadly focused of the new groups. Initially a Douglas Aircraft subsidiary that provided research to the Air Force, RAND became an autonomous nonprofit think tank after World War II, reliant almost entirely on government contracts for support. The government became a direct provider of think tank financial support. RAND became the progenitor of "systems analysis" research for the combined military, "oriented toward the analysis of broad strategies and policy questions, and particularly seeking to clarify choice under conditions of great uncertainty."[36]

The establishment of RAND and the direct involvement of social scientists and think tanks in political decision making reflected a general trend of government intervention to solve social and political problems. The Great Depression had provided evidence that administrative solutions to social problems could be untenable or at least unreliable. Yet with the end of the second World War, a revised consensus arose that government was at least a necessary and appropriate manager of social and political problems, even if it could not solve them. Experts with ideas for this management were crucial. Government had become involved not

---

[34] Smith, *The Idea Brokers*, p. 94.

[35] The total number of nonprofit research organizations that existed to provide support to the military by the immediate post–World War II period is unclear. By some accounts, the number of military research institutes reached as high as 350. As Bruce L.R. Smith points out, however, "There are no data which substantiate this estimate, and idiosyncrasies of definition could in any case substantially expand or contract the number of 'nonprofit organizations.'" Bruce L.R. Smith, *The RAND Corporation: Case Study of a Nonprofit Advisory Corporation* (Cambridge, Mass.: Harvard University Press, 1966), p. 6.

[36] Smith, *The RAND Corporation*, p. 8.

just in administering social welfare programs but in managing the economy generally. Herbert Stein, at the time a think tank economist and later to become chairman of President Richard M. Nixon's Council of Economic Advisors, reflects, "It was a time when sophisticated economics became used in the policy discussion process – mainly Keynesianism and anti-Keynesianism. You began to have economists in the government, so the language of the policy discussion became much more sophisticated, and everybody needed an economist if they were going to participate in the debate."[37]

This prevailing philosophy of government intervention and management favored the efforts and contributions of think tanks. Growth – and belief in growth – in government enhanced institutional demand for independent ideas and experts, which think tanks were equipped to provide. The financial supporters of think tanks favored their taking shape in ways that established their independence. They expected their strict adherence to conventions for social science research.

The Beginnings of Change

With the explicit backing of big business, the Committee for Economic Development (CED) emerged in 1942, representing a new variant on existing think tank models. Anticipating the end of the war, business leaders were concerned with generating high employment in a postwar economy. Marion B. Folsom, one of the CED's founders and treasurer of Eastman Kodak Company, observed: "The problem is to find jobs in the post-war period for eight to nine million more persons than were employed in 1940 and to increase the output of goods and services by 35 percent. . . . To bring about this increase in civilian employment and output in two years time is a most difficult assignment. This is largely the task of private industry."[38]

A research organization like the CED was deemed necessary to provide ideas for this undertaking. Business support of the CED was explicit, with collaborative links to the Chamber of Commerce and the National Association of Manufacturers. The CED's reports were issued by and with the endorsement of the committee of businesspeople overseeing its operation. Yet, if the CED took a slightly different institutional form than conventional think tanks at the time, it did not deviate from the

[37] Interview with Herbert Stein, American Enterprise Institute, Washington, D.C., September 24, 1997.
[38] "Bids Industry Plan for Post-War Jobs." *The New York Times*, 13 February 1943, p. 20.

prevailing orthodoxy about the role of expertise in government. Herbert Stein, an economist at the CED in the 1940s, recalls that the organization supported "managed fiscal policy, and things that the business community actually didn't generally like.... The CED was seen as a kind of maverick in the business community. It became influential because it was a group of business people saying things that business-people didn't ordinarily say, which gave it a kind of credibility."[39]

While perhaps a maverick in the business community, by conforming to prevailing economic ideas and organizing in order to conduct research, the CED was closely akin to other think tanks. It was staffed by a group of economists, mostly trained at the University of Chicago, and it conformed to the standards of systematic data-driven research set by existing think tanks. By measure of its reference in the *New York Times* around the period of its founding, the CED was a quite visible actor in postwar debates, achieving reference in sixty stories between 1943 and 1945. In its seeming success early on, the CED signaled a somewhat broader institutional space for think tanks at that time, one in which organizations might vary from one another and still share credibility and political access.

The American Enterprise Association (AEA) took shape in 1943 with seed money from Louis Brown of the Johns Manville Corporation. More conservative and anti-government than the CED and seemingly at odds with the prevailing ideological environment at the time, the AEA, renamed the American Enterprise Institute in 1960, wallowed in relative obscurity in its first decades of existence. Distant from conventions of the period, both in ideology and in its organization, the AEA gained little notice or support until the 1960s, receiving no references in the *New York Times* in its first seven years of existence.

Shifting Currents: Ideological and Organizational Change in the 1960s

By the 1960s, the established efforts of think tanks to produce ideas and expertise for policy makers in ways that balanced their sustained credibility with efforts to obtain political access were becoming less compatible with an evolving ideological and organizational environment. Most notably, the objective nature and value of expertise in the political process was under question. Until this time, think tanks had more or less consistently provided ideas and social science expertise to advance the development of administrative and managerial – government-based – solutions to

---

[39] Stein interview, September 24, 1997.

public problems. They worked hand in hand with government, growing in number slowly and adapting as government itself expanded between the 1920s and 1960s. The political nature and objective quality of their work varied, but their prescriptions were almost invariably in terms of governmental solutions. In the 1960s, as government itself grew larger and larger, the desirability and possibility of achieving social change through government programs became doubtful. Some of the problems themselves – the lack of civil rights protections for blacks and the Vietnam conflict – were immense and highly divisive. In this context, the relationship between the traditional attributes of think tanks and the demands of the political environment faced new tensions, which were reflected in new organizations of the period.

The Hudson Institute and the Institute for Policy Studies, founded in 1961 and 1963 respectively, shared little by way of mission or outlook. The Hudson Institute had roots in the defense establishment's RAND Corporation, founded a quarter-century earlier. Herman Kahn, Hudson's founder, had spent twelve years at RAND when he decided to form his own organization in collaboration with another RAND researcher and an MIT mathematician. Through its early years, the Institute strongly reflected Kahn's interests and style.

Kahn founded the Hudson Institute soon after the release of his controversial book *On Thermonuclear War*, an analysis of strategies for and likely implications of a full-scale nuclear war.[40] It was a provocative book taken by some, including a reviewer in *Scientific American*, as a "moral tract of mass murder: how to plan it, how to commit it, how to get away with it, how to justify it."[41] Kahn and his many defenders viewed it instead as simply a realistic exploration of the possible scenarios and outcomes involved in a nuclear conflict, scenarios few were willing to consider publicly at the time.

Never shrinking from controversy, Kahn aimed to keep himself and his new Institute in the eye of policy makers. He encouraged his researchers at Hudson to push the boundaries of conventional subjects and analytic approaches. In a 1971 profile, Kahn was described as

engaging, witty, friendly, and frank. . . . Punctuated by occasional stammers, wheezing, snorts, and chuckles, his words flow rapidly and without the slightest trace of self-consciousness. Talking to him is not unlike talking with a hyperactive,

---

[40] Herman Kahn, *On Thermonuclear War* (Princeton, N.J.: Princeton University Press, 1960).
[41] Paul Dickson, *Think Tanks* (New York: Atheneum, 1971), p. 107.

oracular New York cab driver who has both a sense of where he's going and of what he feels he must communicate to you before the ride is over.[42]

With Kahn at the helm, Hudson was supported in its early years by government contracts, primarily through the U.S. Department of Defense, which were relatively abundant in the early 1960s. But Hudson's attention to big and often unconventional ideas, at the expense sometimes of practical detail, made it an occasional target of criticism within government.[43] In one instance, as Dickson recalls:

> Senator Thomas F. Eagleton of Missouri...wrote to his constituents, "Recently...the Hudson Institute, perhaps the nation's best-known think tank, contributed the suggestion [to the Pentagon] that we dig a moat around Saigon....I wonder how much that cost the taxpayers of Missouri?" Arkansas Senator J. William Fulbright, in an August 1969 speech, had similar words for the moat and also commented dryly on a plan to dam up the Amazon. "I understand," he said, "that it did not appeal to the Latin Americans."[44]

Far from insulating itself from ideological conflict, Hudson appeared to its critics and admirers alike to produce studies that reflected preformed values, albeit values that did not always fit neatly into conventional categories. In a 1963 profile of Hudson in the *New York Times Magazine*, Herzog described the bulk of personnel at the Institute as "liberal Democrats."[45] Yet in relation to their research, Hudson was more often characterized as conservative in inclination. In particular, Hudson researchers brought to their work a set of values about the necessity of promoting world order and democracy. Such inclinations were visible, for example, in a late 1960s study of Angola that essentially validated Portuguese colonization and continued rule of the country. As Dickson recalls, "In this case, Hudson's politically Rightist predilection

---

[42] Dickson, *Think Tanks*, p. 109.

[43] Hudson drew fire from the government in a 1968 report in which the General Accounting Office found that "Seven of the 11 study reports submitted by the Hudson Institute under the three contracts were considered either to be less useful than had been expected or to require major revision." Ironically, Hudson fellow George Wittman observed of Hudson around the same period (although not in reference to the GAO report), "We're the product of affluence, and people with money come to us as an oracle because they can afford an oracle and, who knows, they may get something out of it.... [But] if I were in a company and one of my men told me he was going to the Hudson Institute for a study, I'd probably fire him." The GAO report is *Observations on the Administration by the Office of Civil Defense of Research Study Contracts Awarded to Hudson Institute, Inc.* B-133209. 25 March 1968, p. 2. The comment from Wittman comes from Dickson, p. 92.

[44] Dickson, *Think Tanks*, p. 106.

[45] Arthur Herzog, "Report on a 'Think Factory.'" *New York Times Magazine*, 10 November 1963, p. 40.

dictated taking the [research] contract. It is safe to conclude, moreover, that Hudson would not have hired itself out to those trying to rid Angola of Portuguese rule."[46]

Quite different in emphasis and operation, the Institute for Policy Studies (IPS), founded in 1963, reflected both in its organization and operation the liberal and progressive inclinations of its founders, Marcus Raskin and Richard Barnet. Having met while serving in the Kennedy administration, Raskin and Barnet wanted to create an independent intellectual foundation from which to develop ways to promote peace and equality and to end the arms race and the Cold War. IPS used a variety of strategies for achieving social change and disseminating its research, ranging from seminars with congressional staff to grassroots organizing. In a 1969 profile of IPS, senior fellow Arthur Waskow is quoted as characterizing the institution in its early days as

committed to the view that to develop social theory, one must be involved in social action and experiment. Toward this end, he advocated "creative disorder," which, he said, means "to simply keep experimenting and to discover at what point one is neither smashed nor ignored, but creates enough change to move the society." Admitting a "gut preference for disorder," Mr. Waskow said IPS "stands on the bare edge of custom in the United States as to what an education research institution is."[47]

Uninterested in government research and development contracts, IPS began its work with the support of the Ford Foundation and several wealthy liberal benefactors.

As different as they were, both Hudson and IPS broke with some of the institutional conventions associated with think tanks, particularly norms of neutrality and academic objectivity. Neither Kahn nor Barnet and Raskin held Ph.D.s, historically the degree of think tank scholars. And both institutions seemed as concerned with staffing their organizations with creative and aggressive intellectuals as with those who might have obtained a long list of academic credentials. Both organizations doggedly defended – and gained respect for – the quality and accuracy of their research products, but Hudson and IPS were more dogmatic and unrestrained than their think tank forebears. One of Hudson's first brochures

---

[46] Dickson, p. 103. Dickson goes on to observe, "Though the Angola study is more obvious than many, it underscores the fact that Hudson, like most of America's think tanks, is a political entity that, to varying degrees, does all but its most technological thinking along ideological lines. . . . In fairness, however, few show Rightward bias as blatantly as Hudson does."

[47] Shirley Scheibla, "Ivory-Tower Activists," *Barron's*, 13 October 1969, p. 9.

boldly declared, "While the institute will not seek to be foolishly ideal-
istic, it does believe that the existence of large numbers of readily de-
liverable H-bombs and an active arms race make it necessary to devote
serious, detailed, informed thought to such things as disarmament and
world government."[48] IPS fellow Milton Kotler made his more activist,
as opposed to intellectual, interests clear at the beginning of a report
to the Urban Affairs subcommittee of the Joint Economic Committee of
Congress. He began, "At the outset, let me say that this paper is not a
study. It is an argument . . . intending to persuade you toward a course in
urban legislation. . . ."[49]

The success of Hudson and IPS reflected a changing political context
in which confidence in straightforward social science expertise was weakening and the debate over the nation's political ideals was broadening.
By most accounts, the core aspirations of think tanks – credibility and
political access – were being achieved by Hudson and IPS; but in a changing political environment, achieving them was becoming difficult. The
attributes were being demonstrated in different ways.

The debate over the role and effectiveness of government was engaged
by a new think tank voice in 1969 with the founding of the Urban Institute. Often characterized as the "domestic RAND Corporation," the
Urban Institute relied on government contract support to evaluate the
social welfare programs created as part of the Great Society. The Urban
Institute dates back to the addition of legislative language in a U.S. Department of Housing and Urban Development bill in the mid-1960s, explicitly
providing funds for program evaluation. The legislation stated that "the
secretary shall have available to him one percent of all money appropriated for the purpose of evaluating this legislation." From that narrow
beginning, William Gorham, founding president of the Urban Institute, recalls "they tacked [that clause] onto a whole bunch of new legislation, and
that was the beginning of the [domestic] evaluation industry. . . . Money
created the industry."[50] Ironically, though a creation of the Great Society,
the Urban Institute and the "evaluation industry" of which it was a part
uncovered evidence of the failures of many social programs.[51] With the

[48] Herzog, pp. 30, 35.
[49] Scheibla, p. 9.
[50] Interview with William Gorham, The Urban Institute, Washington, D.C., August 1, 1996.
[51] On the research critical of the Great Society, see Henry J. Aaron, *Politics and the Professors:
The Great Society in Perspective* (Washington, D.C.: The Brookings Institution Press, 1978).
On the rationale of researchers during this period, see especially pp. 155–9. On the uneven
quality and depth of this research, see Alice M. Rivlin, *Systematic Thinking for Social Action*
(Washington, D.C.: The Brookings Institution Press, 1971).

government's financial backing, the research actually contributed to the further erosion of confidence in social welfare programs and the expertise that had created their architecture.

A New Wave of Ideological and Organizational Change: The Conservative Swing

At the same time that Hudson, IPS, and the Urban Institute were forming in the 1960s, four broader political developments were setting the context for the proliferation of a disproportionate number of conservative think tanks beginning in the 1970s: (1) the political mobilization of business and corporations, (2) the political conversion and aggressive advocacy of neoconservative intellectuals, (3) the political mobilization of evangelical and fundamentalist Christians, and (4) the ascendance of neoclassical economic theory at universities and among key policy makers. These developments occurred concurrently through the 1960s and 1970s, but they had separate origins and different consequences for the ideological and funding environment in which the number of think tanks expanded. The developments combined to mark a clear turning point for what might be the characteristics and strategies of think tanks in American policy making.

Political Mobilization of Corporate Interests

The events that account for the expansion of corporate involvement in American politics in the 1960s and 1970s are disputed.[52] The widened extent of this involvement is not. Through the 1960s and 1970s, scores of businesses opened new, well-staffed corporate and trade association offices in Washington, D.C.; by one count, the number of trade associations

---

[52] Cathie Jo Martin argues that increased business involvement in the political process through this period had roots in the efforts of Presidents Kennedy and Johnson in the early 1960s to mobilize business leaders in support of free trade proposals. Johnson fostered business involvement in efforts to persuade reluctant members of Congress of the merits of his Great Society housing programs. Martin argues that it was through these mostly friendly interactions between government and business in the 1960s that an organizational foundation, by which business could organize opposition to government regulation and intervention, was created in the 1970s. She observes: "The administrations encouraged firms to create their own public affairs units [and,] although Presidents have always turned to business elites for advice, the sixties mobilization strategy brought the corporate rank and file into the policy process.... The Democratic Administrations, by building coalitions in support of legislative initiatives, helped business to think of their interests in more collective terms, and this moved business toward the organization of class interests." Cathie Jo Martin, "Business and the New Economic Activism: The Growth of Corporate Lobbies in the Sixties," *Polity*, 27 (1994): 49–76.

with offices in Washington jumped from 99 in 1960 to 229 by 1969.[53] And by 1972, with the formation of the Business Roundtable, the CEOs of many Fortune 500 companies became personally involved in Washington policy making. The Business Roundtable acted to advance and protect the shared interests of business.[54]

By all accounts, corporate might was becoming substantial – and increasingly antagonistic toward government – by the mid-1970s.[55] Business leaders were concerned with declining productivity and profits along with stagflation – combined high inflation and unemployment – at a time when government regulation of the business sector was expanding. By the mid-1970s, as Vogel reports,

corporations became highly visible and sophisticated participants in the political process. Attempting to influence the political agenda and policy outcomes, they hired large numbers of lobbyists and lawyers, opened Washington offices, established and funded political action committees (PACs), expanded the size of their governmental relations staffs, developed sophisticated strategies for influencing public opinion, and learned how to mobilize the "grass roots."[56]

A New Cadre of Neoconservatives

Through roughly the same period that business involvement in government decision making accelerated, a new intellectual movement emerged, reflecting a disillusionment with the tenets of socialism and liberalism. Neoconservatism's roots were in the intellectual transformations of a class of primarily New York–based intellectuals. Irving Kristol, Daniel Bell, and Nathan Glazer were prominent among a group whose anti-communist beliefs turned into an aggressive pro-Americanism in the 1960s, in opposition to the disorder and excess created by government and social protest. Many among them were former immigrants who believed that the United States provided rich opportunities for those who were loyal and hardworking to succeed.[57]

Their vision gained voice through *The Public Interest*, a journal founded in 1965 that became an important forum through which prominent

---

[53] Martin, "Business and the New Economic Activism," p. 72.
[54] On the Business Roundtable, see Blumenthal, *The Rise of the Counter Establishment*, pp. 55–80.
[55] David Vogel, *Fluctuating Fortunes: The Political Power of Business in America* (New York: Basic Books, 1989).
[56] David Vogel, *Kindred Strangers: The Uneasy Relationship between Politics and Business in America* (Princeton, N.J.: Princeton University Press, 1996), pp. 5–6.
[57] See Peter Steinfels, *The Neoconservatives: The Men Who Are Changing America's Politics* (New York: Touchstone Books, 1979).

intellectuals could make pronouncements about social and foreign policy that found an attentive readership among Washington policy makers. The articles – and the ideology generally – questioned the premises underlying government policies in a wide range of areas. Although neoconservatism was often characterized as a diffuse ideology, Seymour Martin Lipset captured the essence of it in a 1986 speech describing its origins. He observes:

A number of prominent intellectuals, with roots in the anti-Stalinist left, were dismayed by the rise of the increasingly influential New Left and New Politics tendencies which they perceived as soft on Communism. They were especially critical of the student movement and identified many of the new single issue movements that had developed in the sixties as somehow linked together in undermining resistance to Communism. These reactions gradually led them to concentrate on fighting the anti-anti-Communist left. They continued, however, to favor welfare state policies and support trade unions.[58]

Political Mobilization of Fundamentalist Christians

A third and slightly later change in the political environment involved the political mobilization of fundamentalist and evangelical Christians. Hodgson explains that Christian fundamentalists started to become politically attuned through the 1950s and 1960s, a period when their numbers were also growing, as the Supreme Court handed down decisions that banned prayer in public schools. One response by Christian conservatives was to pull their children out of public schools and place them in independent Christian schools. Another was to mobilize politically to restore what they perceived to be the appropriate role of prayer and spirituality in public education.

Fundamentalist Christians made this choice as high-profile, fundamentalist preachers like Oral Roberts, Pat Robertson, and Jerry Falwell began to unite Christian evangelicals behind a politically active common purpose. As Hodgson summarizes:

Some of the claims made for the influence of televangelism were greatly exaggerated. Underneath all the hype, however, a shift of enormous significance for the future of American politics had taken place . . . It was a decision on the part of many of the most powerful leaders of evangelical Protestantism to become active in politics. This had certain immediate political consequences. More important, it

---

[58] Seymour Martin Lipset, *Neoconservatism: Myth and Reality* (Berlin: John F. Kennedy–Institut für Nordamerikastudien der Freien Universität Berlin, 1988), p. 10. Admittedly, if this is where neoconservatives started, it is not where they ended up. Many of the original cadre of neoconservatives came to reject the label and disagree as well on its meaning.

marked a historic departure for those conservative Christians in America who for several generations had turned their backs on the mainstream culture . . . with its strongly secular belief in liberal reform. The decision was to abandon separatism and get in there and fight.[59]

Besides school prayer, the issues of significance to the newly active constituency included opposition to the women's movement and the Equal Rights Amendment, opposition to a growing gay rights movement, and, most important, hostility toward the Supreme Court's *Roe v. Wade* (1973) abortion rights decision.[60]

The Appeal of a New Economics

The fourth development contributing to a favorable context for conservative think tanks was the ascendance through the 1960s and 1970s of monetarist and supply-side theories of economics, which eventually came to displace Keynesianism. Monetarism, which advocated manipulation of the money supply in order to control inflation, had long-established scholarly roots, but Milton Friedman, a University of Chicago economist, was the principal proselytizer who made the approach fashionable among his contemporaries in the 1950s and 1960s. Friedman's writings on monetarism attracted academic disciples early on. And it was his talent as a political advocate, serving initially as an advisor to the failed Goldwater campaign in 1964 and later for Nixon and Ronald Reagan, that eventually made monetarism a salable political alternative when Keynesian appeared to falter.[61]

In fact, with Richard Nixon's election in 1968, monetarism seemed poised to become the prevailing governing philosophy, but the combined inflation, unemployment, and oil shocks of the 1970s made Nixon

---

[59] Godfrey Hodgson, *The World Turned Right Side Up: A History of the Conservative Ascendancy in America* (Boston: Houghton Mifflin, 1996), p. 174.

[60] Hodgson argues that the decisive mobilizing event prompting evangelical and fundamentalist Christians to become politically active was a 1978 IRS challenge to the tax-exempt status enjoyed by independent Christian schools, charging that these schools functioned to segregate white children from black. According to Hodgson, "This absolutely shattered the Christian community's notion that Christians could isolate themselves inside their own institutions and teach what they pleased. The realization that they could not do so linked up with the long-held conservative view that government is too powerful and intrusive, and this linkage was what made evangelicals active. It wasn't the abortion issue; that wasn't sufficient. It was the recognition that isolation simply would no longer work in this society." Hodgson, *The World Turned Right Side Up*, p. 178.

[61] For Friedman's views, see Milton Friedman, *Capitalism and Freedom* (Chicago: University of Chicago Press, 1962); Milton Friedman and Anna Jacobson Schwartz, *A Monetary History of the United States, 1869–1960* (Princeton, N.J.: Princeton University Press, 1963).

reluctant to experiment with new policies, and he reverted to Keynesian interventionism. Nonetheless, monetarism and free market economics continued to attract supporters through the 1970s, particularly among conservatives and libertarians, and it, along with supply-side doctrine, became the dominant paradigm when Ronald Reagan was elected president in 1980.

The Origins of Conservative Think Tanks

These four specific developments coincided with a growth in conservatism's popularity among the American public through the 1960s and 1970s, as the general appeal of New Deal liberalism began to fade.[62] This growth in public popularity was slow, but these four developments combined to fashion an environment for new think tanks that were more ideological and more marketing-oriented. Conservative think tanks emerged in a friendlier ideological environment, and they formed with the help of new sources of patronage, which advantaged them, in particular. The founding moments of two of the most successful new organizations of this period – the Heritage Foundation and the Cato Institute – illustrate these developments well.

The Heritage Foundation

By the late 1990s, the Heritage Foundation was the largest and best known of the new generation of ideologically conservative think tanks and rated as most influential among think tanks generally. Yet its ascendance to this position was not immediate. Heritage was founded in 1973 by Paul Weyrich and Ed Feulner. Both were working on Capitol Hill in the early 1970s when they identified a need for an independent and aggressive conservative policy organization.

Weyrich was press secretary to Senator Gordon Allott (R.-Colorado) and Feulner was administrative assistant to Congressman Philip Crane (R.-Illinois) when, in 1971, their frustration with a lack of policy-relevant conservative research on Capitol Hill peaked. As Feulner remembers it, the trigger event was a compelling brief about the supersonic transport distributed by the American Enterprise Institute (AEI) to members of Congress after their vote on the matter. Weyrich and Feulner were frustrated. As Feulner recalls, "It defined the debate, but it was one

---

[62] See Howard J. Gold, *Hollow Mandates: American Public Opinion and the Conservative Shift* (Boulder, Colo.: Westview Press, 1992).

day late. We immediately called up the president of [AEI] to praise him for this thorough piece of research – and ask why we didn't receive it until after the debate and the vote. His answer: they didn't want to influence the vote. That was when the idea for the Heritage Foundation was born."[63]

Weyrich and Feulner were motivated to start a new policy organization because they believed that conservative ideas were missing from legislative policy making. They had been inspired by the conservative message of Barry Goldwater's failed presidential campaign in 1964, a campaign that brought conservatives of many stripes into contact with one another for the first time. The organization was formally established when Feulner and Weyrich found financing for it from beer magnate Joseph Coors. Feulner recounts:

Weyrich was working for Senator Gordon Allott, and he received a letter from one of the Senator's major constituents, Joe Coors in Colorado, asking what could be done besides just giving money to candidates to have an effect in politics. Weyrich happened to get the letter because his colleague in the office wasn't in that day. Weyrich followed up with a phone call on the Senator's behalf. After some discussions, Coors met with Weyrich; then Weyrich and Feulner, and Coors and his representatives all met, and the rest, as they say is history. He gave us enough to get it started.[64]

With Coors's assistance, Weyrich and Feulner made connections with several additional wealthy conservative contributors and foundations, and, by 1973, the Heritage Foundation was off the ground, with Weyrich as its first president.[65]

[63] Edwin J. Feulner, Jr., "Ideas, Think Tanks and Governments," *The Heritage Lectures*, Number 51 (1985). For its part, the American Enterprise Institute had developed substantial regard in policymaking circles by 1970 as a credible conservative intellectual enterprise, after operating in relative obscurity in its early years after being founded in 1946. Under the leadership of William J. Baroody Sr., AEI had become an active voice for fiscal conservatism and against government regulation in the 1960s and 1970s. It was, however, reserved in its efforts on Capitol Hill, particularly after congressional investigation of the potentially improper partisan and legislative activities of nonprofit organizations – including think tanks – in the 1960s and after specific examination of AEI's links to the 1964 Goldwater campaign. Baroody and several of AEI's economists were active supporters of and advisors to Barry Goldwater in 1964, raising questions about AEI's political work in light of its tax-exempt status. Even though Baroody and his staff sought to support Goldwater on their own time – without using the institution's resources – AEI came under close scrutiny from the IRS in the years following the campaign. Its tax-exempt status was preserved. AEI was careful to avoid any perception of crossing boundaries toward legislative-issue advocacy in the 1970s, and its research was more often directed at the executive branch as well as academic audiences anyway.

[64] Interview with Edwin Feulner, Washington, D.C., July 30, 1996.

[65] For a more detailed history of the Heritage Foundation, see Lee Edwards, *The Power of Ideas: The Heritage Foundation at 25 Years* (Ottawa, Ill.: Jameson Books, Inc., 1997). On

The successful start of the Heritage Foundation is particularly notable because in the early 1970s conservative philosophies were far from mainstream in political discourse. Consensus around the viability and appropriateness of government management of and solutions to problems – New Deal and Great Society liberalism – was only beginning to break down through the late 1960s and early 1970s as many of the newly enacted public programs of the period came under criticism from conservatives and free marketeers. Events like AEI's intentional delay on the supersonic transport brief and, even more, the free market conservative movement born out of the failed Goldwater campaign were catalysts for the entrepreneurs who founded Heritage, but it took the vision and abilities of entrepreneurs along with the support of new political patrons to bring the Heritage Foundation into existence.

The Cato Institute

The same appears to be true of the libertarian Cato Institute, formed a few years later, in 1977. Ed Crane was the entrepreneurial catalyst in this instance. After beginning his career in Washington, D.C., in the early 1970s, and becoming active in the Libertarian Party, Crane moved to San Francisco by the middle of the decade to work for a capital management firm. Crane quit that job in 1976 to become chairman of the Libertarian National Party and an advisor to the presidential campaign of libertarian Roger McBride. It was in 1977 that Crane decided to found the Cato Institute. He recalls:

When I was working in Washington, I had been very impressed by what I perceived to be the leverage of Brookings and AEI. Back then, in the mid-70s, they were really the only think tanks of any consequence. I just viewed it – and still do today – as a remarkable, highly leveraged way to participate in the national policy debate. For a relatively small amount of money, if it's done properly, you can get your ideas on the table in a national debate through a think tank.[66]

Through contacts he developed with west coast members of the Libertarian Party in the early 1970s, Crane met billionaire Kansas oilman Charles Koch, who would become the patron for his new think tank. Crane remembers, "Since I didn't agree with the philosophy of either Brookings or AEI, I had, at the time, a friend who was a very wealthy industrialist, Charles Koch in Wichita. He and I talked about it. We

the Heritage Foundation, generally, see Niels Bjerre-Poulsen, "The Heritage Foundation: A Second Generation Think Tank," *Journal of Policy History* 3 (1991): 152–72.
[66] Interview with Ed Crane, President, Cato Institute, Washington, D.C., July 12, 1996.

decided it would be good to have a think tank with a libertarian perspective."[67]

Charles Koch provided the bulk of support for the Cato Institute through its first three years. Formed in San Francisco in 1977, Cato moved its headquarters to Washington, D.C., in 1981. By the mid-1990s, the Koch family foundations provided only 3 percent of Cato's annual budget, but they remained key supporters of new free market initiatives, including think tanks.[68] The Cato Institute is today preeminent among the growing group of libertarian and free market think tanks that have formed both in Washington and in state capitals.

Heritage and Cato are two of the 109 conservative think tanks that have been established since the mid-1970s. Evidence indicates that most were formed in much the same pattern of events, although newer think tanks have also been helped directly by more established organizations, like Heritage and Cato.[69]

The Roots of Organizational Imbalance

If entrepreneurs and wealthy patrons help account for the proliferation of conservative think tanks, the absence of the latter diminished opportunities for think tanks of other points of view to form. Three developments, all relevant to the financing of nonconservative think tanks, occurred during the 1960s and early 1970s and hindered their emergence and growth. In 1969, Congress passed a Tax Reform Act (TRA) stiffening restrictions on the political activities of private foundations, historically the main funders of think tanks. Over the same period, the resources of the largest

---

[67] Interview with Ed Crane, 1996.

[68] The Koch foundations typically support initiatives that advance one of two goals: free enterprise and peace. As Richard Fink, an executive of the foundation as well as of Koch Industries, puts it:

Obviously if you have war, it doesn't do a whole lot of good for a whole lot of people, although there are circumstances where all peaceful solutions have failed and therefore war may be justified. Free markets for us have been empirically indications of more housing, more education, more technology, more drugs, more clothing for kids. It has been sort of the most effective social welfare institute that mankind's ever seen. So we support institutions that either advance peace or advance an understanding or implementation of market-based economies.

Interview with Richard Fink, Koch Industries, Washington, D.C., November 6, 1997.

[69] The Heritage Foundation is involved in coordinating a State Policy Network of conservative policy organizations and has been helpful in the sharing of information with many new conservative organizations as they have formed.

private supporter of think tanks, the Ford Foundation, began to shrink, and Ford's interest in financing think tanks dwindled. And, finally, the volume of Department of Defense contract support available to research organizations began to erode. With these three developments, the diversity of sources of support for think tanks shrank, to the detriment of nonconservative organizations. The developments also prompted think tanks overall to become more marketing-oriented actors in American politics.

The Tax Reform Act of 1969

In 1969, Congress passed tax reform that prohibited foundations from supporting any efforts that might "influence the outcome" of legislation or political campaigns. Legal restrictions on the political activities of foundations were not new, but the coinciding breadth and lack of specificity of the new prohibitions were a cause for concern among think tank leaders, who depended upon foundations for the core of their support. By the mid-1970s, the traditional support from foundations for some of the most well-established think tanks (e.g., the Brookings Institution and National Bureau of Economic Research) began to erode.

Since 1934, it had been illegal for tax-exempt foundations to engage in "substantial" activity that might be aimed at "influencing legislation." What constituted "substantial" activity had always been unresolved in the law, however, and few proceedings to punish foundations under this provision had been successful. The reforms of 1969 prohibited *all* attempts to influence legislation, leaving little room for ambiguity about what might be acceptable conduct.[70] The reforms came at the end of several years of investigation and growing hostility within Congress about the appropriate political activities of private foundations.

The attack from Congress actually came on two fronts: one aimed at restricting the political activities of foundations directly and the other intended at revoking the tax-exempt privilege of foundations generally. Led by Representative Wright Patman (D.-Texas), Congress studied the role of foundations in American life for seven years before the reforms were enacted. And by 1969, the frustrations with foundations and eagerness for reform were palpable in a statement by Congressman Patman before the Ways and Means Committee that began, "Put most bluntly, philanthropy – one of mankind's more noble instincts – has been perverted into

---

[70] For a careful and legally contextualized explanation of the new law as it affected the political activities of foundations, see "Political Activity of Foundations," 1971.

a vehicle for institutionalized, deliberate evasion of fiscal and moral responsibility to the Nation."[71]

In pursuing restrictions on the political activities of foundations, Patman and the Congress were reacting most strongly against activities by the Ford Foundation, which had made grants to staff of the late Senator Robert Kennedy (D.-New York) in support of voter registration efforts in Ohio, and for the purpose of experimental school decentralization in New York City, all activities viewed as having explicit political intentions and consequences.[72] By restricting *all* activity that might influence legislation – as opposed to *substantial* activity, as the existing statute had – the new law had its greatest implications for the largest foundations, like Ford, which previously could be confident of few repercussions for efforts that might be construed as political because, by their great size, such efforts could be offset as *insubstantial* in comparison with the overwhelming scope of their "nonpolitical" efforts.

The Ford Foundation along with the Rockefeller Foundation, which was also substantially involved in debates over the legislation, had been among the principal funders of think tanks up until this reform. The Brookings Institution received a large grant of $14 million from the Ford Foundation in 1966 and had been founded earlier in the century with the backing of the Rockefeller family and foundation. Resources for the Future, another growing, environmentally focused think tank at the time, had been formed in 1953 with a single large grant from the Ford Foundation and had enjoyed support from Ford since. The practical effects of the 1969 reforms in restricting foundation contributions to think tanks were uncertain early on (for think tanks also were prohibited from seeking direct influence over legislative debates), but the Tax Reform Act raised some concerns among foundation executives about pursuing social change by supporting organizations seeming to be directly involved in Washington policy making.

---

[71] *Statement of Honorable Wright Patman before House Committee on Ways and Means*, 18 February 1969 (Washington, D.C.: Government Printing Office, 1969), p. 12.

[72] The Ford Foundation made grants totaling $131,069 to eight former members of Senator Robert F. Kennedy's staff in 1968 for the purposes of travel and research. See the *Washington Post*, 10 July 1968. It made grants in 1967 and 1968 totaling $475,000 to the Cleveland Congress of Racial Equality (CORE), portions of which were used to register African-Americans to vote. And the Ford Foundation made several grants to the Ocean Hill–Brownsville demonstration district in New York City and was accused of unfairly organizing school board elections and district lines. See Hearing, pp. 12–55 and 444–57, respectively.

Beyond restricting foundation contributions, the additional aim of reformists in Congress – to revoke the tax-exempt status of foundations – served as a direct threat to some long-established think tanks. Congressman Patman and his committee proposed a tax of 20 percent on foundation income. On the one hand, proponents of this reform were concerned with what they saw as the unfettered growth and autonomy of large bases of private wealth.[73] On the other hand, the proposed tax, which was whittled down to 2 percent through negotiation, was aimed also at preventing middle- and upper-income Americans from sheltering earnings in foundations.[74]

The proposed tax penalties jeopardized think tanks because several of the largest and best-known think tanks were themselves being classified

[73] In a revealing letter, Patman complained of John D. Rockefeller III:

> Mr. Rockefeller took a dim view of most of the proposed foundation reforms and talked at considerable length about the multitude of benefits that foundations bring to our nation and to persons abroad, and how the foundation overlords are motivated primarily by charitable impulses. Then Mr. Rockefeller volunteered this piety: "In my own case, although I have qualified for the unlimited deduction privilege during every year since 1961, I have deliberately paid a tax of between five and ten percent of my adjusted gross income in each of those years." One wonders what reaction Mr. Rockefeller expects from his audience when he makes such a statement – a silence respectful of his family's economic power; hosannahs of praise at his generosity in paying a tax at a rate one-third that of the poorest of us; pleas that he abandon such arduous self-sacrifice and cease paying any tax whatsoever. My own reaction should be no surprise to Mr. Rockefeller. In our society, legality is not necessarily synonymous with morality, and we have come to the point where Mr. Rockefeller and the other persons whose wealth is protected by tax-free foundations need guidelines more specific and binding than personal conscience – in sum, laws that require the rich to pay taxes. My disgust with Mr. Rockefeller's statement is matched in magnitude only by his audacity in offering it as a defense of inequity which this nation should no longer tolerate.

Hearings before the Committee on Ways and Means. *Tax Reform 1969.* 91st Congress, First Session. Part 1 of 15, p. 78.

[74] Members of Congress were concerned by a rise in the number of small foundations cooperatively organized for the benefit of families wishing to shelter college or retirement money from taxation. Patman complained of the proliferation: "Tax-exempt foundations will be as commonplace in this country as bathtub distilleries were during the Prohibition era.... This could be the beginning of complete chaos for the nation's tax structure.... When millionaires set up tax-dodging foundations, that is bad enough, but when foundations become as common as the Model T once was, then the Government's income faces a real and grave peril." In "Treasury Pressed for Closer Check on Foundations," *Congressional Quarterly Weekly Report,* 27 October 1967, p. 2176. On the intersection of these issues with the nonprofit sector, see Peter Dobkin Hall, *Inventing the Non-Profit Sector and Other Essays on Philanthropy, Voluntarism, and Non-Profit Organizations* (Baltimore: The Johns Hopkins University Press, 1992); see also Lester Salamon, *The Nonprofit Sector and the Rise of Third-Party Government* (Washington, D.C.: Urban Institute, 1983).

as foundations. The Brookings Institution, founded in 1916, joined an ad hoc consortium of think tanks and research institutes in the late 1960s to fight proposed revisions of the tax code that would have classified some think tanks as "operating foundations," limiting the amount of contributions they could receive from other private foundations, narrowing the boundaries on their political efforts, and taxing their income. The consortium of groups, calling themselves the "Advanced-Study Institutions" and including, among others, the Carnegie Endowment for International Peace, the National Bureau of Economic Research, the RAND Corporation, and Resources for the Future, all well-established think tanks, wrote letters to members of Congress and testified before hearings to protest the proposed changes.

These opponents were quite vehement about the potential harm such legislation could cause them. Brookings President Kermit Gordon began testimony before the Senate Committee on Finance in September 1969 by stating unequivocally:

To treat the [Brookings] Institution as a foundation under the provisions of the bill would be to place it in a category in which it does not belong. A group of institutions engaged in advanced study and research, of which Brookings is one, is submitting a suggestion for an amendment to the bill that would exclude these organizations from the provisions of the bill. If the proposed exclusion is denied, the bill if enacted would have extremely adverse effects on the future operations of the Brookings Institution.[75]

Joseph Fisher, president of Resources for the Future, went so far as to declare that, "Certain provisions in . . . the Tax Reform Act of 1969 now being considered by the Senate Finance Committee could pose serious difficulties to Resources for the Future to the point of requiring this organization to change drastically its whole method of financing and operation, or even to go out of business entirely."[76] A version of the "Advanced-Study" institution's amendment did pass the Congress, excluding Brookings and the other think tanks from treatment as foundations. Nonetheless, the heightened congressional scrutiny of think tank activities during this period along with the real restrictions placed on many of the foundations upon which they depended for support influenced the levels of foundation support for existing think tanks. In addition, the scrutiny appeared

---

[75] Kermit Gordon, *Committee on Finance Hearing about the Tax Reform Act of 1969 (H.R. 13270),* 7 October 1969, p. 1.

[76] Joseph Fisher, *Committee on Finance Hearing about the Tax Reform Act of 1969 (H.R. 13270),* 7 October 1969, p. 571.

to hinder the formation of new think tanks that might be looking for traditional foundation support.

Shifting Priorities at the Ford Foundation

Limiting options for think tanks further, the Ford Foundation began to decrease support for think tanks in the 1970s and 1980s. Since becoming the nation's largest private foundation in 1950, the Ford Foundation had actively pursued a program supporting "knowledge-creating" institutions; it had become a principal source of support for many think tanks.[77] Through the 1950s and 1960s, the Foundation was itself staffed primarily by academics, and the ethos at the Foundation was to fund research on public problems, rather than on actual programs intended to solve them. Marshall Robinson, a longtime program officer and vice president at the Ford Foundation through the 1960s and 1970s, characterized the norm this way:

When I went there [in 1963], the Foundation was essentially a kind of think tank itself. It wasn't doing research but it was an academic institution. It was staffed by academics, refugees from the universities, and its whole mode of thinking was wrapped up in the academy. You want to do something? Get the universities to study it. If there's a problem, let's study it.[78]

Robinson goes on about the changes undertaken at the Foundation in the late 1970s when then-president McGeorge Bundy was replaced:

When Bundy was replaced by Frank Thomas, the ethic of the place became, "if there's a problem, let's do something about it." What do you do? Well, you find some niche in the thing. You get somebody to take a little Ford Foundation money to create some nonprofit so that people can change things, and the agenda of the Ford Foundation became very much the agenda of the activist part of the American society: troubled about racism, about sexism, about inequality. But [they were] not writing books about it or funding book writers. You couldn't get money [for that] from the Ford Foundation at any time through this period. Research was just a bad word. We've studied too damn much. Let's get on with doing things. So they did that, and that's continued.[79]

---

[77] The Ford Foundation had existed since 1936 but through its first fourteen years gave grants averaging only $1 million annually, primarily in Michigan. The assets of the Foundation reached $474 million by 1950, however, following the deaths of Henry Ford and his son Edsel, and it began making larger and more nationally focused grants. Richard Magat, *The Ford Foundation at Work: Philanthropic Choices, Methods, and Styles* (New York: Plenum Press, 1979).

[78] Interview with Marshall Robinson, formerly of the Ford Foundation, New York City, June 17, 1998.

[79] Interview with Marshall Robinson, 1998. Michael Shuman, at the time a co-director of the Institute for Policy Studies, a liberal think tank, makes a similar point in relation to the

The shifting of priorities came after the Ford Foundation's overall pool of resources had shrunk as well. Between 1968 and 1978, the value of the Ford Foundation endowment declined precipitously, in tandem with the troubled economy and oil shocks. As their ability to meet existing commitments was challenged, their new obligations declined sharply. Symptomatic of the troubles, in a memo closing out a multimillion-dollar long-term grant to the Brookings Institution in 1980, program analyst Peter deJanosi wrote in an interoffice memorandum, "Brookings is now cited as a model for policy research institutes. Be that as it may, the general support grant of 1978 was billed as the last of a series. Given the temper of the times and the Ford Foundation, it is indeed likely to be terminal for a long time."[80]

Decline in Research and Development Dollars

Through roughly this same period, although beginning a bit earlier, a similar decline occurred in Department of Defense research and development expenditures, historically another important source of financing for think tanks. Ever since the Progressive Era movement to professionalize the political process, the federal government had devoted limited resources to policy research. Following World War II, the federal government began substantial new investments in research and development, aimed overwhelmingly at the nation's defense and security during the Cold War. Such commitments declined in the 1960s, for reasons unrelated to challenges to the Ford Foundation and private philanthropy generally, and had substantial consequences for the organizations that depended on them.

Whereas between 1947 and 1967, research and development expenditures by the Department of Defense (DOD) increased in constant 1990 dollars from $2.9 billion to $31.8 billion, between 1968 and 1980, such funds decreased in constant terms, from $30.7 billion to $21.8. The decline reflects a shift in priorities in the 1960s with regard to the total proportion of federal outlays suitable for national defense as well as the proportion of those outlays appropriate for research and development. Whereas roughly 15 percent of the defense budget went to research and development in 1961, only 11 percent was so allocated in 1971.[81]

lack of interest by liberal or progressive foundations generally in supporting knowledge-creating organizations like think tanks. Michael Shuman, "Why Progressive Foundations Give Too Little to Too Many," *The Nation*, 12–19 January 1998, pp. 11–16.

[80] Inter-Office Memorandum, The Ford Foundation, from Peter E. deJanosi to Marion Coolen, 22 February 1980.

[81] Leonard A. Lederman and Margaret Windus, *Federal Funding and National Priorities: An Analysis of Programs, Expenditures, and Research and Development* (New York: Praeger,

Decline in Department of Defense (DOD) research and development expenditures seemed to stem from an increased inability on the part of policy makers to agree in the 1960s on where to place priority in spending. As Lederman and Windus point out:

Although National Security has traditionally had a "first lien on the Treasury," the latter part of the past decade saw increased questioning of the extent of resources devoted to this function. A new willingness emerged to discuss National Security in the context of all priorities, rather than as a thing apart. DOD, whose budget requests had for many years been relatively untouchable, found itself strongly questioned by members of both parties in Congress and by the Bureau of the Budget and under pressure to reduce its own requests. The Democratic Majority Leader in the Senate said it would no longer be simply a matter of: "Ask and you shall receive."[82]

And, indeed, for a period of years after the time that Lederman and Windus wrote, the Department of Defense seemed to lose in the competition for national resources, including those to support research and development.

In the 1960s, think tanks were relatively small players in the research and development establishment. Nonetheless, government contracts were an important source of their support. The RAND Corporation, founded in 1946 to develop strategies for the Air Force, was the largest Department of Defense research and development–dependent think tank. Think tanks also succeeded in capturing a small percentage of NASA and Health, Education and Welfare (HEW) research and development money in the 1960s and 1970s. RAND actually gained approval from the Air Force to tap NASA research dollars as NASA grew in the 1960s.[83] The Urban Institute had formed in 1969 with explicit and substantial backing from HEW to do program development and evaluation. The great dependence of so many think tanks on government contract support left think tanks vulnerable to declines in these funds. The shifting priorities in Congress had many causes in the 1960s; an important consequence was the further erosion of think tank support.

The most obvious constraints posed by the changes in available support were on the continued success of existing think tanks that depended on foundations and government and on the efforts of entrepreneurs

1971), p. 34. The National Science Foundation defines research and development as the total of three activities: basic research, applied research, and development.

[82] Lederman and Windus, *Federal Funding and National Priorities*, p. 13.

[83] Carol H. Weiss, *Organizations for Policy Analysis: Helping Government Think* (Newbury Park, Calif.: Sage, 1992), p. 51.

motivated to form think tanks that might require their patronage. The changes had the combined effect of diminishing traditional sources of support for relatively long-established organizations and giving a boost to more ideological, particularly conservative, institutions, like the fledgling Heritage Foundation, that rejected value-free expertise and could appeal to a clear conservative constituency in the business sector. Organizations that were ideological – and particularly conservative – became institutionally advantaged; those that were not were challenged.

Ronald Reagan's election was a "coming of age" for conservatives. After 1980, conservative think tanks held a certain fundraising advantage given their alignment with politically interested corporations as well as foundations. In the last two decades of the twentieth century, the Fred C. Koch Foundation, the Lilly Foundation, the John M. Olin Foundation, the Smith Richardson Foundation, and the Sarah Mellon Scaife Foundation were among the principal foundations supporting Heritage's efforts. These and seven more foundations contributed almost $9 million to Heritage between 1992 and 1994, according to a report by the National Committee for Responsive Philanthropy.[84] And they contributed in similar ways to the formation and sustenance of other conservative think tanks as well.[85]

Besides corporations and ideologically compatible foundations, Heritage successfully built a broad base of individual support, which accounted for more than half of its budget by the 1990s.[86] Heritage made a self-conscious decision to pursue a diversified resource base. Edwin Feulner, Heritage's president, observes:

One of the first things that we did was decide to create a broader base. I was not going to have to run around having to defend us institutionally, not only for our

[84] This number is based on the NCRP's assessment of IRS forms 990 for twelve conservative foundations for the years 1992 to 1994. The foundations include the Lynde and Harry Bradley Foundation, the Carthage Foundation, the Earhart Foundation, the Charles G. Koch Foundation, the David H. Koch Foundation, the Claude R. Lambe Foundation, the Phillip M. McKenna Foundation, the J.M. Foundation, the John M. Olin Foundation, the Henry Salvator Foundation, the Sarah Scaife Foundation, and the Smith Richardson Foundation. Sally Covington, *Moving a Public Policy Agenda: The Strategic Philanthropy of Conservative Foundations* (Washington, D.C.: National Committee for Responsive Philanthropy, 1997).

[85] See interview with James Piereson, Executive Director, John M. Olin Foundation, February 2, 1999. See also David Callahan, $1 Billion for Ideas: Conservative Think Tanks in the 1990s (Washington, D.C.: National Committee for Responsive Philanthropy, 1999).

[86] All foundation contributions combined accounted for roughly only 30 percent of Heritage's revenue between 1992 and 1994. Heritage's total expenses in those years ranged from $17.6 million to $23.4 million.

ideas, not only for our methodology, but also for being a stooge of a small handful of major fatcats. So we went out with something that was absolutely unheard of for a think tank – and disdained by some of the establishment at the time – and that was with a plan to come up with a broad membership. Now [in 1996] we have 240,000 plus or minus members at any one time.[87]

Heritage's success in this effort was due in no small part to the development of direct mail techniques by conservatives through the 1960s, whereby the ranks of conservative supporters nationwide could be efficiently canvassed.[88]

The Heritage Foundation set a standard for successful fund raising in the new political environment. Their annual budget grew from less than $1 million in 1975 to almost $30 million by 1995, more than a tenfold increase even after adjusting for inflation. The Foundation's success also points to the obvious problem that think tanks not sharing Heritage's conservative ideals faced: Wealthy conservative supporters were generally not available to nonconservative organizations.

Over time, older, nonconservative think tanks learned from Heritage, and they used similar methods to ensure their own continued development. Despite declining foundation support, the annual budget of the Brookings Institution remained more or less stable year to year between 1971 and 1996.[89] Although Brookings enjoys a certain financial stability because of an endowment that typically covers between 20 percent and 33 percent of its annual expenses, it faced a significant shortfall when in 1978 the Ford Foundation phased out what had been $500,000 in annual support. This shortfall was partly compensated for by increased contributions from individuals. In 1977, the Brookings Institution drew 0.5 percent of its support from individual contributions. By 1986, individual gifts had climbed to constitute 2.7 percent of Brookings' revenue. Between 1991 and 1996, the proportion of Brookings' budget coming from individual contributions consistently reached a range of 12 percent to 16 percent, totaling between $2 million and $3 million annually.

Corporate contributions also increased through the 1980s and 1990s. In 1977, Brookings received 1.1 percent of its annual support from corporations. By 1981, this proportion had reached 8.9 percent, and since 1986 corporate contributions have consistently ranged between 10 percent and 15 percent of Brookings' annual revenue. Declaring in its 1986 annual

---

[87] Interview with Edwin Feulner, 1996.
[88] Himmelstein, *To the Right*, 1991.
[89] The Brookings Institution budget grew in real terms from $5.7 million in 1971 to $21.7 million in 1996. Almost all of this growth is accounted for by inflation.

report that "the Institution is working actively to expand its corporate-giving base and to encourage giving from individuals," this goal has been achieved.[90]

Long-established think tanks nurtured corporate contributions by creating a venue for their involvement in and education about policymaking efforts. The Brookings Institution expanded the role of its Center for Public Policy Education (CPPE) in 1985, developing workshops and conferences for "broad audiences" that included a great many corporate representatives. Brookings' 1986 annual report clearly states that one of the benefits of developing the CPPE was that "it provides an opportunity to approach potential funding sources with an overview of the Institution's plans in a particular field, in the hope that they may see the advantages of providing the multi-year funding that enables an... organization such as Brookings both to maintain its tradition of excellence and to break new ground."[91]

The Hudson Institute and the RAND Corporation have been among other older think tanks that have adapted to changing sources of support. Hudson moved from receiving 38 percent of its support from government contracts in 1990, which in itself was far less than a decade before, to receiving less than 3 percent of its revenue from government contracts in 1995 and 1996. Like Brookings, it made up the difference in revenue by cultivating corporate and individual support, by drawing on some of the same conservative foundations as the Heritage Foundation, and by beginning to build an endowment.

Overall federal government support of the RAND Corporation has remained far steadier. RAND drew 82 percent of its 1995 $114 million annual budget from the federal government, representing only a 5 percent decrease in the proportion of its budget from government contract support since 1981. But the end of the Cold War and the shrinkage of military spending generally diminished the proportion of RAND's government support that comes from defense-related projects. RAND's reliance on domestic policy evaluation contracts has increased.[92]

These latter contracts have become more competitive in recent years, however, as the currency of expertise and the merits of government

---

[90] *Brookings Institution Annual Report* (Washington, D.C.: Brookings Institution, 1986), p. 37.

[91] *Brookings Institution Annual Report*, 1986, p. 5.

[92] Preparing for an overall decline in the proportion of financing it may receive from government contracts, RAND has been developing an endowment since 1974 to provide a cushion of autonomous support.

intervention have declined. The Urban Institute was hit particularly hard by these reductions in the 1980s, as support from both government and foundations dropped sharply. UI's overall revenue went from $14.4 million in 1980 to $11.8 million in 1981. UI's revenue declined further in the 1980s to range between $8 million and $10 million in the middle part of the decade, before its diversification of revenue sources enabled its growth in the 1990s. UI became involved in more internationally sponsored research. Former UI President William Gorham recalls the rationale for the diversification of revenue sources:

> Reagan came in and said, quite rationally, that we don't need housing programs so why should we evaluate them. It doesn't matter how they are doing. It doesn't matter if they work or they don't. So basically a lot of our program was just cut. The head of our housing group said to me, "Look, I'm not going to be able to raise any more money from the government. Why don't you let me bid on overseas work? There's a lot of interest in housing overseas." I wanted to keep together a critical mass of analysts and so I turned them loose. And now one-third of our annual budget comes from overseas contracts.[93]

The Emphasis on Marketing Expertise

The changing sources of patronage had consequence not just for the size and ideological character of think tanks. The changes affected the activities of think tanks as well. Think tank strategies have come to more regularly include efforts to market and promote research to achieve high profile and immediate visibility in policy debates. High visibility helps attract funding, and the competition spawned by the increased number of think tanks leads to an increased emphasis on marketing expertise.

The Heritage Foundation set the standard for marketing research, developing an ability to produce timely, short, faxable briefs on any pending issue that might reach Congress. While other, particularly long-established, think tanks are critical of how close Heritage comes to crossing boundaries of appropriate behavior in its pursuit of visibility and access, many of these same older think tanks have begun to emulate features of Heritage's aggressive style.[94] In July 1996, the Brookings Institution launched a new series of *Policy Briefs*, expressly intended to "provide stimulating new ideas to the debate on national and international issues"

---

[93] Interview with William Gorham, Urban Institute, Washington, D.C., August 1, 1996.

[94] For an early critical appraisal of Heritage and conservative organizations generally, see John S. Saloma III, *Ominous Politics: The New Conservative Labyrinth* (New York: Hill and Wang, 1984).

and designed to be "informative, timely, and useful."[95] The five- to ten-page briefs offer the immediate wisdom of Brookings' scholars on current, often contentious policy debates. Soon after beginning the *Policy Briefs*, Brookings created a new position of Vice President for Communications, upgrading what had been a director of public affairs position. In 2001, Brookings built an in-house television studio so that its scholars could be easily arranged as guests on news shows.[96] All of these efforts were aimed at increasing the timeliness and currency of Brookings' contributions to the policy process.

The American Enterprise Institute, the Urban Institute, and the Institute for Policy Studies have sought – and continue to seek – to respond to the changed political environment as well. AEI reformatted and expanded the circulation of its magazine, *American Enterprise*, in the late 1980s. AEI is producing fewer and shorter books and is placing a greater emphasis on monographs and other shorter and more quickly produced publications. Karlyn Bowman, resident fellow and former editor of *American Enterprise*, observes, "We're pretty convinced that people just don't read books in the way that they once did. You can produce things more quickly that are shorter. You can get out a monograph or an occasional paper or something of that sort, and I think you can perhaps be more influential."[97]

Achieving visibility has become a higher priority at the Urban Institute as well. Bill Gorham, UI's former president, reflects, "Increasingly [our researchers] want to see [their studies] out there in public, and I encouraged that.... I, more in the last ten years than earlier, encouraged people to get it out there."[98] Michael Shuman, formerly co-director of the Institute for Policy Studies, agrees. He points out, "Research matters, but transforming that research into usable advocacy is just as important.... Think tanks should be kind of a mid-wife between academia and policy 'wonks' on the one hand, and politicians on the other."[99]

Changes in marketing strategies are connected in part to developments in the revenue sources available for think tanks. As institutions like the Hudson Institute and the Brookings Institution have become as reliant on

[95] Memo from Michael Armacost, "Letter to Our Readers about Brookings Policy Briefs," Washington, D.C.: Brookings Institution, 24 June 1996.
[96] Richard Morin and Claudia Deane, "Live from Massachusetts Ave., It's WONK-TV," *The Washington Post*, 25 September 2001, p. A21.
[97] Interview with Karlyn Bowman, American Enterprise Institute, Washington, D.C., July 23, 1996.
[98] Interview with William Gorham, 1996.
[99] Interview with Michael Shuman, Institute for Policy Studies, Washington, D.C., August 3, 1996.

corporate support as on foundations and the government, the member-
ships of their boards of directors have come to reflect these changes, and
corporate leaders have demonstrated a great concern for visible signs of
immediate policy impact. Former Brookings president Bruce MacLaury
observes of his institution's adjustments:

That was driven by the junction of the trustees and the starting up of the whole
corporate support program that had not existed before. As you go around and
try to ask corporations for bucks, either for projects or for general support of
the institution, you have to justify that you are doing not only credible work but
relevant and visible work, and that you are not just perceived as being knee-jerk
liberal. So funding was an influence.[100]

Funding and publication changes have implications for the internal
organization of institutions as well. One of the principal "brakes" on
older think tanks' quick adjustment to changes in the institutional and
ideological environment has been the resistance of existing staff. An organization's ability to adapt quickly – whether or not such adaptation may
be desirable – is largely contingent on the coordination and flexibility of
leadership, staff, and mission.

In recent years, leaders at the Brookings Institution have considered
what organizational changes might be necessary to make the institution
more responsive to shifting political currents. Brookings' scholars have
historically been Ph.D. researchers, many of whom came to the institution from university settings. Scholars have been coordinated by program
directors but have traditionally had substantial freedom in selecting research projects, projects designed to culminate in books. Unlike university
tenure systems, Brookings scholars are on one-year renewable contracts.

[100] Interview with Bruce MacLaury, formerly of the Brookings Institution, Washington,
D.C., July 18, 1996. Another example of the way funders influence organization is
revealed in the National Bureau of Economic Research's (NBER) wholesale change in
leadership following the Ford Foundation's rejection of its 1966 grant request. After consulting with an advisory group of academic economists, the Ford Foundation declined
NBER's request for $1 million in institutional support, recording in an internal memo,
"the research program [was] diffuse and [was] not carefully thought out; the present
research director is of insufficient stature to occupy that position [and] the president of
the Bureau while certainly a major figure in economics does not seem to have the vigor
and breadth for leading an important research institution...." Marshall A. Robinson,
Interoffice Memorandum: The National Bureau Meeting – June 4, 1966, June 7, 1966.
Over the next two years, NBER underwent substantial internal change, all well documented in a series of lengthy letters to Ford Foundation program officers. In 1969, the
Ford Foundation provided NBER $1 million in support, following a wholesale reorga-
nization. For a report on the development of marketing strategies among think tanks,
see Carol Matlack, "Marketing Ideas," *National Journal*, 8 July 1995, pp. 1552–5.

But the norm has been to renew contracts except in extreme cases of lack of productivity.

The director of Brookings' foreign policy studies program in the late 1990s raised the possibility that the institution's internal organization may need adjustment. Richard Haass, a former George H.W. Bush administration national security advisor, observed early in his tenure at Brookings:

Part of my goal is to change a little bit the culture of the foreign policy studies program. I want to make it a little bit more policy relevant. I want to get people away from the notion that this is All Soul's College, and you come for two years and you largely write a book. I want people to still write books, but I want to slightly shift the percentages and have them put slightly less calories in that and slightly more calories in producing other products along the way... I want Brookings to be connected to policy or one step removed. [Before coming here,] I thought it had become two steps removed.[101]

Haass believed that Brookings should be staffed more by policy practitioners than by university scholars. He suggested that scholars should serve for short lengths of time, writing and reflecting on their experiences in direct service and then returning to it or going somewhere else.[102] Haass himself left Brookings in 2001 to become Assistant Secretary of State for Policy Planning in the new Bush administration but not before helping to change the culture at Brookings. He became president of the Council on Foreign Relations in 2003.

At the Institute for Policy Studies, the potential for increasing visibility with a change in organizational structure has also been raised, although in a far more speculative way. IPS is an institution that is still weathering transitions in funding streams. As a result, possible changes in organization are closely linked to issues of financing. IPS's funding base

---

[101] Interview with Richard Haass, Brookings Institution, Washington, D.C., September 22, 1997. Others have made similar observations about Brookings. In reporting on the appointment of Michael Armacost as Brookings' president in 1995, Paul Starobin reported, "He takes over a place that many of its own residents describe as tired.... With many of its scholars drawn from the Ivy League and with a silk-stocking board of trustees, Brookings is a fixture of the American educational, philanthropic, and corporate elite. But the center ground defined and occupied by this elite is sagging. And so is Brookings" (Starobin 1995: 1875).

[102] Haass believes that "So often people who have recently been practicing public policy are in a good position to write, because they have just had some wonderful experiences. And if they are the kind of people who have been trained and are inclined to write and reflect and come up with lessons, that would be great. And I think that it is good for people here to get out" and work in the fields they write about. Interview with Richard Haass, 1997.

declined in the late 1980s and 1990s as traditional foundation support for its efforts dried up. By 1995, IPS was running with less than a third of its $1.2 million 1986 budget, in inflation-adjusted dollars. Revenues in 1995 were just over $650,000. Individual contributions may be the way for IPS to rebuild financial strength. Former co-director Michael Shuman observes:

> In the end, I think that we are not going to be able to dramatically expand our financial base with foundations. I think we can slightly expand our financial base with foundations, but it's going to come through other means. It will come through development of a membership, which we really never took seriously, and the recruitment of more individual high donors.[103]

Like Brookings, researchers at IPS have substantial autonomy in developing projects. They have the added responsibility of generating their own project support. Shuman sees a turn toward an "elite-level" strategy of policy advocacy, modeled after Heritage's success, as one possible path of reform. Shuman reflects, "I still see this [elite strategy] as a place where we want to go, and if I had $30 million a year, I wouldn't spend as much as Heritage does on the congressional and White House outreach, but I would spend a lot on it."[104]

IPS's current mission and organization are more varied with efforts divided among seeking "elite-level" impact, and efforts to shape public opinion, to challenge and inform grassroots movements, and to launch progressive state- and local-level policy "experiments." With such a mix of efforts, and emphasis more on the last three than the first, Shuman believes that developing an elite marketing-oriented strategy might make the organization more appealing to funders. He points out, "To the extent that we become more of an elite think tank, fundraising becomes easier. That is...the more congress-people and the more people in the White House that we can show ourselves in pictures with, the easier fundraising would get. [Potential funders] would say, okay, they are legitimate."[105]

---

[103] Interview with Michael Shuman, 1996.
[104] Interview with Michael Shuman, 1996.
[105] Interview with Michael Shuman, 1996. IPS's decentralized structure – and its possible disadvantages – are not new. Former Senator George McGovern observed upon joining IPS's board of directors in 1986, "At IPS you have highly intelligent, marvelously motivated scholars who are not well structured, a kind of conglomerate of bright minds going off in various directions without any serious effort to influence public policy. I say this with affection. I wish it weren't true." Sidney Blumenthal, "The Left Stuff: IPS and the Left-wing Thinkers," *The Washington Post*, 30 July 1996, pp. D1–D3.

Conclusion

Think tanks that formed at the beginning of the twentieth century reflected an ideological environment that valued neutral expertise and believed in its potential for devising rigorous solutions to public problems. Those who supported the first think tanks valued their capacity for producing credible research that attracted the interest of policy makers without involving the experts or organizations directly in high-profile controversies or ideologically charged political debates. Sources of support for think tanks changed somewhat through the first half of the century and confidence in social science expertise evolved, but until the 1960s, think tanks generally emerged in a political environment that encouraged and fostered a balancing of organizational credibility and political access.

At the beginning of the twenty-first century, IPS, Brookings, and other older think tanks are confronting an ideological and organizational environment that is substantially changed from the time when each was founded. On the one hand, there have been developments in the political environment in the past three decades that have enabled conservative think tanks to form in numbers far greater than before. Policy entrepreneurs have emerged from the political ascendance of neoconservatism, monetarism and free market economics, and Christian evangelicalism. Activist, particularly conservative think tanks are increasingly engaging in efforts to influence particular policy decisions as well as overall policy directions.

On the other hand, there has been a series of changes in available sources of organizational funding that have hindered the proliferation of nonconservative think tanks and prompted the marketing of the expertise and ideas produced by think tanks generally. New sources of patronage have been made available to think tanks – particularly conservative think tanks – out of the renewed interest and involvement of business in the policymaking process. At the same time, the shifting priorities of the Ford Foundation and government limited what were traditional sources of support for think tanks and prompted a reorientation of think tank activities.

Changes in the ideological and funding environment since the 1960s have stimulated the growth in number of more ideological and marketing-oriented think tanks. The question remains: How are the changes among think tanks – the explosion in their numbers, their more ideological nature, and their greater emphasis on marketing ideas and expertise – affecting the role of think tanks in politics and policy making? In this regard, AEI's Karlyn Bowman has voiced the worry of many: "I wonder what is happening sometimes to the think tank currency, whether it's becoming a little bit like paper money in Weimar – currency without a lot of value because of the proliferation and because of the open advocacy of some of the think tanks."[106] Examining the extent to which she might be right is the subject of the rest of the book.

[106] Interview with Karlyn Bowman, 1996.

3

Political Credibility

Expertise plays a substantial role in American policy making. The variety of it available to decision makers is enormous, having expanded considerably since 1970, over the same period as the number of think tanks has grown. In their 1974 reforms, Congress established the Congressional Budget Office (CBO) and Office of Technology Assessment (OTA) and expanded the roles of already existing research agencies (e.g., the Congressional Research Service and General Accounting Office). These congressional agencies counterbalanced the proliferating numbers of trained experts staffing the Executive Office of the President and bureaucratic agencies. In more recent years, both have been complemented by growing numbers of for-profit consulting firms (e.g., the Advisory Board) and research groups within traditional interest groups (e.g., the Public Policy Institute of the AARP). The expanded presence of experts reflects a realization shared by many in Washington that "you can't really play in the policy game unless you have a study."[1]

But what is the added value of expertise? And, even more, given the volume of its purveyors, how do its producers affect the chance of particular expertise having value in the "policy game"? In this and the next two chapters, I evaluate the behavior of think tanks as well as other experts in American policy making and their success in achieving policy influence. I begin by taking stock of perceptions of think tanks among two audiences that are their frequent targets: congressional staff and journalists. Congressional staff and journalists are a useful focus because they are

[1] Author interview with Henry Aaron, Senior Fellow, The Brookings Institution, Washington, D.C., 11 February 1999.

key actors in the policymaking process; they are audiences with whom most think tank personnel – and sources of expertise generally – seek to cultivate close relationships. I explore results from a survey of these groups that gauges their views on the influence and credibility of think tanks. In the legislative process, members of Congress and their staffs depend on expertise for confirmation and support of pre-existing views, as evidence in persuading colleagues, and, occasionally, for insights into new policy directions.[2] Journalists, an important intermediary in the policy process, also seek out expertise in order to understand and explain policy debates and to validate conclusions in already-planned stories.[3] If expertise can be important to both, it is worth considering how they view think tanks, as one of its purveyors.

More important than their views is how congressional staff and jour-nalists actually use think tank expertise. And assessing that use is the focus of the rest of this chapter. I examine the visibility of think tanks in congres-sional hearings and in major newspapers. I consider whether differences among think tanks matter for how visible their work is among policy makers. Do the self-conscious strategies of organizations that produce and promote expertise affect the visibility of their work? Affecting their own visibility appears to be no small challenge for think tanks with audi-ences whose demands for expertise are understood as principally driven by the prerogatives of congressional leaders and news cycles.

In fact, think tanks not only are cumulatively viewed as influential by congressional staff and journalists but seem capable of affecting how that influence is derived, at least in the form of visibility. Think tanks that are ideological or aggressively marketing-oriented obtain different kinds of visibility with congressional staff and journalists than those that appear to be of no identifiable ideology or are more staid in their behavior. Overall, quite contrary to the predictions of some, the intentional efforts of experts appear to affect how they are viewed and how their work is received by policymaking audiences.

My assessment of think tank visibility is followed in the next two chap-ters by a more concrete examination of their policy influence, for visibility

[2] David Whiteman, *Communication in Congress: Members, Staff, and the Search for Information* (Lawrence: University Press of Kansas, 1995); Carol H. Weiss, "Congressional Committees as Users of Analysis," *Journal of Policy Analysis and Management* 8 (1989): 411–31; Bruce Bimber, *The Politics of Expertise in Congress: The Rise and Fall of the Office of Technology Assessment* (Albany: State University of New York Press, 1996).

[3] Carol H. Weiss and Eleanor Singer, *Reporting of Social Science in the National Media* (New York: Russell Sage Foundation, 1988).

and even perceptions of influence do not guarantee that the substantive work of think tanks is affecting the views of policy makers or the content of policy proposals. I examine the efforts of think tanks compared with alternative sources of expertise in three contentious policy debates between 1991 and 2001: those over health care reform, telecommunications reform, and tax cuts. In the context of so many and such diverse sources of expertise available to policy makers, I evaluate differences in how particular types of issues accommodate think tanks and variation within issue debates in how think tanks and experts generally succeed in achieving some type of influence.

Perceptions of Think Tanks

In their day-to-day activities, members of Congress are said to use expertise most often to support already-held views. By the time members of Congress are collectively attentive to an issue, Weiss finds, "by all accounts, the most common form of legislative use [of expertise] is as support for preexisting positions."[4] Research can also help to inform policy development among specialists on issues, but overall, members of Congress and their staff are typically too busy to pay much attention to the sources of research. They balance the demands of packed legislative schedules, constituents, and interested groups.[5] They choose to use research based on whether it helps them justify points of view or provides ammunition for fights with opponents.

Likewise, journalists are understood to draw on expertise that is relevant to timely subjects for stories that are often already in the works. In more than two-thirds of newspaper, newsmagazine, and broadcast news segments with reference to social science in 1982, Weiss finds that studies were mentioned because their "topic was related to matters already in the news" or because they offered insight on topics that were "interesting or trendy."[6] Weiss does find some evidence that specific sources of expertise that are well known to journalists – or that make themselves known through press releases and phone calls – may have advantages in gaining

---

[4] Carol H. Weiss, "Congressional Committees as Users of Analysis," p. 425.

[5] See Michael Malbin, *Unelected Representatives: Congressional Staff and the Future of Representative Government* (New York: Basic Books, 1980).

[6] Weiss, *Reporting of Social Science*, p. 32. The other most common reasons that studies were cited related to their perceived importance and likelihood of provoking controversy.

coverage, but she observes that journalists rarely dwell on differences in the quality of their sources of expertise.[7]

These characterizations suggest that those on Capitol Hill and in the news media may have limited ability to evaluate think tanks. To be sure, they receive think tank products, and they are aware of some of the big organizations. But they are so busy on a regular basis that they principally look at the work of think tanks and other experts from the point of view of whether it might be helpful to them, with only a peripheral interest in what its source might be. Only those who specialize in the area of a think tank's research would likely know it, and then only if their particular responsibilities provide time to evaluate studies, a rare luxury for congressional staff and journalists.

This understanding of Congress and the news media frames my survey of 125 congressional staff and journalists about their perceptions of think tanks. The survey, administered in the summer of 1997, includes responses from 71 congressional staff, split between committee and personal staff, Republicans and Democrats, and 54 Washington, D.C.–based journalists, split between journalists with national circulation publications and those with regional papers from around the country. Details about how the survey was administered are provided in Appendix A.

Perceptions of Think Tanks, Collectively

Whatever their distractions, both congressional staff and journalists not surprisingly expressed widespread recognition of think tanks as an organizational form. And almost all shared the belief that think tanks are influential in contemporary policy making (93.6 percent). Most viewed them as "somewhat" as opposed to "very" influential, but influential nonetheless.[8]

Interestingly, congressional staff and journalists were split on the question of what type of think tank is more influential: ideological or not. Respondents were asked, "Which do you think are more effective overall in influencing policy, those think tanks with a distinctive ideological

---

[7] Weiss, *Reporting of Social Science*, p. 51.

[8] The only notable difference between responses from journalists and congressional staff related to the magnitude of this perceived influence. More than a quarter (28 percent) of respondents from national publications viewed think tanks as "very influential," whereas only 11.4 percent to 17.1 percent of those interviewed in the other response categories (journalists with local newspapers; Republican and Democratic congressional staff) viewed think tanks as "very influential." The overwhelming majority of respondents overall rated think tanks as "somewhat influential."

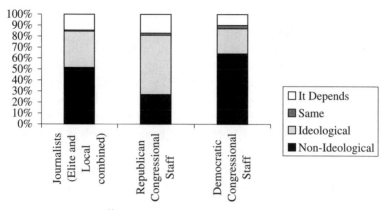

FIGURE 3-1. Most effective think tank at being influential by respondent group

perspective or those that are nonideological?" Almost half of respondents (46 percent) rated nonideological think tanks as most effective. A bit more than one-third (36 percent) viewed ideological think tanks as most effective. Of the remaining respondents, 3 percent saw ideological and nonideological think tanks as equally effective, and 14 percent viewed effectiveness as contingent on the specific policy issues under consideration.

In fact, all respondent groups except for Republican congressional staff tended to view nonideological think tanks as more effective at influencing policy than ideological think tanks. As Figure 3-1 illustrates, more than half of Republican staff (54 percent) viewed ideological think tanks as more effective than nonideological think tanks. Only 27 percent of them rated nonideological think tanks as more effective, compared with more than half of journalists and Democratic congressional staff who responded to the survey.

This difference reflects the times and the disproportionate number of conservative think tanks that exist. Many Republican congressional staff followed up their response by observing the strength of ideologically conservative think tanks in the "current political environment" – that of the summer of 1997. In the words of one staff member, "in the current political climate with Republican control of Congress, the leadership of the House and Senate give places like Cato and Heritage a bigger voice." And, indeed, when it comes to *ideological* think tanks, conservative think tanks were viewed by congressional staff and journalists generally as having more influence than liberal think tanks in policy making – by an overwhelming margin. In response to a question asking respondents to compare conservative and liberal think tanks, almost three-quarters of respondents (72 percent) identified conservative think tanks as having greater influence than liberal think tanks; only 4 percent viewed liberal think tanks as having greater influence than conservative think tanks.[9]

What is meant by think tank "influence" is left undefined in the survey, and the variation in responses across groups of respondents suggests that not only might the quantity of influence by think tanks be perceived differently by different groups, but the quality of influence – what stands as influence – might be understood differently as well. Congressional staff and journalists were asked to compare think tanks with advocacy organizations, and they were split in how they viewed the comparison. Half of respondents (50 percent) saw no distinction between think tanks and advocacy organizations; 40 percent perceived a clear difference between the two. Interestingly, the responses from journalists and congressional staff were notably different. Journalists most often did see a distinction between think tanks and advocacy organizations, whereas congressional staff most often did not. Overall, 54 percent of journalists saw a clear distinction, with 33 percent perceiving no clear distinction. By contrast, only 29 percent of congressional staff recognized a clear difference between them; almost two-thirds (63 percent) saw no clear distinction.

Together with the response on what types of think tanks are viewed as influential, the split on this question may reflect the contrasting nature of the jobs of journalists and congressional staff – and resulting variation in how think tanks might be helpful to their work. Journalists often need experts to clarify technical issues in their reporting.[10] It may be for this purpose that journalists most often turn to think tanks. If so, think tanks that are not ideological may be most useful to them. These think tanks tend to produce more technical research and to have closer ties to academia, whose studies think tanks can sometimes interpret for journalists. If these think tanks are most helpful, and therefore images of them come to mind when journalists are asked about think tanks, then it is no surprise that journalists tend to view think tanks as different from advocacy organizations. Congressional staff, by contrast, often need research

[9] The remaining respondents believed either that conservative and liberal think tanks have equal influence or that the strength of think tanks of one ideology over another depends on the specific policy issue under consideration.

[10] See Timothy E. Cook, *Governing with the News: The News Media as a Political Institution* (Chicago: University of Chicago Press, 1998).

to bolster existing proposals or justify policy positions.[11] For this, ideological think tanks may be most helpful. And yet the work of ideological think tanks more closely resembles that of advocacy organizations. If their image comes to mind when questions are asked about think tanks, then it makes sense that congressional staff less often see a distinction between think tanks and advocacy organizations.

Whatever the explanation, congressional staff and journalists agree that think tanks are on the whole more credible than advocacy organizations. Three-quarters of respondents (75 percent) cited think tanks as having more credibility than advocacy organizations. No one viewed advocacy organizations as more credible than think tanks.[12]

Perceptions of Think Tanks, Individually

Even more revealing than their views of think tanks generally are some of the perceptions of congressional staff and journalists about specific, well-known think tanks. The survey had respondents reflect on a selection of think tanks in relation to their influence, credibility, and ideologies. The differences of opinion among congressional staff and journalists in assessments of the overall influence of ideological versus nonideological think tanks carry through to judgments about specific think tanks.

Two think tanks emerged most consistently in response to the question "Which three think tanks would you say have the greatest influence on the formulation of public policy in Washington these days?": the Heritage Foundation and the Brookings Institution. More than three-quarters of congressional staff and journalists (80 percent) named the Heritage Foundation as among the three most influential think tanks; more than half (56 percent) named the Brookings Institution among their top three. While respondents were not asked to rank their top three choices, 41 percent of respondents named Heritage first and 33 percent named Brookings first. Behind Heritage and Brookings, the next most frequently named think tanks were the Cato Institute (35 percent), the American Enterprise Institute (32 percent), the Progressive Policy Institute (10 percent), and

---

[11] See Carol H. Weiss, "Congressional Committees as Users of Analysis," *Journal of Policy Analysis and Management* 8 (1989): 411–31; David Whiteman, *Communication in Congress: Members, Staff, and the Search for Information* (Lawrence: University Press of Kansas, 1995); Nancy Shulock, "The Paradox of Policy Analysis: If It Is Not Used, Why Do We Produce So Much of It?" *Journal of Policy Analysis and Management* 18 (1999): 226–44.

[12] Fewer than one-fifth (16 percent) viewed think tanks and advocacy organizations as equally credible.

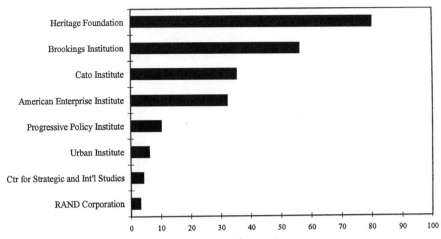

FIGURE 3-2a. Think tanks assessed as most influential in 1997

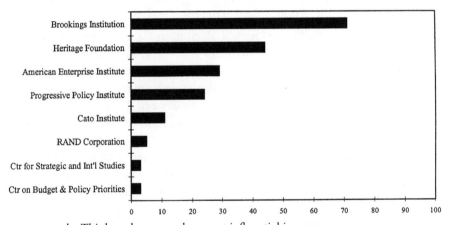

FIGURE 3-2b. Think tanks assessed as most influential in 1993

the Center on Budget and Policy Priorities (6 percent). The eight most frequently named organizations are illustrated in Figure 3-2a.

These findings are comparable to those derived from a 1993 survey of congressional staff and journalists about think tanks conducted by Burson-Marsteller. That survey followed a similar format and methodology to those of the 1997 survey. While the data available for reanalysis are less refined than those for the 1997 survey, results from the 1993 survey on the question of influence are included in Figure 3-2b.[13]

---

[13] In 1993, fifty congressional staff and twenty-five journalists were interviewed. For that survey, the congressional staff interviewed included "aides from both political parties and

TABLE 3-1. *Brookings and Heritage influence by respondent group*

	Republican Congressional staff	Journalists with elite publications	Journalists with local papers	Democratic Congressional staff
Brookings Institution	39%	56%	72%	58%
Heritage Foundation	90%	94%	75%	65%
n	40	18	36	31

The most notable difference between the 1997 results and findings in the 1993 survey is a flip-flop in perceptions of Brookings versus Heritage. Almost three-quarters of respondents in 1993 (71 percent) named the Brookings Institution among the three most influential think tanks. Fewer than half of respondents (44 percent) named the Heritage Foundation. As in the 1997 survey, the American Enterprise Institute (29 percent), the Cato Institute (11 percent), the Progressive Policy Institute (24 percent), and the Center for Budget and Policy Priorities (3 percent) are among the next most frequently named institutions; the relative ranking of each shifted, however, with the Cato Institute overtaking the American Enterprise Institute and the Progressive Policy Institute. The ascendance of Heritage and Cato in perceptions of the influence of think tanks from 1993 to 1997 almost certainly reflects the ascendance of Republicans to control of Congress in the intervening years. Heritage is avowedly conservative; Cato is libertarian.[14]

The variation among respondent groups in their rankings of Heritage and Brookings in the 1997 survey is interesting. As illustrated in Table 3-1, all groups of respondents – congressional staff and journalists – named the Heritage Foundation as most influential with greater frequency than

both houses of Congress, evenly divided between those responsible for major domestic issues and those responsible for defense/foreign affairs issues." The journalists were "generally bureau chiefs, editors, or others responsible not only for reporting in their own areas of expertise but for managing assignments of other reporters as well." The slight differences in background between those surveyed in 1993 versus 1997 may account for some systematic variation in otherwise comparable responses between the two years. The 1997 survey, for example, contains more responses from journalists with elite publications than the 1993 survey. Furthermore, the areas of substantive expertise among congressional staff vary between the two surveys. For these reasons, I make relatively few comparisons with the 1993 survey.

[14] The American Enterprise Institute is conservative as well, and it experienced a 3 percent jump in the frequency with which it was named, even though the Cato Institute passed it up. The Progressive Policy Institute is centrist, and the Center on Budget and Policy Priorities is liberal.

the Brookings Institution. But journalists from national publications and Republican congressional staff did so with much greater frequency than did journalists with local newspapers and Democratic congressional staff, both of whom named Brookings almost as often as Heritage. These findings with regard to the influence of Heritage and Brookings are confirmed in results of respondents' scaling of the influence of twenty-seven different think tanks, reported in Appendix A.

In a political environment in which so many think tanks and other types of organizations compete for the attention of policy makers – and some think tanks are known to aggressively promote themselves – the survey permits me to consider whether the aggressive efforts of some think tanks to achieve influence in the policy process may be at the expense of continued organizational credibility. Respondents were asked to name the think tank that "comes to mind as most credible in the political process," and then to rate twenty-seven think tanks, including most of the largest and best-known institutions, on a 1–5 scale ranging from not credible to extremely credible. In fact, the think tank perceived as having the second greatest influence in the policy process is also the organization most often named as most credible: the Brookings Institution. As recorded in Table 3-2, in rankings of twenty-seven think tanks included in the survey, the Brookings Institution receives the highest score overall for credibility, and it scores the highest among all respondent groups, including Republican congressional staff. The Heritage Foundation, on the other hand, scores as the ninth most credible think tank overall, well below Brookings. And whereas the Brookings Institution's high credibility rating is stable across respondent categories, the Heritage Foundation's mean credibility score varies considerably from one respondent group to another. Heritage's mean score places it sixth in terms of credibility among Republican congressional staff. By contrast, it ranks fourteenth among journalists with national publications and eighteenth among Democratic congressional staff.

One note about these rankings: The third column in Table 3-2 records the percentage of eligible respondents who provided a rating for each organization. Lower response rates usually reflected a respondent's lack of familiarity with the think tank named, and those think tanks with lower response rates were also frequently those with lower credibility ratings. This may suggest that to some extent respondents link their assessments of organizational credibility to their familiarity with think tanks.

Whatever the case, differences in the perceived credibility of think tanks, particularly between Republican and Democratic congressional

TABLE 3-2. *Rank ordering of think tanks by ratings of credibility in 1997*

Think tank	Ideological cluster	% of n responding
1. Brookings Institution	NI	93
2. RAND Corporation	NI	88
3. American Enterprise Institute	C	93
4. Council on Foreign Relations	NI	69
5. Carnegie Endowment for Int'l Peace	NI	71
6. Center for Strategic and Int'l Studies	NI	72
7. National Bureau of Economic Research	NI	52
8. Center on Budget and Policy Priorities	L	78
9. Heritage Foundation	C	94
10. Cato Institute	C	95
11. Hoover Institution	C	74
12. Urban Institute	NI	86
13. Progressive Policy Institute	NI	74
14. Hudson Institute	C	68
15. Joint Ctr. for Political & Economic Studies	L	40
16. Economic Policy Institute	L	58
17. Resources for the Future	NI	33
18. Institute for International Economics	NI	40
19. Competitive Enterprise Institute	C	50
20. Center for National Policy	L	46
21. Institute for Policy Studies	L	51
22. Worldwatch Institute	L	52
23. Manhattan Institute	C	45
24. Reason Foundation	C	41
25. Economic Strategy Institute	NI	37
26. World Resources Institute	L	29
27. Progress and Freedom Foundation	C	44

C – *conservative cluster think tank*
L – *liberal cluster think tank*
NI – *centrist or no identifiable ideology cluster think tank*

staff, seem to relate to the perceived ideologies of the various organizations. Respondents scaled the twenty-seven think tanks from 1 to 5 in terms of their perceived ideological orientations, with an additional choice of rating organizations as nonideological. In the results, illustrated in Figure 3-3, the Heritage Foundation, Cato Institute, and American Enterprise Institute are consistently rated among the most conservative organizations. The Urban Institute, Worldwatch Institute, Progressive Policy Institute, and the Center on Budget and Policy Priorities are ranked among the most liberal. In the credibility ratings, think tanks scaled as

Urban Institute

  Worldwatch Institute

    Center on Budget and Policy Priorities

    Progressive Policy Institute

    Institute for Policy Studies

      Brookings Institution

      Economic Policy Institute

        World Resources Institute

          Economic Strategy Institute

            Joint Center for Political and Economic Studies

              Carnegie Endowment for International Peace

              Council on Foreign Relations

              Center for National Policy

              RAND Corporation

              Resources for the Future

                Institute for International Economics

                  Center for Strategic and International Studies

                  National Bureau of Economic Research

                  Progress and Freedom Foundation

                  Reason Foundation

                  Manhattan Institute

                  Hudson Institute

                  Hoover Institution

                    Competitive Enterprise Institute

                    American Enterprise Institute

                    Cato Institute

                    Heritage Foundation

FIGURE 3-3. 1997 ideology scores for think tanks from congressional staff and journalists

conservative are often those viewed as more credible by Republican congressional staff, whereas think tanks scored as liberal tend to be those
viewed as more credible by Democratic staff.[15]

Interestingly, think tanks were rarely scored as nonideological. Only
two think tanks were perceived by any respondents as nonideological:
the Brookings Institution and the RAND Corporation, and these organizations received nonideological ratings in only 5 percent and 11 percent
of responses, respectively. The Cato Institute – scaled as the second most
conservative think tank – was specifically labeled as a libertarian organization by approximately one-quarter of respondents.

Visibility with Congress and Journalists

Cumulatively, the perceptions of congressional staff and journalists about
think tanks offer a foundation for evaluating their actual visibility and effect on policy decisions. Given the small number of respondents (125)
and variation in many of the responses, the survey results are inconclu-
sive. But think tanks are clearly recognized as active and influential by
congressional staff and journalists, however that influence is understood.
And think tanks are viewed as a motley bunch.

The clear recognition by busy congressional staff and journalists that
think tanks are an influential organizational form, along with the variety
in their perceptions of particular think tanks, adds to my rationale for
assessing their real visibility and policy influence. In the remainder of
the chapter, I examine whether the characteristics and behaviors of think
tanks are important not just for how they are perceived by congressional
staff and journalists but also for how they are used by them. I analyze
instances of congressional testimony offered by think tank personnel and
newspaper citations obtained by think tanks. My question is: How do
the intentional efforts of think tanks affect their visibility with these key
audiences? Overworked congressional staff and journalists have little time
to react to the demands of their jobs; they are prone to use research that fits
their needs. Within that context, can experts at think tanks independently
affect the visibility their work receives?

In fact, it is not clear that members of Congress prefer receiving expertise that has been produced to address explicitly the political questions
facing them. In his assessment of the Office of Technology Assessment

---

[15] Scores and details about the ideology results are in Appendix A. The results correlate at
0.81 with my independent coding of the same institutions along with the 276 other think
tanks that I discuss in Chapter 1.

(OTA), Bimber actually finds that the production of neutral expertise by the OTA and its presentation in a restrained manner led to its frequent use by members of Congress and to the OTA's organizational survival until 1995.[16] I consider whether the same holds for think tanks, or whether the efforts of the more aggressively marketing-oriented think tanks pay off, at least in terms of visibility. In fact, the intentional efforts of think tanks do appear to affect their visibility, but more the content than the quantity of it.

Assessing Visibility

My findings are based on an analysis of data on congressional testimony and newspaper citations collected for a sample of sixty-six nationally focused think tanks. The sample is varied with regard to the ideologies of the think tanks (conservative, liberal, or no identifiable ideology) and think tank location (Washington, D.C.–based or not).[17] The data represent counts of the frequency with which think tank personnel testified before congressional hearings and were cited in newspaper stories between 1991 and 1999.[18] The dependent variable in the first analysis is the number of times personnel from a think tank testified before House and

---

[16] Bimber, *The Politics of Expertise in Congress*. Bimber's analysis also points to the importance of considering the organizational attributes and functions of sources of expertise in assessing the role of expertise in policy making. Bimber finds that the organizational imperatives on the OTA as a support agency of a partisan and contentious Congress provide incentive for it to behave as a neutral arbiter of expertise.

[17] The sample selected is a one-third, stratified, random sample of the 200 nationally focused think tanks identified as operating in American politics in 1996. Forty of the sampled think tanks (61 percent) are based in Washington, D.C., with the rest based elsewhere in the country. Nineteen of the think tanks included in the sample (29 percent) are broadly conservative; 17 are liberal (25 percent); and 30 are centrist or of "no identifiable ideology" (46 percent). Judgments on the ideologies of each think tank are the same as those described in Chapter 1, made from a review of think tank mission statements and annual reports.

[18] Data on the frequency of congressional testimony were drawn from the Congressional Masterfile CD service and from Congressional Universe, a service of Nexis. Data on the frequency of newspaper citations of the sixty-six think tanks were drawn from the *New York Times*, the *Washington Post*, and the *Wall Street Journal* for the odd-numbered years between 1991 and 1999. Articles were accessed through the Nexis and Dow Jones databases. Portions of the media dataset are drawn from a collaborative project with R. Kent Weaver in which we examine the factors that account for the media visibility of think tanks. See Andrew Rich and R. Kent Weaver, "Think Tanks in the National Media," *Harvard International Journal of Press/Politics* 5 (2000): 81–103. See also Andrew Rich, "The Politics of Expertise in Congress and the News Media," *Social Science Quarterly* 82 (2001): 583–601.

Senate hearings in each year between 1991 and 1999.[19] The dependent variable in the second analysis is the number of articles in which substantive mention is made of a think tank in each newspaper in each year – that is, stories in which think tank studies or commentary are referenced.[20]

The independent variables in my analysis fall into three categories: (1) those associated with the marketing strategies and ideologies of think tanks, (2) those principally related to the biases of congressional staff or journalists, and (3) those essentially autonomous of both the suppliers and consumers of expertise. I operate from the assumption that the reception of expertise from an organization should be highly dependent on its size. The expertise of a think tank with a $10 million annual budget should be greater – and should be used more by Congress and the media – than that of one with a budget of only $1 million. And the effects of budget size on the reception of think tanks may be intensified by other variables. For example, Washington, D.C.–based think tanks may receive more invitations to testify or more media citations *for every dollar spent* than non-D.C.–based think tanks. As a result, I consider not only the direct effects of budget size on think tank visibility but also its effects in interaction with other variables of interest.[21] The variables associated with the first category of explanation include the marketing strategies and ideologies of think tanks.

I code think tanks as marketing-oriented or not for my analysis based on assessments of their organizational philosophies, products, and recent efforts. A third category of think tanks, which I break out from those that are non–marketing-oriented, are contract research think tanks. Besides being non–marketing-oriented, contract research think tanks often have what approach proprietary client relationships with government agencies, whereby those supplying their support (government agencies) prefer and may even require that they not publicize their results.[22]

---

[19] The total number of cases in the analysis is 323.

[20] Excluded from these counts are stories in which think tanks are mentioned for other reasons (e.g., obituaries or wedding announcements). With 66 think tanks, three newspapers, and three years, the total number of cases is 969. Both models are analyzed using a random effects generalized least squares regression technique.

[21] Budget figures are adjusted for inflation to constant 1991 dollars.

[22] The RAND Corporation, in particular, which is an organization with a $120 million budget, often fulfills contracts with the government whereby its results are not highly publicized, either in the media or on Capitol Hill. RAND alone can swing results in the analysis. In an analysis not reported here, the contract research think tanks were included in the non-marketing-oriented group, and their inclusion shifted the non-marketing-oriented result in the same direction as the contract research variable in the results presented here.

With a recognition of the penchant among congressional staff and journalists for, respectively, politically supportive and timely research, ideological and marketing-oriented think tanks may have an advantage because they may satisfy these preferences better than their counterparts. Working against this notion, however, is the possibility that policy makers and journalists prefer to "politicize" research themselves and make it timely on their own initiative. While their time to sort through research is short, in selecting sources for information, members of Congress and journalists might prefer sources that appear to provide the most credible information, with appeal to the broadest possible audience. The Office of Technology Assessment sustained a broad and supportive constituency among members of Congress so long as its research was viewed this way.

In the survey, congressional staff and journalists both consistently named think tanks styled as non–marketing-oriented as most credible. More than three-quarters of journalists and more than half of congressional respondents offered non–marketing-oriented institutions in response to the open-ended question "In terms of credibility, what think tank comes to mind as most credible in the political process?" More than two-thirds of journalists and Democratic congressional staff also named think tanks classified as of no identifiable ideology as most credible. Only Republican congressional staff more often viewed ideological think tanks – conservative think tanks – as the most credible institutions. These results, confirmed in scores of in-depth interviews, make these variables all the more interesting. They posit the credibility of non–marketing-oriented think tanks and organizations of no identifiable ideology against the aggressive promotion by marketing-oriented think tanks and many ideological think tanks.

My second category of variables considers the location, age, and research scope of the organizations; these are factors that play to the possible biases of congressional staff and journalists, who are known to be extremely busy, often preoccupied with deadlines. In her study of the mass media and American politics, Graber observes that journalists, as a result, rely extensively on personal networks and established contacts for information.[23] Gans concurs in his study of network news and news organizations, observing, "staff and timing being in short supply, journalists actively pursue only a small number of regular sources who have been available and suitable in the past, and are passive toward other

---

[23] Doris A. Graber, *Mass Media and American Politics* (Washington, D.C.: Congressional Quarterly Press, 1993), p. 112.

TABLE 3-3. *Characteristics of Think Tank Sample*

Think tank	Founding	1996 budget	Ideology	Org'al strategy
D.C.-based, nationally focused				
American Enterprise Institute	1943	$13,033,786	Conservative	non-marketing
American Foreign Policy Council	1982	$373,315	No Identifiable	marketing
Atlantic Council	1961	$2,701,366	No Identifiable	non-marketing
Brookings Institution	1916	$21,944,000	No Identifiable	non-marketing
Cato Institute	1977	$11,264,791	Conservative	marketing
Center for Defense Information	1972	$1,564,569	Liberal	marketing
Center for Immigration Studies	1985	$413,638	No Identifiable	non-marketing
Center for Law and Social Policy	1969	$1,243,505	Liberal	marketing
Center for Security Policy	1988	$863,393	No Identifiable	marketing
Center for Women Policy Studies	1972	$1,045,848	Liberal	marketing
Child Trends, Inc.	1979	$2,460,722	No Identifiable	non-marketing
Competitive Enterprise Institute	1984	$1,734,297	Conservative	marketing
Cong. Institute for the Future	1979	$290,948	No Identifiable	marketing
Council on Hemispheric Affairs	1975	$80,201	Liberal	marketing
Economic Strategy Institute	1989	$1,890,756	No Identifiable	marketing
Environmental Law Institute	1969	$5,269,422	Liberal	non-marketing
Ethics and Public Policy Center	1976	$1,098,349	Conservative	marketing
Group of Thirty	1978	$507,591	No Identifiable	non-marketing
Heritage Foundation	1973	$24,195,189	Conservative	marketing
Hispanic Policy Develop. Project	1981	$288,211	Liberal	non-marketing
Inst. for Energy and Environmental Rsch.	1985	$565,976	Liberal	non-marketing
Institute for International Economics	1981	$4,200,736	No Identifiable	marketing
Institute for Policy Studies	1963	$1,333,996	Liberal	non-marketing
Inst. for Research on the Econ. of Taxation	1977	$627,381	Conservative	marketing
Institute for Science and Int'l Security	1993	$297,300	No Identifiable	non-marketing
Institute for Women's Policy Research	1987	$856,116	Liberal	non-marketing
Jamestown Foundation	1983	$1,044,811	Conservative	marketing
Jewish Inst. for National Security Affairs	1976	$797,709	No Identifiable	marketing
Joint Ctr. for Political & Economic Studies	1970	$7,046,206	Liberal	marketing
National Academy of Social Insurance	1986	$1,510,032	No Identifiable	non-marketing
Nat'l Ctr. for Public Policy Research	1982	$4,031,925	Conservative	marketing

Think tank	Founding	1996 budget	Ideology	Org'al strategy
National Strategy Information Center	1962	$626,826	No Identifiable	marketing
Pacific Inst. for Research and Evaluation	1975	$13,120,049	No Identifiable	contract rschr
Progress and Freedom Foundation	1993	$1,770,817	Conservative	marketing
Progressive Policy Institute	1989	$3,259,023	No Identifiable	marketing
Tax Foundation	1937	$1,148,780	Conservative	marketing
Urban Institute	1968	$36,643,687	No Identifiable	contract rschr
Washington Center for China Studies	1990	$217,207	No Identifiable	non-marketing
World Priorities, Inc.	1977	$116,676	No Identifiable	marketing
Worldwatch Institute	1974	$2,171,743	Liberal	marketing

Non–D.C.-based, nationally focused

Think tank	Founding	1996 budget	Ideology	Org'al strategy
Center for Education Reform	1993	$632,560	Conservative	marketing
Center for the New West	1989	$1,785,511	No Identifiable	marketing
Center for the Study of Popular Culture	1988	$2,654,596	Conservative	marketing
Committee for Economic Development	1942	$3,865,706	No Identifiable	non-marketing
Family Research Institute	1982	$83,524	Conservative	marketing
Foundation for Economic Education	1946	$1,629,772	Conservative	non-marketing
Hastings Center	1969	$2,236,815	No Identifiable	non-marketing
Hoover Institution	1919	$19,500,000	Conservative	non-marketing
Inform, Inc.	1974	$1,593,263	Liberal	non-marketing
Institute for Agriculture and Trade Policy	1986	$1,122,405	Liberal	non-marketing
Institute for Contemporary Studies	1972	$3,056,900	Conservative	marketing
Institute for Food and Development	1975	$647,516	Liberal	marketing
Institute for Policy Innovation	1987	$611,713	Conservative	marketing
Institute for Puerto Rican Policy	1982	$381,808	No Identifiable	non-marketing
Interhemispheric Resource Center	1979	$285,490	Liberal	marketing
Manhattan Institute	1978	$7,042,492	Conservative	marketing
Manpower Demonstration Rsrch. Corp.	1974	$18,341,419	No Identifiable	contract rschr
National Bureau of Asian Research	1989	$843,184	No Identifiable	non-marketing
Political Research Associates	1981	$391,710	Liberal	marketing
Population Council	1952	$56,852,426	No Identifiable	non-marketing
RAND Corporation	1946	$117,606,889	No Identifiable	contract rschr
Rockford Institute	1976	$1,511,994	Conservative	marketing
Rocky Mountain Institute	1982	$4,118,927	Liberal	marketing
Southern Center for International Studies	1963	$1,609,868	No Identifiable	non-marketing
W. E. Upjohn Institute	1945	$6,136,284	No Identifiable	non-marketing
World Institute on Disability	1983	$3,979,751	No Identifiable	marketing

possible news sources."[24] Congressional staff, not to mention members of Congress themselves, are under equally onerous time pressures. If factors related to the strategies and ideologies of think tanks are unimportant, the biases of congressional staff and journalists may lead them to favor Washington, D.C.–based think tanks that are close at hand, older think tanks that may be better known, and think tanks with broad research missions that may be convenient for "one-stop shopping" on a variety of issues.

Finally, my third category of variables includes a series of interaction terms that take account of important political developments and the think tanks that might have been associated with – and advantaged by – them. In particular, I include a term for think tanks with expertise in Middle East affairs in 1991, the year of the Gulf War, and one for think tanks with economic forecasting expertise in 1991, the year of a domestic recession. I also include a variable for think tanks with links to Bill Clinton's election as president in 1992 and 1993, and one for think tanks with ties to the Republican takeover of Congress in 1994 and 1995.[25] Appendix A includes details on the coding of variables in the analysis. Table 3-3 lists the think tanks in my sample along with their locations, ideologies, size, marketing strategies, and founding years.

Results on the Frequency of the Use of Expertise

The results of a regression analysis, listed in Table 3-4, suggest that the variation in marketing strategies and ideologies of think tanks does make some difference for the frequency with which their expertise is called upon overall by Congress and media outlets, but the biases of congressional staff and journalists and particularly the demands of political events seem more

---

[24] Herbert J. Gans, *Deciding What's News* (New York: Vintage Books, 1980), p. 116.
[25] In the analysis of media citations, three terms are used to measure the differences among the three media outlets. Two dummy variables are included to assess overall differences in the frequency with which think tanks are cited by the three newspapers (for the *New York Times* and the *Wall Street Journal*, with the *Washington Post* serving as the excluded case). An interaction term is included to assess whether the *Wall Street Journal*, known for its conservative editorial page, shows a particular preference for the products of conservative think tanks (*Wall Street Journal* times conservative think tanks). Combinations of other ideological clusters and specific newspapers were considered, but there was little substantive basis for including them in the final equation. When tested in the equations, interaction terms of conservative and liberal think tanks with the *New York Times* and *Washington Post* and liberal think tanks with the *Wall Street Journal* were not significant. That is, there appeared to be no significant differences in the frequency of their citation compared with think tanks of no identifiable ideology.

TABLE 3-4. *Regression results*

	Congressional testimony		Media citations	
Producer variables				
Budget (in millions)	0.19	(0.05)	0.09	(0.09)
Marketing Orientation	−0.29	(0.78)	−2.10	(1.52)
Contract Researcher	−3.86[a]	(2.26)	0.54	(3.92)
Conservative	1.42[a]	(0.84)	3.93[b]	(1.64)
Liberal	0.01	(1.03)	−0.10	(1.88)
Budget × marketing	−0.19	(0.21)	0.18	(0.33)
Budget × contract	0.13[b]	(0.06)	0.16[a]	(0.10)
Budget × conservative	−0.38[b]	(0.16)	−3.25[c]	(0.27)
Budget × liberal	−0.19	(0.46)	0.56	(0.77)
Consumer variables				
D.C. location	1.76[c]	(0.56)	2.11[b]	(1.04)
Research focus	−0.41	(1.28)	0.80	(2.32)
Age	−0.94	(0.72)	−0.63	(1.34)
Budget × D.C.	0.20[c]	(0.06)	0.42[c]	(0.10)
Budget × Research Focus	0.93[c]	(0.15)	4.40[c]	(0.26)
Budget × Age	0.26[b]	(0.13)	−0.13	(0.26)
New York Times			−1.72[c]	(0.54)
Wall Street Journal			−4.20[c]	(0.62)
WSJ × conservative			5.11[c]	(1.03)
Political Events Variables				
Gulf War	25.58[c]	(5.37)	28.05[c]	(6.23)
1991 Recession	5.65	(3.72)	3.09	(4.40)
Clinton Election	1.80	(2.61)	9.77[c]	(3.09)
Republican Congress	32.09[c]	(2.71)	17.49[c]	(2.24)
	$r^2 = 0.74$		$r^2 = 0.78$	
	$n = 323$		$n = 969$	

[a] $p < 0.10$ [b] $p < 0.05$ [c] $p < 0.01$

important. Non–D.C.-based, older, specialized, non–marketing-oriented think tanks with no identifiable ideologies represent the baseline case in the analysis.

Congressional Testimony

There are slight statistical differences in the frequency with which think tanks of different marketing strategies and identifiable ideologies testify before Congress, with some additional effects in interaction with budget size. Conservative think tanks start out with an advantage in obtaining opportunities to testify before Congress, compared with the baseline think tanks of liberal, centrist, or no identifiable ideology, receiving, on average, almost one-and-a-half more opportunities to testify than otherwise similar think tanks (1.42). The strength of this conservative advantage diminishes, however, as the sizes of think tanks increase (−0.38 per $1 million in budget). In other words, small conservative think tanks are more efficient in obtaining opportunities to testify than their nonconservative counterparts, but this advantage declines against other think tanks as organizational size increases.

In terms of marketing, whether a think tank is marketing-oriented or not appears to make little difference, but contract research think tanks do have a difficult experience. By comparison with both marketing and non–marketing-oriented think tanks, contract research think tanks start out with a sizable disadvantage in obtaining opportunities to testify before Congress (−3.86), but the disadvantage is overcome slowly as organizational size increases (0.13 per $1 million in budget). Contract research think tanks lack the efficiency of other think tanks – especially ideologically conservative think tanks – in obtaining opportunities to offer congressional testimony.

Some of the variables that reflect the preferences of Congress are also important for understanding think tank opportunities to testify. Think tanks based in Washington, D.C., receive more chances to testify than think tanks based elsewhere (1.76), an advantage that also increases with the size of organizations (0.20 per $1 million in budget). Think tanks that are newer have a slight advantage (0.26), and those that are focused on a broad range of policy issues receive more opportunities to testify before Congress than those that specialize in a narrow set of topics, all else being equal (0.93).

Finally, the independent influence of political events outweighs in importance all other explanations for congressional testimony. In 1991, the year of the Gulf War, think tanks with Middle East expertise testified an average of more than twenty-five more times than otherwise comparable think tanks (25.58). In 1995, the year Republicans took control of the House and Senate, identifiably conservative think tanks were called to testify an average of thirty-two times more than other think tanks (32.09).

Selection of think tanks with a Middle East expertise and, even more, the choice of think tanks with conservative proclivities is, of course, to a substantial extent an expression of preferences by congressional staff. But such choices represented as well a reaction by Congress to the imperatives of political events. Once the Republicans had won Congress, their reliance on conservative think tanks in the early days of 1995 represented not just a preference but also a recognition of their obligation to deliver on a conservative platform of policy reforms, for which conservative think tanks could be helpful. The variables for the new Clinton administration in 1993 and the economic recession in 1991 were not significant, suggesting that these developments had few immediate or short-term implications on the selection of experts for hearings in a Congress already led by Democrats.

Newspaper Citations

The results for total substantive newspaper citations are similar to those for congressional testimony. Independent political events remain most important in accounting for the frequency with which think tank expertise is cited. Think tanks with Middle East expertise received more than twenty-eight additional citations in 1991 than otherwise comparable think tanks (28.05). Conservative think tanks with links to the Republican takeover of Congress received an average of close to eighteen more citations than their baseline counterparts (17.49). In this analysis, the Clinton election variable was also significant, with think tanks linked to the Clinton election receiving almost ten more citations than their baseline counterparts (9.77).

The marketing strategies of think tanks make no difference for the frequency of their citation. As with congressional testimony, conservative think tanks start out with significantly greater media visibility than their nonconservative counterparts (3.93), but that advantage erodes quickly as the size of otherwise comparable organizations increases (−3.25 per $1 million in budget). Conservative think tanks do not hold onto their efficiency in attracting media visibility as the sizes of think tanks increase.

The remaining significant coefficients reflect the nonsubstantive biases of journalists. Washington, D.C.–based think tanks receive more visibility than non–D.C.-based think tanks, at the baseline (1.76) and as the size of organizations grows (0.20 per $1 million in budget). Likewise, as the size of think tanks with broad research missions grows, they secure media visibility at a substantially faster rate than comparable but more narrowly focused think tanks (4.40 per $1 million in budget).

Between publications, there are two specific media effects. First, the *Washington Post* demonstrates a greater overall propensity for citing think tanks than the *Wall Street Journal* and the *New York Times*.[26] Second, the *Wall Street Journal* shows a remarkably strong preference for ideologically

---

[26] In part, these results reflect differences in the extent to which think tanks are a "source of choice" in particular newspapers, but they also reflect, at least as it relates to the *Wall Street Journal*, the simple arithmetic of how frequently newspapers are published (e.g., the *Wall Street Journal* only five days a week) and how many column-inches of news and opinion coverage each carries.

conservative think tanks, citing them on average five more times per year than the other newspapers and than think tanks of other ideologies on their own pages (5.11).

Discussion of Regression Results

Cumulatively, these results suggest that the marketing strategies and ideologies of think tanks have an effect on how often their expertise is tapped by Congress and the news media, but not a strong one. Conservative think tanks begin with an advantage in securing media visibility and opportunities to testify before Congress over nonconservative baseline think tanks. But this efficiency diminishes as organizations grow in size. Contract research think tanks have the opposite experience, at least with regard to obtaining opportunities to testify before Congress.

On first appearance, the general absence of more significant results among this first category of variables suggests limits to the ability of think tanks – of experts – to affect their own visibility. The results suggest that at least as it relates to media and congressional visibility, the ability of think tanks to affect their own treatment is secondary to the preferences of those that choose to rely on them – journalists and congressional staff. The results suggest that a Washington, D.C., location is helpful for obtaining opportunities to testify and for gaining visibility in the news media. And while the initial choice to locate in Washington may belong to the think tanks, over time, even the preeminence of D.C.-based think tanks reflects more the preferences of Congress and the news media than that of the think tanks themselves. Washington-based think tanks, like think tanks with full-service missions, appear to better satisfy the biases of congressional staff and national media than their counterparts. It is these biases and especially the independent effects of political events that appear to best explain the frequency with which think tank expertise is drawn on by Congress or journalists. Overall, and in contrast to findings in the survey, these results are relatively consistent across Congress and the news media.

The results do not close the door to the possibility that think tanks and experts can affect their own visibility and influence, however. First, media citations and appearances before congressional hearings are in some respects crude measures of visibility, not to mention influence. What does the appearance of think tanks in newspapers or before congressional panels really mean? It is not immediately clear whether media and congressional visibility relates to debates over final legislative enactment on policy issues, to developing public understanding on new topics headed for the policy-making agenda, or perhaps ultimately to meaningless lipservice paid by journalists, Congress, and think tanks alike to topics that have little hope of becoming policy priorities. Whether visibility pertains to one or another of these purposes suggests quite varied possible implications for the substantive importance of think tanks.

Even more, the absence of advantages for think tanks that aggressively market their work raises the possibility that there may be complicated drawbacks – or tradeoffs – for think tanks that assume an aggressive marketing posture. On some topics and in some venues, more restrained efforts at promoting research might make sources appear more credible and believable, and therefore make them more desirable. There may be a tradeoff for think tanks between cultivating political access and fostering credibility. If such a tension exists, it might be revealed in an analysis of *how* think tanks are portrayed in the news media and *with whom* think tank personnel are invited to testify before Congress. An analysis of the frequency of congressional and media visibility is only half the story; the other half relates to the content of that visibility.

The Uses of Expertise from Think Tanks

Congressional Testimony
The strongest indication that think tanks with different strategies and ideologies experience different treatment in congressional hearings comes from an examination of the panels upon which think tank personnel are placed. Congressional committee appearances were coded for the chamber and committee before which personnel testified and the affiliations of others with whom think tank personnel testified (e.g., interest groups, universities, other think tanks) between 1993 and 1999 (1,075 cases). In addition, the specific institutional affiliations of those testifying were sorted when staff from more than one think tank testified together; this latter step permits comparison of the strategies and ideologies of the think tanks whose personnel appeared together at congressional hearings.

Table 3-5 reports the frequency with which those from think tanks with different marketing strategies sat on panels with various other types of witnesses. Representatives of interest groups are the single group with whom think tank personnel from all types of organization most often testify.[27] But whereas almost half of the personnel with whom marketing-oriented

---

[27] Witnesses labeled as interest groups in this analysis include everything from trade association officials to union representatives, corporate CEOs to public interest groups. As a result, it is not surprising that this is the group most frequently represented on hearing panels with all kinds of think tanks.

TABLE 3-5. *Think tank congressional testimony, organizational forms by affiliations of others testifying*

| | Affiliations of other personnel testifying | | | | | | |
	University	Government	Interest group	Journalist	Think tank	Other	n
Marketing-Oriented Think tanks	11.9%	14.0%	49.1%	1.2%	17.8%	6.1%	251
Non–marketing-Oriented Think tanks	19.0%	14.8%	30.4%	1.3%	22.8%	11.8%	191
Contract Research Think tanks	19.1%	21.2%	32.5%	0.0%	17.7%	9.4%	51

think tank researchers are grouped on congressional panels come from interest groups (49.1 percent), fewer than one-third of those from non–marketing-oriented and contract research think tanks are grouped with interest groups (30.4 percent and 32.5 percent, respectively). Instead, non–marketing-oriented and contract research think tanks are often grouped with university officials, at a much greater rate than personnel from marketing-oriented think tanks.[28] These results begin to confirm the suspicion that think tanks may be judged differently – and therefore meet with different kinds of opportunities – based on their strategies. Think tanks that remain more reserved in their approach to promoting work (whether by choice or necessity) and that do not typically package their work for fastest or easiest consumption are more often grouped with others similar to themselves – university scholars – that are also typically viewed with greater credibility than those from interest groups.

If one disaggregates by ideology instead of by organizational form, similar patterns become visible. While interest groups are still the most frequent partners of think tank personnel on congressional panels, staff from conservative and liberal think tanks, as noted in Table 3-6, are more often grouped with those from interest groups (43.9 percent and 42.7 percent, respectively) than are think tanks of no identifiable ideology (35.9 percent). And staff from think tanks of no identifiable ideology testify slightly more often with university personnel (17.7 percent) than

---

[28] Differences of proportion in this and all of the tables in this section of the paper pass chi squared tests for statistical significance.

TABLE 3-6. *Think tank congressional testimony, ideological clusters by affiliations of others testifying*

	Affiliations of other personnel testifying						
	University	Government	Interest group	Journalist	Think tank	Other	n
Conservative Cluster	13.8%	14.4%	43.9%	1.4%	18.8%	7.7%	259
Liberal cluster	9.7%	25.0%	42.7%	0.8%	12.9%	8.9%	27
No Identifiable Ideology cluster	17.7%	15.1%	35.9%	0.7%	21.1%	9.5%	207

do those from the conservative and liberal think tanks (13.8 percent and 9.7 percent, respectively).[29]

Newspaper Citations
I gauge how expertise is used in newspapers by coding the nature of references made to think tanks. References to think tanks are coded into four categories based on whether they refer to (1) articles written by think tank personnel (often op-eds), (2) the findings of studies produced by think tanks, (3) substantive or political commentary by the "experts" at think tanks in news stories, or (4) some other topic (ranging from obituaries and wedding announcements to television listings of appearances

[29] The patterns in how personnel from think tanks that testify together on congressional panels are grouped suggests additional confirmation that differences in the strategies of think tanks carry over to affect their visibility. Personnel from think tanks tend to testify most often with researchers from think tanks with similar strategies and ideologies. Marketing-oriented think tank personnel testify most often with staff from other marketing-oriented think tanks, and non–marketing-oriented think tanks share panels most frequently with other non–marketing-oriented think tanks. The pattern is not as strong in connection with the ideologies of think tanks. Most of the period of my analysis (1993–9) falls after the Republicans won control of Congress, and beginning in 1995, all think tank personnel testified most often with personnel from conservative think tanks, who testified most, overall, before Congress.
    There is one additional and important note about these results. Two categories of think tanks are extremely small: think tanks that are contract researchers in form and think tanks that are liberal in ideology. The think tanks with which personnel from contract research think tanks share panels are almost evenly split between those that are marketing-oriented and those that are non–marketing-oriented. Personnel with think tanks in the liberal cluster are much more often grouped with conservative think tanks than with organizations of no identifiable ideology, suggesting that, along with facing opportunities in a Republican Congress, ideological think tanks – even with opposing outlooks – testify together more often than do conservative or liberal think tanks with think tanks of no identifiable ideology.

TABLE 3-7. *Think tank media citations, organizational forms by type of mention*

	Article written by think tank personnel	Article references think tank study	Article references commentary by think tank staff	n
Marketing-oriented Think tanks	17.7%	27.3%	55.0%	2,424
Non–marketing-oriented Think tanks	18.3%	16.1%	65.7%	3,419
Contract research Think tanks	5.5%	48.6%	45.9%	996

by think tank personnel on Sunday morning talk shows). The "other" category captures all references to think tanks that are not expressions of the knowledge or expertise of think tanks; they are excluded from my analysis.[30]

As shown in Table 3-7, a significantly greater proportion of references to non–marketing-oriented think tanks is to commentary compared with marketing-oriented think tanks, and the marketing-oriented think tanks receive a greater proportion of references to studies and research. These results are at first curious. If the non–marketing-oriented think tanks appear to be more credible, shouldn't their research receive more attention? In fact, the answer may be that the reduced visibility for their studies may stem precisely from their less effective marketing of it.

On the one hand, the think tanks in the non-marketing cluster are typically also some of the older and more broadly focused institutions. Consistent with Weiss's finding that journalists prefer sources that they know well and can rely on with some regularity, the think tanks in the non–marketing-oriented cluster may be preferred by journalists when they are looking for comment on topics about which they already intend to write.[31] On the other hand, the greater attention to the research of the

---

[30] My interest is in the first three categories of citations, but it is interesting that a full one-quarter of all citations to the think tanks in my sample are part of this "other" category – not reflecting the expertise or research produced by think tanks (1,311 references). The percentage of "other" references is roughly proportional across categories of think tanks grouped by form and ideology.

[31] A content analysis of a sample of these stories suggests that the think tank personnel from the non–marketing-oriented think tanks provide general technical and expert background for stories in this capacity.

more marketing-oriented think tanks suggests that they are succeeding in securing attention for exactly that which they care to: their expertise and ideas. The self-conscious strategy of marketing-oriented think tanks is to package and promote their research in ways that attract greater attention for it. These results suggest that they are succeeding.

One last note about the results in Table 3-7: The contract research think tanks receive the greatest proportion of attention to their research of any strategic category of think tanks. This significant attention to contract think tank research has to be understood, however, in the context of what is proportionally much less media visibility overall received by these think tanks than those that are marketing- or non–marketing-oriented.

The results recorded in Table 3-8 reveal more about how the media apportioned visibility and the extent to which it might be affected by the deliberate efforts of think tanks. Table 3-8 groups the content of visibility by think tank ideology. The interesting result here is the significantly greater proportion of references to conservative think tanks for articles written by their personnel than is the case for liberal think tanks and organizations of no identifiable ideology. Almost 30 percent of references to conservative think tanks were to articles written by think tank staff, compared with less than 8 percent of the references to think tanks of liberal, centrist, or no identifiable ideology. As the lower half of Table 3-8 reveals, many of the articles written by conservative think tanks were published in the editorial pages of the *Wall Street Journal*. Almost half of the references to conservative think tanks in the *Wall Street Journal* (47.1 percent) were to articles written by think tank personnel. By comparison, in the *New York Times* and *Washington Post*, fewer than one-fifth of references made to conservative think tanks were in relation to articles written by think tank personnel during this same period.

The conservative bias of the editorial page of the *Wall Street Journal* is visible again in connection with the placement of references in the newspapers. References were coded for whether they appeared in the news sections (national, international, local, or business), opinion sections, or other sections (e.g., style, book review) of newspapers. Almost one-third of substantive references to conservative think tanks appear in the opinion pages of the three newspapers. Two-thirds of these are in the *Wall Street Journal*. By comparison, less than 20 percent of references to liberal think tanks and organizations of no identifiable ideology appeared on opinion pages. So proportionally, conservative think tanks were more likely not only to write articles that appeared on editorial pages but also to be cited by others on these pages for their research and views.

TABLE 3-8. *Think tank media citations, ideological clusters by type of mention*

All Three Newspapers	Article authored by think tank personnel	Article refers to think tank study	Article refers to commentary by think tank staff	n
Conservative Cluster	29.1%	21.6%	49.3%	2,690
Liberal Cluster	7.9%	32.5%	59.6%	391
No Identifiable Ideology Cluster	7.8%	26.3%	65.9%	3,758

Wall Street Journal	Article authored by think tank personnel	Article refers to think tank study	Article refers to commentary by think tank staff	n
Conservative Cluster	47.1%	19.9%	33.0%	1,010
Liberal Cluster	0.0%	37.3%	62.7%	51
No Identifiable Ideology Cluster	6.2%	27.1%	66.7%	827

New York Times and Washington Post	Article authored by think tank personnel	Article refers to think tank study	Article refers to commentary by think tank staff	n
Conservative Cluster	17.9%	22.6%	59.5%	1,680
Liberal Cluster	9.1%	31.8%	59.1%	340
No Identifiable Ideology Cluster	8.3%	26.0%	65.7%	2,931

Accounting for Visibility

In the end, these results suggest that differences in the strategies and ideologies of think tanks may indeed affect both how their work is perceived
and how it is used by Congress and the news media, even if these factors
do not affect the overall frequency of their visibility. These last results,
in relation to the news media, suggest that the think tanks most successful at conveying their ideas, at least through national newspapers, are
conservative, marketing-oriented think tanks. Marketing-oriented think

tanks generally are more successful in having their research cited, and conservative think tanks have good fortune in obtaining space in which to promote their work, at least in the pages of the editorially sympathetic *Wall Street Journal.*

The results with regard to congressional testimony suggest that the success of conservative and marketing-oriented think tanks in obtaining visibility may be tempered by its potential for impairing the perceived credibility of their work. The same think tanks that are most successful at obtaining substantive visibility for their research and ideas in the news media are also most likely to be grouped with officials from interest groups, as opposed to academics, for congressional hearings. These results are consistent with those of the survey, where those who were most likely to view ideological think tanks as influential also viewed them as little different from advocacy organizations.

Whatever the case, cumulatively, these results suggest reason to take seriously the possibilities for experts based at think tanks to self-consciously affect their chances of obtaining attention. In this chapter, the nature of that attention has been forms of visibility. Visibility is far different from influence, however, and the types of visibility analyzed here might at times be quite different from that which has substantive bearing on policy. But the strength of the results nonetheless lay the foundation for my direct examination of the policy influence of think tanks in the next two chapters. The results suggest the possibilities for think tanks, as policy experts, to be quite politically engaged in policy making; the results suggest the possibilities for think tanks to affect, if not determine, the dimensions and extent of their political engagement. And the results suggest the tensions that surface when policy researchers seek to balance political activity with the maintenance of credibility for their work and themselves in the eyes of policy makers. These tensions have been central to the dilemma for think tanks and for policy experts generally.

4

The Policy Roles of Experts

When President Bill Clinton signed welfare reform into law in 1996, he codified a range of ideas for changing government assistance to the poor that had been emanating from think tanks and the broader research community for several decades. Especially since Charles Murray's book *Losing Ground* was published in 1984, written while Murray was affiliated with the New York–based Manhattan Institute, the merits of a cash-based government entitlement for single mothers with children had been under heavy assault, criticized as a system that promoted overdependence on government support and a propensity toward having children out of wedlock.[1] The welfare law enacted in 1996 had features that responded to Murray's by then twelve-year-old critique, along with many elaborations on it published by him and others in the succeeding years.[2] The new law's general approach and many of its specific provisions were informed by the work of think tanks. The final law was the synthesis of work by experts, advocates, and ideologues during the 1980s and 1990s, many based at think tanks that embodied the spirit of all three.[3]

[1] Charles Murray, *Losing Ground: American Social Policy, 1950–1980* (New York: Basic Books, 1984).

[2] Murray's book set an initial context for the welfare reform debate, and the work of Robert Rector, a scholar at the Heritage Foundation, was called upon frequently by lawmakers as they crafted specific provisions of the welfare reform law. See R. Kent Weaver, *Ending Welfare as We Know It* (Washington, D.C.: The Brookings Institution, 2000), pp. 213–17. This work was offset, to a limited extent, in the final law by the work of more liberal researchers, some of whom were leading proponents of the idea of imposing time limits on welfare recipients. See, for example, David T. Ellwood, *Poor Support: Poverty in the American Family* (New York: Basic Books, 1988).

[3] For a thorough discussion of the role of policy research in the welfare reform debate, see Weaver, *Ending Welfare as We Know It*, pp. 135–68. For a longer-term perspective on social

The welfare reform debate of the mid-1990s was one clearly open to the contributions of policy researchers. The work of those who fashioned themselves experts on the issue was tremendously important in bringing critiques of the cash assistance system to the attention of policy makers in the 1980s; many of the reform ideas developed in books and articles during the late 1980s and early 1990s formed a foundation for early policy proposals. And after deliberation over a new law had begun in earnest in the mid-1990s, policy experts based at think tanks and elsewhere were a central source of advice on how to formulate technical aspects of the legislation. In his analysis of the politics of welfare reform, Weaver observes that policy research was often contested "with multiple purveyors and limited agreement among policy elites on 'whom you can trust' in the policy research community. But policy research did produce a number of broadly accepted 'fire alarms'" about the problems with the current policy regime that formed an intellectual foundation for reform.[4] Despite frequent discrepancies among specific analytic findings, research made important contributions to the final law.

Policy debates are not always as concerned with nor as accommodating of the work of policy experts as was the welfare debate in the 1990s. This chapter examines the dimensions of the policy process that create favorable and unfavorable conditions for think tanks and policy experts generally. Building on the findings in Chapter 3 which suggest that think tanks, by their characteristics and behavior, can affect the type of attention received, I investigate the next logical question: Specifically when and how do think tanks and policy researchers make themselves influential? In this chapter, I consider "when," as opposed to "how." I examine the conditions of the domestic policy process that advantage or disadvantage think tanks and policy experts generally. What types of issue debates provide clear opportunities for policy research to be important and influential? What types of issue debates are less suited to contributions of research? The findings of Chapter 3 indicate that political events and attributes of the policy environment can affect opportunities for policy experts. In this chapter, I consider when that occurs. In the next chapter, I build on these findings to examine *how* think tanks and other policy experts achieve policy influence. I consider the characteristics and behaviors of think tanks

science research about poverty, see Alice O'Connor, *Poverty Knowledge: Social Science, Social Policy, and the Poor in Twentieth-Century U.S. History* (Princeton, N.J.: Princeton University Press, 2001).

4 Weaver, *Ending Welfare as We Know It*, p. 367.

and policy experts within particular issue debates that advantage some and disadvantage others in their efforts to affect preferences and decisions. My analysis in these chapters focuses not just on the activities of think tanks but on the work of policy experts generally. "Think tanks and policy experts generally" is a phrase used perhaps all too often here. But as I move beyond an examination of the origins and evolution of think tanks to consider their policy influence, think tanks cannot be evaluated in isolation. Far from operating in a vacuum, think tanks participate in the policy process alongside a range of sources of research that also include academics, private-sector consulting firms, interest groups, and government bureaus. Think tanks are among the most numerous organizational forms devoted to policy research, and they are often among the most focused and visible sources of ideas and analysis in contemporary policy making. But it is precisely because they are so numerous and visible that considering their efforts in relation to other sources of policy research is desirable. I am concerned with both their individual and, if it exists, cumulative advantage in policy making as an organizational form. So despite its rote quality, "think tanks and policy experts generally" it is in the pages that follow. The power and position of think tanks are best assessed in relation to these other actors.

The analysis also operates from the premise that even in the best of circumstances, policy research, including the work of think tanks, is no more than one in a panoply of sources of information and influence on any issue navigating the policy process. Weaver observes that in the welfare reform debates of the mid-1990s, public opinion, interest groups, and electoral pressures were essential forces.[5] But still policy research was important – more so, in fact, than in debates over many other policy issues. My purpose is not to suggest that there are some issue debates in which policy research plays the dominant role but rather that some issue debates provide better opportunities for policy research than others.

In this chapter, I focus on the opportunities for and role of policy research in three issue debates of the past ten years: health care, telecommunications, and tax policy. The experiences of policy research in each reveals much about what issues and what conditions generally privilege research. I begin the chapter by enumerating how I selected the cases and

[5] See Weaver, *Ending Welfare as We Know It*, pp. 364–85. Weaver also points out that the influence of research was mitigated by disagreements in the research, with research supporting multiple points of view, and by fundamental conflicts in policy makers' values. Policy makers came to the debate with different entrenched preconceptions about the appropriate role of government in providing welfare support.

the framework within which their analysis is placed. I turn to an examination of the three issue debates, and the chapter ends with a consideration of the mutable role of policy researchers in a quite variable policy process. Four features of issue debates emerge as especially relevant to the opportunities experts have to play a meaningful and sometimes influential role in the policy process. On the one hand, experts can have a greater chance of affecting the broad outlines of policy debates in instances where an accumulation of policy research supports similar conclusions as a new issue debate gets underway. Then the role of experts tends to be greater in debates that take on a high public profile, that move at a relatively slow pace, and that do not elicit the mobilization of organized interests with much to lose in the decisions under consideration.

Issues That Can Use Experts

Making policy about any particular issue occurs not in a single moment, by a single decision, with a consistent set of actors but rather over a series of moments in a lengthy period that typically involves scores of different actors and different types of decisions. The policy process is conventionally analyzed in relation to stages of policy development[6]: *Agenda setting* is the period – lasting weeks to decades – when policy proposals are generated and issues work their way toward becoming the priorities of policy makers. *Policy deliberation* is the period when public officials – elected decision makers – are collectively engaged in discussing issues. *Policy enactment* is the point when policy makers resolve decisions by accepting or rejecting new legislation or regulation. The period of *policy implementation* begins once a law or regulation is enacted and refers to the administration of policies and programs and the tinkering that may be associated with efforts to ensure their effectiveness. Issues cycle through the stages, with frequently changing attributes, constituencies, and prospects.[7]

My interest is in how think tanks – and experts and expertise generally – become important and influential at different points in the policy process.

---

[6] See John W. Kingdon, *Agendas, Alternatives, and Public Policies, Second Edition* (New York: Longman, 1995); Arthur Maass, *Congress and the Common Good* (New York: Basic Books, 1983).

[7] The stages heuristic has been the subject of considerable criticism in recent years for its limits in explaining policy outcomes. Even if limited in its explanatory power, it remains the most useful way for operationalizing the policy process. See Peter deLeon, "The Stages Approach to the Policy Process: What Has It Done? Where Is It Going?" in *Theories of the Policy Process*, ed. by Paul A. Sabatier (Boulder, Colo.: Westview Press, 1999).

Besides obtaining visibility with Congress and journalists, expertise is understood to play active, important – but quite different – roles in each stage of the policy process. During agenda setting, expertise is useful as *warning* to policy makers of impending problems and as *guidance* to decision makers on how to revise policy.[8] Expertise, at this point, can "alter people to the extent [that] a given situation affects their interests or values."[9] As Rochefort and Cobb point out, policy research can help to define the boundaries of problems and the dimensions of interventions before issues even receive serious debate.[10]

Once an issue is under deliberation and headed toward policy enactment, from the point when policy makers are collectively involved until final decisions are imminent, elected officials are positioning themselves on issues, and expertise becomes valuable as *ammunition* in policy battles and as *support* for policy makers' already-developed views. As Lindblom and Woodhouse observe of this point in the policy process, "Not usually an alternative to politics, analysis commonly operates as an indispensable element in politics. . . . Rather than making frontal attacks on policy problems, it more often meets certain needs of people, especially officials, to control others in political interaction."[11] At this point, policy research often plays little substantive role, but it is not unimportant either. As Jenkins-Smith and Sabatier observe, policy makers "can seldom develop a majority position through the raw exercise of power. Instead, they must seek to *convince* other actors of the soundness of their position concerning the problem and the consequences of one or more policy alternatives."[12] Policy research, as they point out, is useful – often vital – in this process.

Finally, when issues are resolved and especially after new programs have been created, research becomes useful for those implementing policies and programs. At this stage, policy research can serve as *assessment*

---

[8] See Carol H. Weiss, "Congressional Committees as Users of Analysis," *Journal of Policy Analysis and Management* 8 (1989): 411–31, for an enumeration of these roles for research. For an earlier formulation, see Carol H. Weiss, *Using Social Research in Public Policy Making* (Lexington, Mass.: Lexington Books, 1977).

[9] Hank C. Jenkins-Smith and Paul Sabatier, "The Dynamics of Policy-Oriented Learning," in *Policy Change and Learning: An Advocacy Coalition Approach*, ed. by Paul A. Sabatier and Hank C. Jenkins-Smith (Boulder, Colo.: Westview Press, 1993), p. 45.

[10] David A. Rochefort and Roger W. Cobb, *The Politics of Problem Definition: Shaping the Policy Agenda* (Lawrence: University Press of Kansas, 1994), pp. 10–15.

[11] Charles E. Lindblom and Edward J. Woodhouse, *The Policy Making Process, Second Edition* (Englewood Cliffs, N.J.: Prentice-Hall, 1980), p. 28. See also Aaron Wildavsky, *Speaking Truth to Power* (Boston: Little, Brown, 1979).

[12] Sabatier and Jenkins-Smith, *Policy Change and Learning*, p. 45.

and further *guidance*.[13] Assessment is work that might point to desirable adjustments to the administration of programs. This work directs policy and guides policy actors toward new issues. Research at this point provides substantive guidance on where and how policy makers might proceed next.

The stages-based model of the policy process is helpful for organizing an analysis of issue debates. But it is just an organizing tool. Within the different stages of the policy process, decision making on any particular issue can take on many distinctive features and follow many different twists and turns. Each stage in the policy process can take on radically different attributes depending on the issue under debate, the path by which the issue came up for discussion, and the range of actors who have a stake in how it is decided. This variation may carry over to affect the opportunities for think tanks and other policy experts to be influential; in other words, it may affect the chances for research to inform the views and actions of decision makers.

In a classic formulation of how issues prompt different types of decision-making processes, James Q. Wilson enumerates four styles of policy making. These styles, which vary based on the perceived distribution of costs and benefits on issues, are: (1) majoritarian politics, which is characteristic of issues with distributed costs and distributed benefits; (2) client politics, which is characteristic of issues with distributed costs but concentrated benefits; (3) entrepreneurial politics, which is characteristic of issues with concentrated costs but distributed benefits; and (4) interest group politics, which is characteristic of issues with both concentrated costs and benefits.[14] The categories were helpful in selecting issues to use in evaluating the possibilities for experts. My three issues – health care, telecommunications, and tax reform – each fall into different categories of Wilson's typology.

The movement for universal health care coverage in the early 1990s is most characteristic of entrepreneurial politics, albeit perhaps in a perverted form. While the actual costs of the proposed health care reform would have been broadly distributed, the health insurance industry along with the medical community perceived themselves as most at risk by the

[13] Daniel Mazmanian and Paul Sabatier, *Implementation and Public Policy* (Lanham, Md.: University Press of America, 1989). See also Jeffrey Pressman and Aaron Wildavsky, *Implementation, Third Edition* (Berkeley: University of California Press, 1984).

[14] See James Q. Wilson, "The Politics of Regulation," in *The Politics of Regulation*, edited by James Q. Wilson (New York: Basic Books, 1980). Wilson's typology has been the subject of substantial debate and elaboration since it was first developed.

reform proposals – both financially and professionally. They took up the fight against health care reform and created the perception among policy makers that the costs of reform would be unjustly shouldered by them. The industries sought to convince the general public that it would suffer reduced or more costly service under the proposed reforms. It was an issue generally perceived as having broadly distributed benefits for the public, however, if perhaps at a high cost. So health care reform became an issue that eventually featured characteristics of entrepreneurial politics, although it began as an issue with majoritarian attributes with broad-based benefits and an expectation of broadly distributed costs.[15]

Telecommunications reform is a textbook illustration of interest group politics. Depending on how the final legislation was formulated, some narrow set of corporate interests stood to gain or lose. The long-distance carriers were seeking to compete in local service markets. If successful, they would be winners and the local phone companies would be losers. The cable industry and broadcasters were among many other industry segments that also had an interest in winning new business opportunities in the high-stakes battles.

Finally, the debate over a tax cut in 2001 is an example of majoritarian politics at work, or at least one that was perceived as majoritarian. The issue was promoted as one that would have broadly distributed benefits for the American people, who would enjoy tax reduction, and the costs of a tax cut in 2001 would be broadly distributed. In fact, as initially conceived, the costs of the tax cut were to have been negligible because revenue reductions were to have come from the return of a budget surplus to the American people.

The differences in the distribution of costs and benefits associated with the three issues provides one source of variation in the cases under examination here. To classify the three issues as characteristic of entrepreneurial, interest group, and majoritarian politics respectively, however, only begins to take note of how different the politics surrounding the debates over the issues were from one another, from the point when they worked their way to policy maker attention to their passage (or demise). Issues can reach policy makers after long efforts by advocates or organized interest groups to have them be heard. They can emerge quite suddenly out of public

---

[15] Wilson points out that the dynamics of particular issues can sometimes be characterized by more than one style of politics, and issue debates can sometimes switch from one type to another in mid-debate, if public and policy makers' perceptions of costs and benefits change. That happened with the health care reform debate.

crises or shifts in public opinion. Issues can develop momentum during election campaigns or in the corridors of Congress. Overall, major policy change is infrequent in Washington, with incremental reform the norm.[16] But the paths that issues take to reach policy makers – even similar issues at different points in time – vary tremendously.

So it is with the three issues under analysis here. The 1993–4 attempt at comprehensive health care reform and the 2001 tax cut emerged as debates through events of the national electoral process. After health care reform's unanticipated success as an issue in Harris Wofford's 1991 election to the U.S. Senate from Pennsylvania, it became a central topic of debate among presidential hopefuls in 1992. Organized proponents and opponents of health care reform used aggressive strategies to sway the opinions of policy makers.[17] The 2001 tax cut had been a centerpiece of President George W. Bush's 2000 presidential campaign. By the end of the campaign, he and his Democratic opponent, Vice President Al Gore, were no longer debating whether a tax cut would be enacted but rather what its size and focus should be.

Telecommunications reform, by contrast, enacted in the Telecommunications Reform Act of 1996, became law without attracting much notice by the general public. It was interest group driven and would be decided "inside the Beltway." It was promoted for years by well-organized interested parties before it was decided. These interested parties intentionally encouraged policy makers' concern for the issue through a hard-fought but low-profile process.

How issues emerge and become defined can have important consequences for how they are ultimately resolved because policy makers can understand most issues as stemming from more than one cause. The early definition of a problem's "cause" can dictate much about what policy solution is pursued. As Rochefort and Cobb point out, "At the nexus of politics and policy development lies persistent conflict over where problems come from and, based on the answer to this question, what kinds of solutions should be attempted. . . . Every retrospective analysis in problem definition is also a look ahead and an implicit argument about what

---

[16] See Frank R. Baumgartner and Bryan D. Jones, *Agendas and Instability in American Politics* (Chicago: University of Chicago Press, 1993); Charles E. Lindblom, "The Science of Muddling Through," *Public Administration Review* 19 (1959): 79–88.

[17] See Mark A. Peterson, "The Politics of Health Care Policy: Overreaching in an Age of Polarization," in *The Social Divide: Political Parties and the Future of Activist Government*, ed. by Margaret Weir (Washington, D.C.: Brookings Institution Press, 1998).

government should be doing next."[18] So the substance of problem definition can have consequences for the substance of proposed policy solutions.
In addition, how an issue is defined can affect the political processes by
which issues and solutions are deliberated and decided; it can dictate the
profile of the debate and the advantages for different interests.[19] And
differences in the origins and definition of issue debates can affect the
opportunities for think tanks and policy experts generally.

The three issues considered here reached policy makers by different
paths and were deliberated under different conditions. A striking example
of the differences in profile of the three issues: The *New York Times* published ten times the number of articles about health care reform (1,648) as
it did about telecommunications reform (169) between 1990 and 1996 –
ironic because telecommunications reform was enacted while comprehensive health care reform failed. The *Times* published more than 2,200 articles (2,262) about the debate over the tax cut in just the eighteen-month
period before it was enacted in June 2001.[20]

The differences in profile of the three issues are indicative of their
very different policy histories. The issues involve different sectors of the
economy. They were initiated in the 1990s by different sets of actors,
and different strategies were associated with the passage of two and the
ultimate defeat of one. The points of contrast among health care, telecommunications, and the tax cut, as issues and as issue debates, are useful for
comparing the possibilities for think tanks and policy experts generally in
policy making.

The Debate Over Health Care Reform

Setting the Agenda

Presidential efforts to reform the health care system were hardly original to the Clinton administration in the 1990s. As with most issues,
the efforts on health care reform that grew out of the 1992 presidential

---

[18] David A. Rochefort and Roger W. Cobb, *The Politics of Problem Definition: Shaping the Policy Agenda* (Lawrence: University Press of Kansas, 1994), p. 3.

[19] See Mark P. Petracca, *The Politics of Interests: Interest Groups Transformed* (Boulder, Colo.: Westview Press, 1992).

[20] These numbers are based on NEXIS searches by the author. All three of the case studies focus on issues that were significant in their legislative implications. All are the kinds of issues that would qualify as "notable laws" under David Mayhew's coding scheme in *Divided We Govern*. See David R. Mayhew, *Divided We Govern: Party Control, Lawmaking, and Investigations, 1946–1990* (New Haven, Conn.: Yale University Press, 1991).

election built on a long history of previous policy developments, in this case a history that included efforts to overhaul the country's health care system during the administrations of Presidents Harry Truman, Lyndon Johnson, Richard Nixon, and Jimmy Carter. The basis for and content of reform proposals varied with each administration.[21] Only Johnson met with notable success in these efforts, winning enactment of Medicaid and Medicare. The successive casualties and occasional successes of efforts at health care reform since World War II formed the foundation for renewed interest in the 1990s.

The impetus for reform in the last decade of the twentieth century lay in the rapidly growing numbers of the uninsured and the quickly escalating costs of health care through the late 1980s.[22] The event that cemented the issue on the political agenda was Harris Wofford's 1991 upset in Pennsylvania's special U.S. Senate race, beating Richard Thornburgh. Wofford's advocacy of health care reform was seen as the key to his election, and his win made health care a clear priority for presidential hopefuls in 1992.[23] The general public seemed to be showing signs that health care reform was a central concern. Presidential candidates became eager to respond with enthusiasm. They needed the assistance of research – and researchers – to formulate concrete proposals, even in broad terms, for the campaign.

By the early 1990s, health care research was available from many sources on many fronts. Especially since the creation of Medicare and Medicaid in the 1960s, a large and diverse community of what are known as "health services researchers" had developed in the United States. These researchers, who analyzed all aspects of the health care market, were based at universities and consulting firms and often at think tanks and in government agencies. The legislation that created the Great Society programs in the 1960s had also appropriated substantial resources for program evaluation. So in large part with government support, a series of large and

---

[21] See Paul Starr, *The Social Transformation of American Medicine* (New York: Basic Books, 1982), book two, Chapters 3 and 4.

[22] Estimates of the number of uninsured jumped from less than 30 million in 1980 to more than 40 million in 1992. By 1994, health care costs had reached $3,300 a year per person, twice as much as was spent on education and three times that which was spent on national defense. See Sherry Glied, *Chronic Condition: Why Health Reform Fails* (Cambridge, Mass.: Harvard University Press, 1998), Chapter 1.

[23] Jacob S. Hacker, *The Road to Nowhere: The Genesis of President Clinton's Plan for Health Security* (Princeton, N.J.: Princeton University Press, 1997). For another account of the Clinton health care reform effort, see Theda Skocpol, *Boomerang: Clinton's Health Security Effort and the Turn Against Government in U.S. Politics* (New York: W. W. Norton, 1996).

small research studies of the health care market had been launched and completed in the 1970s and 1980s. Among the most notable was an evaluation of the effects of insurance deductibles on the demand for health care, done by the RAND Corporation in the 1970s and 1980s.[24] This study and many others produced results that were widely accepted in the health services research community by the time the 1990's round of health care reform was heating up. The cumulative weight of this work created an information-rich context for debates over reform as the issue emerged anew.

Health care reform emerged as an important electoral issue, but Bill Clinton, who would eventually champion it, was not the first candidate to formulate a reform proposal. Senator Bob Kerrey (D.-Nebraska), who was competing with Clinton for the Democratic presidential nomination, moved first. Kerrey introduced the "Health USA Act" in the Senate in July 1991 and soon after announced a run for the presidency with health care reform as the cornerstone of his campaign. Health USA proposed a state-financed, single-payer health system, funded with a new payroll tax, with private insurers taking on the role of providing mostly supplemental coverage.[25]

Kerrey, along with Senator Paul Tsongas (D.-Massachusetts) – Clinton's other principal primary opponent, who was more loosely and less aggressively touting a version of managed competition – pressured Clinton to stake out at least the outlines of a health care position.[26] A "play or pay" proposal became the plan Clinton espoused early on. Clinton chose play or pay in the fall of 1991, more for rhetorical purposes than out of deeply held convictions. A play or pay system required that employers provide insurance for their employers or pay a tax to support a publicly funded health care system.[27] During the presidential primaries, play or pay was a strategic middle ground between the positions of Kerrey and Tsongas. It was also a popular Democratic proposal in Washington at the time. A version of play or pay had been introduced in the Senate

[24] See Joseph P. Newhouse and the Insurance Experiment Group, *Free For All? Lessons from the RAND Health Insurance Experiment* (Cambridge, Mass.: Harvard University Press, 1993).
[25] See Robert Kerrey, "Why America Will Adopt Comprehensive Health Care Reform," *The American Prospect* 6 (Summer 1991): 81–92.
[26] Kenneth J. Cooper, "Focusing More on Cost than Compassion: In Health Care Debate, Democratic Rivals Generally See Link between Greater Access and Control." *The Washington Post*, 6 February 1992, p. A16.
[27] On play or pay, see Henry Aaron, *The Problem That Won't Go Away* (Washington, D.C.: Brookings Institution Press, 1996).

in 1991 by a group of Democratic senators after having been given new life as a product of the congressional Bipartisan Commission on Comprehensive Health Care, known as the Pepper Commission, which had completed its work in 1990.[28]

By the fall of 1991, all three of the Democratic presidential candidates had embraced an approach to reform, each with the help of health care experts. Senator Kerrey's version of the single-payer plan was the product of UCLA Professor Richard Brown. Brown, a longtime single-payer advocate, was approached by Gretchen Brown, Kerrey's health care aide and a graduate of UCLA's public health program, to meet with Kerrey and eventually develop a plan for him.[29] Tsongas was drawn to the work of Alain Enthoven and others, who had developed the concept of managed competition in the previous two decades. Enthoven, who had been an assistant secretary of defense during the Kennedy and Johnson administrations, was at the Stanford business school in the 1970s when Joseph Califano, Carter's secretary of Health, Education and Welfare, asked him to develop a market-based health care reform proposal for the administration. His product, managed competition, involved grouping people into health care cooperatives, which acted as insurance-purchasing agents for large groups.[30] The Carter administration did not embrace Enthoven's

---

[28] The Democratic senators were Mitchell, Kennedy, Riegle, and Rockefeller. See Mark A. Peterson, "Momentum toward Health Care Reform in the U.S. Senate," *Journal of Health Politics, Policy, and Law* 17 (1992): 553–73.

[29] Senator Kerrey met with Richard Brown and some of his colleagues while on a visit to Los Angeles. In early 1991, Kerrey was relatively inexperienced on the health care issue. When he decided to write legislation, Gretchen Brown set up a series of seminars with health policy experts for the senator around the country, of which the session in Los Angeles was one. While he was in California, Richard Brown spent a whole day with the senator, at the end of which he offered to write a memo outlining principles for a health care proposal that the senator might endorse. The principles that Brown sent Kerrey several weeks later were adapted from a proposal he had previously drafted for the state of California on behalf of Health Access, a state-focused consumer coalition that he helped lead. In April 1991, several months after sending his proposal to Senator Kerrey, Gretchen Brown contacted the UCLA professor and said that the senator wanted to turn his proposal into legislation. Information comes from author interviews with Gretchen Brown and Richard Brown.

[30] The cooperatives, which could group people previously uninsured, would negotiate with insurers or health plans to offer their subscribers a menu of options among different insurance plans with information on each plan's quality of care and price. Managed competition was intended to make health insurance more price competitive at the same time that it incorporated the previously uninsured through cooperatives. See Alain C. Enthoven, *Health Plan* (Reading, Mass.: Addison-Wesley, 1980). Enthoven's ideas were an extension of little-known work by Scott Fleming that circulated during the Nixon administration. See Hacker, *Road to Nowhere*, p. 47.

plan, but, in the years that followed, his ideas gained substantial visibility and were the subject of frequent discussion among policy makers and many within the health services research community.[31]

The first version of Clinton's play or pay proposal was drafted by Ron Pollack, executive director of Families USA, in December 1991. Families USA combined grassroots organizing and information lobbying to promote a "consumer's perspective" in health care reform. Pollack's work came to the attention of the Clinton campaign with an article he cowrote in *The American Prospect* in the summer of 1991 in which he endorsed play or pay as a "politically feasible" alternative to a single-payer, government-administered health care system.[32] Pollack drafted Clinton's first statement on health care, which was reworked by Bruce Reed, issues director for the campaign. The written plan was intentionally vague. It was elaborated upon and defended in the months that followed by a group of Washington-based health policy experts, led by Bruce Fried, a health care consultant with the D.C.-based Wexler Group and a longtime Democratic activist. The group involved many of the researchers who had been involved with the Pepper Commission, including Judy Feder, who had been the commission's staff director and author of its final report.

With the primary season over, pressure to articulate a detailed position on health care mounted for the Clinton campaign. By August 1992, President George H.W. Bush, who had been late to articulate a health care reform proposal of his own, was effectively lambasting what he perceived as the likely costs associated with Clinton's vague play or pay proposal. Bush had endorsed what was seen as an incremental reform

---

[31] For discussion of the Enthoven plan's subsequent development, see Thomas R. Oliver, "Health Care Reform in Congress," *Political Science Quarterly* 106 (1991): 453–77. Enthoven continued to revise and publicize his proposal through the 1980s and co-wrote a reformulated version of his ideas in a pair of 1989 *New England Journal of Medicine* articles. Alain Enthoven and Richard Kronick, "A Consumer Choice Health Plan for the 1990s," parts I and II, *New England Journal of Medicine* 320 (5 and 12 January 1989): 29–37, 94–101. With rising numbers of uninsured and quickly escalating health care costs, Enthoven was keenly aware of the potential for health care to become a central policy issue in the 1990s; writing the *New England Journal of Medicine* articles was part of a strategy for making his ideas part of the debate. These sentiments are apparent in a telephone interview with Jacob Hacker on December 21, 1994. I am grateful to Jacob Hacker for sharing with me and permitting me to cite transcripts of several of his interviews with members of the health care policy community that he did for his book, *The Road to Nowhere*, in 1993 and 1994.

[32] Ronald Pollack and Phyllis Torda, "The Pragmatic Road Toward National Health Insurance," *The American Prospect* 6 (Summer 1991): 92–100. Author interview with Ronald Pollack, Families USA, 1 April 1999.

plan, which relied on new tax incentives, a small dose of government regulation, and malpractice reform as means to extend coverage to the uninsured. The Bush administration proposal had little effect on those insured by their employers but relied on a system of tax credits for those below 150 percent of the poverty threshold.[33] With rhetoric that Clinton's plan would create new taxes and regulation, Bush was gaining ground on the issue by the summer in public opinion polls. During the summer, the Clinton campaign finally focused serious attention on defining a more specific health care position. In the process, it moved away from a play or pay approach and toward managed competition.

Following his inauguration in 1993, President Clinton's ideas for health care reform became the principal focus of attention in Washington. Democratic members of Congress, in particular, some of whom had introduced health care reform bills in the previous Congress, stayed in the shadows of the issue in 1993 awaiting the president's pronouncements. His proposal for health care reform was formally announced in September of that year, after an arduous series of meetings through the winter and spring of 1993, as a 500-person task force headed by First Lady Hillary Rodham Clinton worked out the details of the administration's plan.

Throughout the presidential campaign and into the first year of the new Clinton administration, health care reform was a high-profile public issue. The president was sidelined first with budget negotiations and then with a crisis with U.S. troops based in Somalia, but the First Lady's involvement kept the issue close to the spotlight.[34] Policy research was useful in providing a foundation for the debate, especially analyses of the gaps and problems in the private health insurance market. On these subjects, scores of studies were in the public domain before the debate was underway, and they served as general guidance to those within the policy and advocacy communities setting to work on specific policy provisions in 1993. The dilemma for policy makers attentive to the work of health services research was the lack of consensus among the many studies and reports that confirmed problems in the health care system on

---

[33] Bush's plan was partially inspired by Alain Enthoven's ideas and also by University of Pennsylvania professor Mark Pauly. Neither was involved in its drafting, which was essentially done by Richard Darman, Bush's OMB director, as part of the 1993 budget bill. See Michael Abramowitz, "Pushing Bush to a Market-led Health Solution: Enthoven Sees Competition as Best Antidote for Rising Costs," *The Washington Post*, 26 January 1992.

[34] See Haynes Johnson and David S. Broder, *The System* (Boston: Little, Brown, 1997), pp. 96–136, 181–93.

what the appropriate policy intervention might be. There were advocates for single-payer plans, play or pay, managed competition, incremental reform, and many variants of each that in many cases drew on the same foundational research to reach different conclusions. The president embraced a variant of managed competition in his proposal to Congress, a version more regulatory than that developed by Alain Enthoven. The inspiration of the president's proposal had instead been the work of John Garamendi and Walter Zelman, the California Commissioner and Deputy Commissioner for insurance, respectively, who had developed plans for a managed competition system for Californians.[35]

Policy Deliberation

Once the president's proposal was released in late 1993, attention turned to the Congressional Budget Office (CBO), which had responsibility for "scoring" the budgetary effects of the president's proposal for members of Congress. Both proponents and opponents of the president's plan came to see the estimates that came out of CBO as critical to how they would defend their case for or against the president's plan.[36] Outside of government, only two groups had the capacity to produce large-scale microsimulations of health care reform proposals, which were essential for estimating the costs of proposals: the Urban Institute and Lewin-VHI, a health care consulting firm based in Arlington, Virginia.[37] In contrast

---

[35] For more on the substance of the Garamendi–Zelman plan, see John Garamendi, "Taking California Health Insurance into the 21st Century," *Journal of American Health Policy*, May–June 1992, pp. 10a–13a. For details on how the plan reached President Clinton, see Hacker, *The Road to Nowhere*.

[36] Johnson and Broder, *The System*, pp. 282–7.

[37] Each ran models during 1993–4 for different audiences and different purposes. The Urban Institute was working on contract, as it had for many years, with the Department of Health and Human Services to run and support HHS's "transfer income model." The model simulated how the welfare population reacts to labor market initiatives and changes in public programs. The model was maintained not within the Urban Institute's "Health Policy Center" but rather in its "Income and Benefits Policy Center." Working on contract with the federal government, the Income and Benefits Policy Center produced analyses on demand for officials at HHS and the OMB. Their products were intended for internal use as the executive branch produced estimates of the president's proposal. Lewin-VHI played a very different role. Lewin was a for-profit consulting firm and, by the early 1990s, had spent a decade and several hundred thousand dollars developing a micro-simulation model of the health care system. As the health care reform debate heated up in 1992 and 1993, Lewin was serving curious members of the business community who were concerned about how reform might affect them. Then in December 1993, little more than a month after its public release, Lewin produced the first full, publicly available estimate of Clinton's health care proposals.

to the guidance that came from the large-scale evaluation studies that preceded the health care reform debate, calculated predictions of the effects of reform were hard to come by.

If the number of micro-simulated estimates of health care proposals was limited in 1993 and 1994, sources of variously informed commentary on the health care debates were substantially more abundant. Virtually every interest group and trade association released some type of commentary on the Clinton proposal or its alternatives in early 1994. Think tanks were especially active in releasing policy briefs and voicing commentary on the president's proposals as well. Elizabeth McCaughey at the Manhattan Institute (later the Republican lieutenant governor of New York) was one of the first critics. McCaughey, a lawyer by training, wrote a point-by-point critique of the Clinton health plan in an op-ed in the *Wall Street Journal* at the end of September 1993 and then expanded it as an article in *The New Republic* in February 1994.[38] Her articles elicited an immediate hostile written response from Ira Magaziner, the director of President Clinton's health care initiative, as well as other health policy experts.[39] McCaughey then wrote a rejoinder that followed the next week.[40] The series of *New Republic* articles is just an example of the kind of highly charged exchanges circulated at the time.[41] Cumulatively, the commentary from think tanks, interest groups, and elsewhere was useful precisely as ammunition in what became a highly politicized debate over health care reform. Much of it took the form of criticism of the Clinton plan. Some of it was support for alternative health care reforms. All of it contributed, along with enormous interest group mobilization, to the ultimate demise of the reform effort.

[38] Elizabeth McCaughey, "Health Plan's Devilish Details," *The Wall Street Journal*, 30 September 1993, p. A18; Elizabeth McCaughey, "No Exit," *The New Republic*, 7 February 1994.

[39] Magaziner wrote a widely circulated response to McCaughey in the week following its publication, and two Yale University health policy researchers wrote a scathing reply two weeks later in *The New Republic*. Theodore R Marmor and Jerry L. Mashaw, "Cassandra's Law," *The New Republic*, 14 February 1994, p. 20.

[40] Elizabeth McCaughey, "She's Baaack!" *The New Republic*, 28 February 1994, p. 17.

[41] In this instance, the responses from inside the administration raised the profile of McCaughey's arguments; as one congressional staffer put it in reflecting on the McCaughey exchange: "What really put it over the top was when Magaziner posted his reply to McCaughey. . . . First of all, it wasn't very well done, and, secondly, it immediately raised the stature. So instead of a piece that a few geeks would have seen in the *New Republic*, it suddenly became something everybody knew about, and she came back with a very well written rejoinder. And then she was invited up [to Capitol Hill], and she was talking to Republican senators and House members." Author interview with Doug Badger, 30 March 1999.

By June 1994, the chances of enacting comprehensive health care reform appeared quite slim. Research and commentary were no longer important. Proposals were stalled in both chambers. Senate Democrats spent the summer trying to broker a compromise within their ranks. Senate Republicans, under Dole's leadership, meanwhile spent the summer reaching a political compromise on an alternative that forty of the forty-four Senate Republicans could support. But his plan was outside the range of what President Clinton would consider. Politics trumped substance in the alternative's formulation. With the exception of the CBO, outside experts had no role by this point. By the summer of 1994, both the House and the Senate had contended with – and mostly cast aside – a wide range of alternatives.[42]

Failure to Enact Reform

The House spent most of the summer waiting to see if the Senate would act. Just before July 4, the Senate Finance Committee reported out a much-weakened bill. Despite this optimistic sign for proponents of reform, Republicans were prepared to block a Democratic proposal from reaching the Senate floor. After intense political efforts through July and August, Majority Leader George Mitchell (D.-Maine) declared health care reform dead on September 26, 1994, almost a year to the day after President Clinton had presented his proposals before a joint session of Congress.

The Debate Over Telecommunications Reform

Setting the Agenda

It was a wintry day in Washington when, on February 8, 1996, President Clinton signed the Telecommunications Act of 1996 into law. The lavish Library of Congress signing ceremony, which included the actress Lily Tomlin playing telephone operator Ernestine, followed by a week passage of the legislation by overwhelming majorities in both houses of Congress. Only sixteen members of the House and five members of the

---

[42] Most of these alternatives have been discussed in this chapter; a few have not been. Representative Pete Stark (D.-Calif.), chairman of the Ways and Means health care subcommittee, offered a proposal to extend Medicare to all Americans. His plan, known as "Medicare C," represented Stark's long-held views. Stark, along with his staff, was familiar with many of the health care experts in Washington. Stark's proposal was eventually adapted and become the House version of President Clinton's plan. On the Stark plan, see Johnson and Broder, *The System*, pp. 396–436.

Senate voted against the final conference report.[43] In signing the new law, President Clinton enthusiastically remarked, "Today, with the stroke of a pen, our laws will catch up with our future. We will help to create an open marketplace where competition and innovation can move as quick as light."[44] Unlike the health care legislation in 1994, telecommunications reform, with the administration's ultimate support, had been enacted. The Telecommunications Act became law by a very different path from that forged in the unsuccessful efforts toward health care reform.

While President Clinton and Vice President Gore proudly heralded the passage of the new telecommunications law, the issue did not trace its origins, as health care had, to their presidential campaign. In fact, where health care reform had been a high-profile, hot-button campaign issue, full-blown telecommunications reform made its way to the congressional agenda without the help of a presidential candidate and with hardly any notice by or much interest from the general public. Like health care reform, telecommunications reform had the potential to rewrite regulation of one-seventh of the U.S. economy. But in public opinion polls in the five years preceding the new act's passage, whereas health care typically remained among the top five priorities mentioned by the public, no telecommunications issue of any kind was cited as a major public concern.[45]

The nature of the issues involved in telecommunications reform and the path toward a new law created a very different set of opportunities for think tanks and policy experts generally than had been available in health care reform. The opportunities and the cumulative influence of research were greater during agenda-setting moments on telecommunications reform than was the case for either health care reform or the tax cut. The influence came in the form of a scholarly consensus on the desirability of telecommunications competition, a topic on which there was substantial

[43] The final conference report for the bill, PL 104–104, 110 Stat. 56 (1996), passed in the House 414–16, and in the Senate 91–5. For the vote, see *Congressional Quarterly Almanac*, 104th Congress, 2nd Session, Volume LII (Washington, D.C.: CQ Press, 1997), pp. H8–H11, S3.

[44] Dan Carney, "Telecommunications: Indecency Provision Attacked as Clinton Signs Bill," *Congressional Quarterly Weekly Report*, 10 February 1996, p. 359. Since the 1992 campaign, President Clinton and especially Vice President Gore had been reminding audiences of the importance of investing in an "information superhighway." In the signing ceremony, the Telecommunications Act was portrayed by the administration as a vital paving stone for that highway.

[45] This is in response to the question "What do you think is the most important problem facing this country today?" drawn from the Gallup Poll. See *The Gallup Poll Monthly*, Number 364 and Number 328, January 1996 and January 1993, pp. 34 and 32, respectively.

agreement among decision makers by the 1990s. The remaining specifics of reform, however, were contested. They were of overriding importance to – and aggressively negotiated from the latter agenda-setting moments right up to policy enactment by – the industries affected; in these negotiations, experts were of less consequence.

Telecommunications reform took on steam during the 1980s and early 1990s thanks to the persistent lobbying efforts of interested parties. The list of these parties was long. In its final provisions, the Telecommunications Act of 1996 created substantial new business opportunities for local telephone companies (the Baby Bells or regional Bell operating companies, known as "RBOCs"), long-distance carriers (e.g., AT&T, MCI, Sprint), and cable television companies to compete in one another's markets. With profound anxieties during the law's development about how it would provide such opportunities, members of each of these potentially affected industries as well as those from publishing, broadcast, radio, burglar alarm, and cellular-telephone industries played an active role in lobbying over the legislation's content.[46]

In the decade ending December 31, 1994, leading into the first round of debate over reform in the 1990s, telecommunications companies contributed almost $40 million to candidates and political parties.[47] The size of political contributions and the scope of involved lobbyists in telecommunications reform, while less visible to the public, rivaled the size and scope of efforts associated with health care reform, and the efforts began much earlier in the policy debate.

---

[46] Summing up the politics surrounding telecommunication reform in 1995, as legislative proposals wound their way through Congress, *National Journal* reported that one might

call it the World Series of lobbying. Sure, other issues get more attention in the news media, but the battle over sweeping telecommunications legislation is in a league of its own. Quick, name any other public policy debate for which more long-ball hitters – the heaviest of the heavy weight lobbyists – have been retained. Or try to come up with another issue in which various industries have so consistently thrown such bucket loads of loot at lawmakers. Billions of dollars are riding on how Members of Congress redraw the lines governing competition among the various colossal industries in the communications business – from cable TV to local telephones to long-distance service to publishing. A strong case can be made that the war over telecommunications reform has done more to line the pockets of lobbyists and lawmakers than any other issue in the past decade.

Kirk Victor, "They're in a League of Their Own," *National Journal*, 27 May 1995, p. 1307.

[47] "Robber Barons of the '90s," *Common Cause Report*, June 1995. The FCC reported that the seven individual Bell companies combined to spend $64 million on state and federal lobbying expenses in 1993, up from $41 million in 1992. Mike Mills, "The New Kings of Capitol Hill," *The Washington Post*, 23 April 1995, p. H1.

Along with contributions, the American telecommunications industry also used a series of mergers, buyouts, and court cases in the years leading up to the 1996 Act to generate attention from lawmakers. The Baby Bells, long-distance companies, and cable operators were doing all they could in the face of court supervision and restrictive regulation to enter one another's businesses. By all appearances, the combined pressures worked. Telecommunications reform was not like health care reform, where ambitious policy makers staked out positions early for the sake of political advantage. Rather, it was an issue that evolved from the efforts of the industries affected, and policy makers became involved in articulating positions and developing legislation at the last possible moment. In the midst of escalating merger and buyout activities, Representative Edward Markey (D.-Massachusetts), chairman of the House Energy and Commerce Subcommittee on Telecommunications and Finance, finally made his concern for the issue known in a February 1993 letter to the acting chairman of the Federal Communications Commission, James Quello, arguing that he saw it as "critical for policymakers to wrestle with the tough choices now, before the market and the industry get ahead of the regulators."[48] These were heartening words for telecommunications companies anxious for regulatory relief.

Markey's letter came on the heels of President Clinton's election and shortly before Vice President Gore, a longtime telecommunications policy activist, was designated to lead the administration's program in the area.[49] Gore's enthusiasm and Markey's concerns were early signals that congressional reexamination of the telecommunications laws might be close. In fact, by the latter half of 1993, the first round of comprehensive telecommunications reform legislation was being drafted by Congress. Representative Markey was among the first co-sponsors, and the path toward enactment of the 1996 Telecommunications Act had begun in earnest.

At the core of the telecommunications reform agenda, as it began its trek toward becoming law, was the debate over the conditions under which the Baby Bells and long-distance carriers might be permitted to enter one another's markets. But once it got underway, a number of additional side issues surfaced as well. Lawmakers became concerned with provisions for continuation of universal service, which guaranteed every

---

[48] Kirk Victor, "Road Warriors," *National Journal*, 20 March 1993, p. 681.
[49] See Graeme Browning, "Search for Tomorrow: A Conversation with Vice President Gore about the 'Information Superhighway,'" *National Journal*, 20 March 1993, pp. 676–7.

American access to telephone service at "reasonable" rates. They looked at cross-ownership restrictions between the telephone and cable sectors. They examined foreign ownership restrictions on telephone and broadcast companies. These were by no means the only side issues at stake as telecommunications reform began, but they were among the most contentious. Far more than with health care reform, which was fundamentally a debate over conflicting philosophies for how to provide quality, affordable health care to the greatest number of Americans, telecommunications reform came to take on a piecemeal quality with one core element and scores of separately negotiated side issues.

As disjointed as the issues involved in the telecommunications reform debate turned out to be, for researchers and experts contributing to the discussions, points of view tended to fall along two basic continua as the debate began. They varied based on experts' views about the appropriate market structure in telecommunications industries and their views about the necessity of government regulation to accommodate that structure. Eli Noam argues that in the 1970s and 1980s, economists and lawyers essentially fell into four groups with regard to these questions. In relation to market structure, experts were either monopolists or pro-competitive. Toward achieving a fair and efficient monopoly or balanced and effective competition, experts favored either more or less government regulation.[50]

By the early 1990s, there were few economists or lawyers left who credibly espoused a view favoring a monopolistic structure for the telecommunications industries. And the cumulative weight of research supporting a competitive marketplace was helpful to proponents of reform. But what level of regulation was required to promote competition? It was over this question that most of the battles in telecommunications reform were fought once the issue was on the agenda. Some argued that near-complete deregulation of telecommunications industries was appropriate, permitting full cross-ownership and unregulated customer fees. Others made the case that given what were existing asymmetries in size among potential telecommunication competitors, along with an obligation to ensure universal telephone service, substantial government regulation and supervision were essential for creating and sustaining a competitive environment. These two general views set a context for the remainder of experts'

---

[50] Eli M. Noam, "Beyond Telecommunications Liberalization: Past Performance, Present Hype, and Future Direction," in *The New Information Infrastructure: Strategies for U.S. Policy*, ed. by William J. Drake (New York: The Twentieth Century Fund Press, 1995).

contributions to the telecommunications reform debate, to both the core and the many side issues involved.

Policy Deliberation

In fall 1993, the first serious bills to reform the telecommunications industries were introduced in the House. The first of two bills introduced on November 22, 1993, came from John Dingell (D.-Michigan), chairman of the House Commerce Committee, and Jack Brooks (D.-Texas), chairman of the Judiciary Committee. Dingell and Brooks introduced legislation prescribing conditions for lifting the court-ordered modified final judgment (MFJ) regulating the Baby Bells. They did so on the same day that Markey, chairman of the Commerce Committee's telecommunications subcommittee, and Jack Fields (R.-Texas), the subcommittee's ranking Republican, introduced legislation creating a regulatory context for competition among telephone and cable service providers. Both bills were drafted by committee staff, with little or no assistance from or contact with outside experts or advocates.[51]

The two House bills were introduced at the end of 1993 and set the stage for serious legislative progress in 1994. In February, Senator Ernest Hollings (D.-South Carolina), chairman of the Commerce, Science, and Transportation Committee, joined the debate in earnest on the Senate side, introducing a bill with John Danforth (R.-Missouri) that replaced telecommunications reform legislation introduced by Danforth and Daniel Inouye (D.-Hawaii), the Commerce telecommunications subcommittee chair, in the previous year.[52] Hollings was spurred into action by the House legislation and by two high-profile speeches by Vice President Gore, one at the National Press Club in December and another at the Academy of TV Arts and Sciences in Los Angeles in January.[53] Gore

---

[51] The desire to remove Judge Greene from authority over the Baby Bells was what brought Dingell and Brooks, longtime personal friends, together despite rivalries over the relative jurisdictional authority their committees had on telecommunications regulation. Dingell and Brooks reached agreement on introducing a bill after nine months of closed-door staff negotiations. The negotiations, once they began, relied very little on outside experts. The senior counsels to Dingell and Brooks worked out the content of the bill during the spring and summer of 1993. They operated behind closed doors, with both knowing what they wanted to accomplish with the legislation, if they could find common ground and then line up political support. Interviews with congressional committee staff, Washington, D.C., May 7 and 27, 1999.

[52] See "Not Enough Regulatory Parity," *Communications Daily*, 10 June 1993, p. 4.

[53] Despite the rhetoric of their campaign, Gore and Clinton had been relatively quiet on plans for the information superhighway through 1993, taking until August to nominate

and Hollings had been friendly rivals in the Senate, and Hollings's view was that if the vice president was going to pronounce early 1994 as a time to move telecommunications legislation, he wanted to be an independent leader in the effort.

The Commerce Committee counsel at the time had worked with Inouye in drafting his 1993 bill. Now he worked with Hollings, using the Inouye–Danforth bill as a baseline, to develop legislation that the chairman could introduce. The counsel and his staff solicited the views of a number of industry lobbyists in writing the legislation, many of whom had actually formerly worked for the committee. Like the House drafters, though, they did not rely on think tank or other non-industry experts during the drafting of legislation in the Senate.[54]

In the House, the Brooks–Dingell and Markey–Fields bills were debated in a series of ten hearings over a two-week period at the end of January and beginning of February 1994. Of sixty-nine witnesses, none came from think tanks and only five were researchers of any kind. Most of the rest came from interest groups and corporate offices of the industries concerned. The committees passed the legislation in the middle of March, and, after some compromise with industry, the House passed both bills by overwhelming margins on June 28, 1994.[55] In passing the legislation by such wide margins, House members hoped that their relatively unified action might encourage the Senate to act quickly on Hollings's companion bill. Senate passage was not to be, however.

The Senate Commerce Committee passed a modified version of the Hollings legislation on August 11, 1994, by a vote of 18–2. The committee

an FCC chairman. On Gore's speeches, see "Endorses Brooks-Dingell: Gore Endorses Lifting MFJ Restrictions," *Communications Daily*, 12 January 1994, p. 1.

54 Interview with congressional committee staff, Washington, D.C., May 27, 1999. In its content, the Hollings–Danforth bill combined elements of both House bills but created higher hurdles for the RBOCs before they could extend service into cable, long distance, and manufacturing. In the House bill, the RBOCs had a date-certain waiting period, after which they could compete in cable, long distance, and other industries within their service areas. In the Senate version, there was an entry test for the RBOCs rather than a date-certain; the RBOCs had to meet conditions of "actual and demonstrable competition" in local telephone service before they could enter new markets. The Senate bill, as introduced in February 1994, was originally co-sponsored by Inouye, Danforth, and nine additional Commerce Committee members. "Senate Telecommunications Leadership Introduces New Bill," *Communications Daily*, 4 February 1994, p. 1.

55 On committee passage, see "Bill Advances in House on Telecom," *The New York Times*, 17 March 1994, p. D2. The Brooks–Dingell bill (HR3626) passed 423–5, and the Markey–Fields bill (HR3636) passed 423–4. See "House Passed Telecommunications Legislation by Big Margins," *Communications Daily*, 29 June 1994, p. 1.

vote came after Hollings thwarted a proposed alternative.[56] With a bill reported out of committee, passage of legislation by the full Senate seemed possible as Congress adjourned for its summer recess. But Senator Bob Dole (R.-Kansas), the Senate minority leader, had other plans.

In late August, Dole entered the debate with his own draft alternative, which he circulated among colleagues. Dole thought the Hollings bill created hurdles that were too onerous for the Bell companies to jump before they could enter long-distance competition. Dole's alternative was written by his telecommunications staffer, David Wilson, along with Donald McClellan, a Washington-based counsel for the Intel Corporation and previously a telecommunications aide for Senator Conrad Burns (R.-Montana).[57] They wrote the Dole draft – never more than roughed out – over the course of two weeks in consultation with the Bell companies, which were hoping for a better deal than they had negotiated in the Hollings bill, and in consultation with Sprint, a Kansas business familiar to Dole.[58] The Dole draft called for the unconditional elimination of the court-administered MFJ two years after enactment of the law and for immediate removal of entry barriers to telephone competition.

Dole never formally introduced his bill. It was intended merely to stop Hollings, who by early September was running out of time for bringing his bill to the Senate floor before an October recess for the election. With

---

[56] Only Packwood and Senator John McCain (R.-Ariz.) opposed it. Final committee approval followed negotiations on two issues: handling of the entry test for the Baby Bells into long-distance, and provisions for continued universal service in rural areas. The goal in hammering out a deal on Baby Bell entry into long-distance service was to find a compromise on which both sides could agree. In the first week of August, Commerce Committee staff sent versions of the compromise language to representatives of both the Baby Bells and the long-distance carriers and then met with them to work out their objections. Kirk Victor, "Nope, These Baby Bells Aren't Tykes," *National Journal*, 20 August 1994, p. 1996. The universal service concerns came from a group of six senators from rural states; this self-labeled "farm team," along with the senators' staffs, had worked over a period of four months through the late spring and early summer of 1994 to devise an alternative provision on universal service for the Hollings bill. They had been helped in their drafting by the rural phone carrier associations. All but one of the six, a bipartisan group, sat on the Commerce Committee, and after a six-hour consultation involving both members and staff, Hollings agreed to the farm team's provisions. Interview with Chris McClean, Telecommunications Aide to Senator James Exon (D.-Nebraska), 12 May 1999; Interview with Katie King, Telecommunications Counsel to Senator Larry Pressler (R.-S.D.), 13 May 1999; "Senate Panel Sets Markup on 191-page Telecommunications Bill," *Communications Daily*, 10 August 1994, p. 1.

[57] McClellan became co-counsel to the Senate Commerce Committee when Republicans took control of the Senate in 1995.

[58] Sprint's headquarters were in Kansas City, with portions of their workforce in Missouri and portions in Kansas.

a slim Democratic majority, Republicans could have filibustered or placed a hold on the legislation, which is what Dole threatened. As David Wilson recalls, "We figured that we had 15 or 16 days worth of cloture votes that we could, if we wanted, rake them over the coals with. So theoretically, there was not time for them to fool around with us. And, even though we were in the minority at the time, that is why they had to come to us and say, what's it going to take to get it out on the floor and take a vote."[59]

Unwilling to compromise, on Friday, September 23, 1994, Chairman Hollings announced that no telecommunications reform bill would pass the Senate in 1994. He blamed Senator Dole, along with the Baby Bells, for preventing it. Dole put forward non-negotiable demands, and Hollings said he "simply cannot and will not be forced to agree to accept provisions that fundamentally undermine the provisions that the committee overwhelmingly approved just last month."[60]

Moving Toward Enactment

With sweeping electoral victories in both the House and the Senate, the Republicans took control of the congressional agenda in January 1995. While not a part of the House's Contract with America, which had been the platform of House Republicans during the 1994 election, telecommunications reform was one of the first issues out of the starting blocks in both chambers. Thomas Bliley (R.-Virginia) became chairman of the House Energy and Commerce Committee, and Larry Pressler (R.-South Dakota) took control of the Commerce Committee in the Senate.

The Senate began to act first, with extensive meetings among Commerce Committee members and leadership staff literally the day after the election in November. Pressler realized that running out of time had killed reform the previous year, so he set a goal of having a telecommunications bill passed in the Senate by Easter. On November 9, 1994, the day after the election, he and Dole convened a conference call of Commerce Committee Republicans in which they committed to an accelerated process of bill writing.[61] Through the end of November and December, the

---

[59] Interview with David Wilson, Telecommunications Aide to Senator Bob Dole, Washington, D.C., 6 May 1999.
[60] "Fingers Pointing Everywhere: Hollings and Dole Promise Action on Telecommunications Next Year," *Communications Daily*, 26 September 1994, p. 1.
[61] Interview with Donald McClellan, Co-counsel to Senate Commerce Committee, Washington, D.C., May 18, 1999; Interview with Katie King, Co-counsel to Senate Commerce Committee, Washington, D.C., 13 May 1999.

committee staff spent their mornings meeting with industry representatives and Republican senatorial staff. Their afternoons and evenings were spent drafting a bill. Democrats were excluded from the process entirely. Experts were not much involved either.[62]

With the new Congress sworn in, Pressler held his first hearing on telecommunications reform on January 9, well before a bill was even ready for discussion. On the last day of January, after closed-door negotiations, draft legislation was distributed personally by Pressler to every committee Democrat as well as to Vice President Gore. The Pressler bill was similar to the previous Hollings legislation in many respects but tended to be more deregulatory. Given two weeks to comment on the Pressler draft, Democrats came back in the middle of February with their own alternative bill, more similar to the Hollings bill from the previous Congress. After negotiations that lasted through the first part of March, by a vote of 17–2, the committee passed on March 23 a bill that deregulated the cable industries, lifted cross-ownership bans between the telephone and cable businesses, and enumerated a checklist for Baby Bell entry into long-distance service.

In the House, as in the Senate, Republican committee staff began conversations on a telecommunications bill the day after the election. But there were only preliminary talks in the House during November. Distracted by the Contract with America, committee Republicans did not work in earnest on a telecommunications reform bill until January. In late January, Commerce Committee Republicans held two days of closed meetings with forty-three CEOs from local, long-distance, cable, and broadcast firms. The meetings were intended to provide Republican members with a better understanding of how proposed reforms would affect the companies, and they gave executives the opportunity to communicate their business plans and regulatory concerns privately.

Then, through February and March, the co-counsels for chairman Bliley worked in closed sessions with Dingell's counsel to draft a bill. As in the Senate, the staff spent substantial time meeting with industry representatives as their bill took shape. Bliley had traditionally been an ally of AT&T and liked the idea of regulated competition. In committee,

---

[62] McClellan and King had the old Hollings bill as well as the Dole draft as foundations for their effort. Their interest was in moving the legislation from the previous Congress in a more deregulatory direction and adding cable deregulation to it. They were – and were made to be – keenly aware of the boundaries of what the affected industries would be willing to accept.

Bliley held sway, and after two days of debate over amendments, the House Commerce Committee approved a bill favored by the long-distance industry by a vote of 38–5.[63]

In the 1995 iteration, the bill-drafting process through the end of the committee process involved little more think tank or general expert participation than had been the case in 1993–4.[64] Senate floor consideration of the Pressler telecommunications bill began in the second week of June.[65] After a week of debate, the amended bill passed the Senate by a vote of 81–8. It included the fourteen-point checklist for Bell entry into long distance, date-certain cable deregulation, and provisions for cable and telephone competition. Following the Senate passage, the House returned to the issue in late summer. After extensive debate, the full House passed an amended telecommunications reform bill by a vote of 305–117.

Following passage in both chambers, only the work of the conference committee remained. But reconciling differences between the House and Senate versions and, more important, contending with increasingly mobilized competing interests was no small task. The contentious conference process began in late October, and, with only one day off through Christmas, the staffs of the conferees, particularly committee staff, worked with legislative counsel to find a bill acceptable to both chambers. Side issues, like wiring classrooms and regulating the Internet, were as hard fought as core telephone and cable concerns. By comparison with the spring and summer, commentary and studies by experts were even more infrequent and little noticed. During the conference process,

---

[63] "House Commerce Panel Passes Telecom Bill," *Communications Daily*, 26 May 1995, p. 1.

[64] The only bill drafter in either the House or Senate for whom think tanks were of some consequence was Donald McClellan. McClellan was the more ideological of the two Senate Commerce Committee co-counsels, a true believer in deregulation. He called frequently on Thierer, Gattuso, and Peter Huber for help in sustaining his intellectual understanding of the reform issues, particularly as he negotiated through March with his Democratic counterparts. As he recalls, "They gave intellectual rigor and foundation to the atmosphere that had been created by the election . . . [and] they were good at offering specific suggestions – sometimes specific legislative language; sometimes more historical context to sort out how to be looking at these issues." Interview with McClellan, 18 May 1999.

[65] A number of side issues gained public attention during the course of debate, some far more than the core competition issues in the bills. Most notably, Senator James Exon (D.-Nebraska) introduced a controversial amendment banning pornography from the Internet. The amendment passed and was part of the final legislation (although overturned in part by the Supreme Court in 1997). Experts played no role in the provision's development. Interview with Chris McLean and Senator Exon, Washington, D.C., 12 May 1999.

debates were technical and industry-dominated.[66] On February 1, 1996, the conference report was approved by both chambers of Congress, making way for the president's signing ceremony on February 8.

The Debate Over the Tax Cut

Setting the Agenda

A sizable tax cut was a top priority for George W. Bush from the moment he emerged as the Republican frontrunner in the 2000 presidential campaign. And by the time he was inaugurated on January 20, 2001, a bill-signing ceremony for the tax cut he had promised was less than five months away. Bush took office after a hotly contested election the denouement of which many thought would impair his legislative potential, but his new administration drew lessons from the failed experiences of the Clinton administration on health care reform. The Bush administration moved quickly and boldly and won passage of a $1.35 trillion tax cut by Memorial Day 2001.

The tax cut was passed quickly, but the issue's speed in 2001 was made possible in part by the many years of failed attempts to cut taxes that preceded it. The ideas for tax reduction embodied in the final law were not new to lawmakers in 2001. The core components of the tax cut ultimately enacted were: (1) a reduction in marginal income tax rates, (2) an elimination of the so-called "marriage penalty," so that two-income families would not be taxed more than single-income families, and (3) a phaseout of the estate tax. The latter two provisions had been passed in 2000 without becoming law, and all of the ideas had been evolving among policy makers and researchers for years before the 2001 tax cut was enacted. Like health care, tax policy was an issue area that occupied a great many think tanks and policy experts, including many working on the potential fiscal and economic effects of various tax cuts. Years of research – and, even more, the producers of that research – stood ready to advise and help policy makers as the tax cut debate picked up steam. The issue gained momentum in the late 1990s when the Congressional Budget Office began projecting the first federal budget surpluses in decades.

No issue excites the passions of conservative lawmakers more than tax cuts. The presidential campaign notwithstanding, the 2001 tax cut

[66] Senator Dole nearly scuttled the process at the beginning of January 1996, objecting to a provision that gave broadcast spectrum away to television networks to support their launch of high-definition television. The question of spectrum allocation was ultimately removed from the bill, however.

debate began to take shape in earnest with the Senate's rejection of cuts in marginal tax rates in 1998, followed soon after by projections of federal surpluses. In the next year, conservatives were eager to fashion tax cut proposals that could win their colleagues' support. Republicans were also anxious to achieve a legislative victory that would put the Clinton impeachment and their losses in the 1998 midterm elections behind them.[67] But Republicans had trouble reaching agreement within their ranks on what form of tax cut could and should pass. In 1999, some Republicans argued for continuing the fight for cuts in marginal tax rates.[68] Others supported a variant of President Clinton's position that surplus revenues should be used to protect Social Security and Medicare before devoting them to tax reduction. Under this plan, whatever was left could be used for targeted tax cuts.

As the debate over tax cuts began to take shape, it provided different opportunities for experts and expertise than either health care or telecommunication reform. The general debate was framed more by ideological differences than by research. Nothing like the consensus around telecommunications competition existed on the issue of tax cuts. As specific proposals took form, first in Congress and then in the presidential campaign, relevant expertise was found within the ranks of congressional staff and campaign advisors, many of whom were drawn from think tanks and the ranks of academia. They made the content of research relevant in the agenda-setting moments of the issue. But the research did little to build agreement among decision makers. And once the successful round of deliberation began on the issue following President Bush's election, decisions were made so quickly that there was little time for any last-minute contributions, from experts or even interests. Despite the myriad sources of research available on tax policy, in the end, experts played less of a role in the tax cut debate than they had during both health care and telecommunications reform – with one notable exception: An idea developed by researchers resurfaced as helpful for amending the tax cut in the last moments before its final passage; the added provision won the support of key moderate Republican senators for the overall legislation.

[67] Congress also had experienced difficulty in enacting a new budget in 1998, and the slow progress of the budget process had stalled efforts on a tax cut. In addition, budget rules made it difficult to return budget surpluses as a tax cut.

[68] The political fight for a reduction in marginal income tax rates was becoming difficult, however, because analyses were being released and promoted that illustrated that almost two-thirds of the savings in an income tax cut would go to those earning the top 10 percent of incomes.

Despite disagreements within their ranks, projected federal surpluses helped Republicans pass tax cuts totaling $792 billion over ten years in both the House and Senate in 1999. The tax cut passed by party-line votes just before Congress's August recess. President Clinton vetoed the tax cut in September, and with their time consumed by a bruising budget battle, members of Congress could not return to the issue until 2000.

Looking ahead to elections later in the year, Republicans in 2000 pursued a new strategy focused on cutting marginal tax rates, the estate tax, and the marriage penalty in three separate bills, with hopes of winning enactment of one before Election Day. Both the House and the Senate had passed the latter two provisions by late July. But again, both were vetoed by President Clinton in August, setting the stage for the election and the 2001 debate. Throughout the battle over tax cuts in Congress in 1999 and 2000, legislation was drafted by committee staff, with little advice welcomed from outside experts. Staff were experienced on the issue and sensitive to the priorities of the Republican leadership.

As tax cuts failed in the face of Presidential vetoes, the idea was gaining momentum in the latter stages of the presidential campaign. George W. Bush was touting his commitment to the three major tax cut ideas debated by Congress – cuts in marginal income tax rates, the marriage penalty, and the estate tax. He outlined the parameters of his tax cut plan in December 1999. In a major speech, he called for tax cuts totaling $483 billion over five years that benefited individuals, families, and small business ahead of large corporations. During the campaign, Bush refrained from commenting on the tax cut fights in Congress, but he could not avoid a debate with campaign opponents who took different views on the issue. Since first running for president in 1996, Steve Forbes had made the flat tax in particular and tax simplification in general the core elements of his platform. Senator John McCain (R.-Arizona), who emerged as Bush's strongest primary opponent, made tax cuts a much less central priority of his campaign. He proposed far more modest tax cuts than Bush, focusing on lowering taxes for a segment of middle-class Americans by lowering their tax bracket. Whereas candidate Bush's proposed tax cuts reduced government revenues by 5 percent, McCain's reduced revenues by less than 1 percent. In the general election, Vice Presidental Al Gore favored a targeted approach to tax cuts, much as President Clinton had. He called for Universal Savings Accounts, which would provide retirement credits for those who could not save with an IRA or 401(k) program. He also favored increases in the Earned Income Tax Credit program for families and a more modest reduction in the marriage penalty than that supported by Bush and congressional Republicans. With the exception of Steve Forbes, whose campaign never picked up steam, Bush was the clearest and strongest proponent of tax relief during the 2000 campaign. All of the major candidates had sources of advice on their tax cut proposals. Bush's principal advisor on economic issues during the campaign was Lawrence Lindsey, a strong proponent of tax cuts who had previously served in Bush's father's administration and had been a Federal Reserve Board governor. In the late 1990s, Lindsey was a fellow at the American Enterprise Institute. He became Bush's chief economic advisor in spring 1999 and coordinated Bush's positions on economic issues and advice that he received from a wide range of prominent economists based at universities and think tanks. Bush enjoyed counsel from many of the economists at the Hoover Institution, in particular, who had previously advised his father and President Ronald Reagan.[69] Steve Forbes had been a longtime disciple of a flat tax, promoting it previously in his moderately more successful 1996 run for president. His ideas were adapted from the work of two Stanford University economists, who had devised outlines for a flat tax in the early 1980s.[70] McCain, who waited until January 2000 to release a tax cut proposal, relied to a large extent on his Senate staff and longtime advisors for economic ideas.[71] Gore's principal advisor on the issue was Ronald Klain, who had been his vice-presidential chief of staff and was Washington issues director for the Gore campaign.

For as much attention as the tax cut issue received during the campaign, it was generating surprisingly little enthusiasm among the American people. Support for tax cuts was not as broad-based among the general public in 2000 as public interest in health care reform had been in 1991 and 1992. Americans expressed an interest in tax cuts, but they tended to support tax cuts only after Social Security and Medicare were protected and portions of the national debt were retired.[72] In a period of economic prosperity, the public did not view tax relief as a high priority.

---

[69] John Maggs, "Tax Cuts, Big and Small," *National Journal*, 7 August 1999, pp. 2286–9.
[70] Susan Dentzer, "Arrest Him, He Stole my Flat Tax!" *U.S. News and World Report*, 12 February 1996, p. 56.
[71] Bruce R. Bartlett, "There's Room for McCain on the Right," *The Los Angeles Times*, 9 February 2000, p. B7.
[72] Peter G. Gosselin, "Tax Cuts Seen as Spoiler in Boom Times," *The Los Angeles Times*, 26 August 2000, p. A1; T. Christian Miller and Maria L. LaGanga, "Voters Unswayed by Candidates' Tax Cut Push," *The Los Angeles Times*, 19 January 2000, p. A14; James A. Barnes, "Making the Case for Tax Cuts," *National Journal*, 16 September 2000, pp. 2902–3.

With tepid public interest and after a disputed election result, few expected the president-elect to pursue tax cuts that were as large as those he campaigned on, and few expected him to fight for them as aggressively as he did. But tax cuts became the first priority for the new president, and he signaled his intent to support cuts as large as those he had proposed during the campaign, totaling $1.6 trillion over ten years. He told congressional and business leaders who came to meet with him in Texas during the transition that, despite their warnings, he intended to push hard for his full tax cut. The outlines of the president's plan were in place before he took office. During his transition to office, he appointed Lindsey assistant to the president for economic policy.[73] Lindsey was tasked with coordinating the effort to translate the president-elect's campaign promise on taxes into legislative proposals. The president-elect and his advisors worked assiduously during December and January to have specific tax cut proposals ready once Bush took office.

Policy Deliberation

As Inauguration Day approached, Bush received news that had positive implications for his tax cut proposals. Economic indicators through December and early January suggested that what had been a red-hot economy might be slowing down. Fears of a recession served as a new rationale for enacting tax cuts. Tax cuts could help those Americans experiencing tough times, the thinking went, and it could contribute to a return to or continuation of economic prosperity. The president-elect's aides began publicly justifying tax cuts by reference to economic sluggishness. By early January, even Democratic congressional leaders were conceding room for tax cuts – in light of economic indicators. On January 3, House minority leader Richard Gephardt (D.-Missouri) stated, "I don't know the exact size; it may be that it has to get bigger because the recession is looming."[74] There was more good news for proponents of the tax cut soon after Bush's inauguration. The Congressional Budget Office in early February increased its estimates of the projected ten-year budget surplus to $5.6 trillion. Tax cut proponents could argue that the economy needed a boost and the government had the money to provide it.

---

[73] The American Enterprise Institute experienced considerable success in placing its scholars in the new administration. See Dana Milbank, "White House Hopes Gas Up a Think Tank," *The Washington Post*, 8 December 2000, p. A39.

[74] Daniel J. Parks, "Bush May Test Capitol Hill Clout Early with Expedited Tax-Cut Proposal," *Congressional Quarterly Weekly Report*, 6 January 2001, p. 41.

With deliberation over a tax cut set to begin in earnest between the president and the new 107th Congress, there were few opportunities for experts to make contributions. The president already had his proposal, and his advisors inside the executive branch were ironing out the details. Congress had been working on tax cuts for years, and, even though new chairmen took over both chambers' tax writing committees, experienced and knowledgeable staff on tax issues worked for the House Ways and Means and Senate Finance committees. Points of view among decision makers were well established on the issue as well. When Congress debated health care reform in the early 1990s, it took most members of Congress (as well as the president) considerable time to become familiar with technically complex reform proposals, even if they already had well-formed general preferences on the role of government in health care policy. By contrast, the tax cut was an easier issue for members, and one on which they had been considering for some years detailed proposals similar to those that came from the new Bush administration.

Two days after President Bush's inauguration, a version of his tax cut was introduced in the Senate by Phil Gramm (R.-Texas) and Zell Miller (D.-Georgia). Because he was a Democrat, Miller's sponsorship of the tax cut was a symbolic victory for the new president, but real victory in the Senate would have to wait. The tax cut moved through the House first. President Bush formally submitted his tax cut to Congress on February 8, after three days spent traveling the country to launch and promote it. Bush had agreed to a request from Speaker Dennis Hastert that the tax cut be taken up in parts in the House. That approach led to quick success for the Bush administration. The House passed the first portion of the president's plan exactly one month later, on March 8, 2001. By a vote of 230–198, along almost straight party lines, the House passed a cut in marginal income tax rates totaling $958 billion over ten years.[75] The House went on to pass the remaining core portions of the president's tax cut – reduction in the marriage penalty and elimination of the estate tax – in the last week of March and the first week of April. This was record time for such major legislation; all three bills passed with little real debate in committee or on the floor. The Democrats were angry, but work on the tax cut was nearly finished in one chamber.

The Senate would be more difficult. The Senate first took up the tax cut in debate over the annual budget resolution. Senate Republican leaders

[75] Lori Nitschke, "Tax-Cut Bipartisanship Down to One Chamber," *Congressional Quarterly Weekly Report*, 10 March 2001, pp. 529–32.

had delayed considering the tax cut until after resolving the budget resolution because the budget resolution could have protected debate over the tax cut from filibusters. The budget resolution was passed in early May, and in it, the Senate instructed its Finance Committee to draft a tax cut valued at roughly $1.35 trillion over eleven years, a portion of which was designated as a tax rebate for the current year.[76]

Final Enactment

The new Finance Committee Chairman, Charles Grassley (R.-Iowa), and his ranking Democratic counterpart, Max Baucus (D.-Montana), had been waiting for passage of the budget resolution to begin action in their committee. While waiting, they had produced a jointly written outline for a tax cut valued at exactly $1.35 trillion and released it on May 11, one day after the Senate passed its budget resolution.[77] Once the budget resolution was passed, the Senate had to work quickly in order for the tax cut to be considered under rules of the budget resolution, which limited floor debate to 20 hours and prohibited filibusters. After negotiations to win support from enough moderate senators to pass the tax cut, the legislation moved to the floor for full debate, which began on May 17. The Senate approved the tax cut on May 18. Democrats were ready to offer more than 150 amendments during the Senate debate, but they chose to forgo offering most of them after the first dozen failed.[78]

The tax cut went to conference committee, where the priorities of Senate moderates were paramount.[79] Many of the moderates had supported the Senate version of the tax cut only because it was smaller than what the president had proposed. And the Senate version of the tax cut

---

[76] David Baumann, "Budget Resolution Belatedly Approved," *National Journal*, 12 May 2001, p. 1420.

[77] Lori Nitschke and Bill Swindell, "Grassley–Baucus Tax Blueprint Heads for Rough and Tumble Markup," *Congressional Quarterly Weekly Report*, 12 May 2001, pp. 1069–70; Lori Nitschke, "Scaled-Down Version of Bush Tax Plan Taking Bipartisan Form at Senate Finance," *Congressional Quarterly Weekly Report*, 5 May 2001, p. 1003.

[78] A dozen Democrats supported the final tax cut agreed to in the Senate, which passed by a vote of 62–38.

[79] The House actually had to re-pass the tax cut in order for it to be taken up in conference, because the House had not passed the initial bills under budget reconciliation orders. The House vote was *pro forma* along party lines, 230–197. Commenting on the accommodation of Senate moderates, Republican Don Nickles of Oklahoma, who was the Senate majority whip at the time, commented, "This is loaded towards low-income people. We've done a whole heck of a lot both in size and composition to accommodate many of the moderate influences that we now have in the Senate." Lori Nitschke, "Tax Cut Deal Reached Quickly as Appetite for Battle Fades," *Congressional Quarterly Weekly Report*, 26 May 2001, pp. 1251–5.

was different in content from the House legislation as well. Early in the debate, Senate moderates had been pushing hard for the inclusion of a "trigger" for the tax cut, whereby the tax cut would be suspended if targets for debt reduction were not met.[80] That provision failed. But during final negotiations, moderates were also concerned about the general bias in the tax cut, favoring the wealthy. Senator Olympia Snowe (R.-Maine) championed a provision to expand the doubling of the child tax credit, already included in the legislation passed in the House, to working families that effectively paid no tax.[81] This last-minute idea was developed by think tanks and other experts and formed the basis for a compromise that won the tax cut the support of moderates. Over objections from House conservatives, that provision was included in the final conference report in order to keep Senate moderates in line. In addition, to conform with budget rules, the entire tax cut was set to "sunset" or expire on January 1, 2011, at which point tax rates would revert to pre–tax cut levels unless Congress intervened. The final tax cut was smaller than what the president had originally desired. It reduced revenues by the Senate's amount: $1.35 trillion over ten years. But with agreement reached, the House and Senate adopted the conference report on May 26. President Bush made his signature campaign issue law on June 7, 2001, with a White House signing ceremony.

Opportunities for Experts in Policy Making

The experience of experts in all three of the issue debates considered suggests that the opportunities for experts to be substantively influential are greatest early in the policy process. Early on, policy research can offer warning of problems with government programs, and it can serve as guidance for policy change. The cumulative weight of many research findings can help trigger the process whereby issues receive new deliberation. The "payoff" by way of policy change for research that is influential in this way can take years, if not decades, to become evident. It can be diffuse

---

[80] A group of eleven Senate moderates – five Republicans and six Democrats – made their interest in a trigger public in March. The Bush administration and Republican leaders in the Senate opposed a trigger, and, interestingly, some more liberal constituencies expressed doubts about a trigger's viability. The Center on Budget and Policy Priorities released a study critical of triggers as easily evaded on the day before the moderate senators held a press conference announcing their proposal. Glenn Kessler and Juliet Eilperin, "Tax Cut Is Given Hurdle to Clear," *The Washington Post*, 8 March 2001, p. A1.

[81] Glenn Kessler and Juliet Eilperin, "Pressure Rises for Tax Deal," *The Washington Post*, 25 May 2001, p. A1.

and difficult to trace. But the foundational work of researchers combined often becomes some of the most substantively useful contributions to the policy process. Research and expertise can play a critical role in how issue debates take shape and are initially defined.[82]

Experts are not always or even often influential in the early agenda-setting moments of issue debates. But the substantive prospects typically only get worse as issues become subject to more intense deliberation and interest. Experts sometimes still play an important role, but that role is less frequent and often of less substantive importance. As policy debates heat up, experts often produce work that becomes window dressing in battles where sides are clearly drawn and outcomes are oftentimes all but decided.

The cases confirm that the greatest substantive opportunity for experts is early in policy debates, with diminishing opportunities to be influential as issues heat up. But my focus in this chapter has been on differences in the opportunities for think tanks and experts generally *across* issue debates. On this front, the three cases point to at least four characteristics of issue debates that matter for experts: (1) the nature and extent of pre-existing research in the issue area, (2) the path the issue takes to the policy agenda, (3) the speed with which the issue travels through the policy process, and (4) the level of concern from organized interests about the outcome of the debate.

The Substance of Expertise

In a book generally about the power of experts to independently affect their role in policy making, it makes sense to begin my analysis of the three cases by considering how the numbers and pre-existing products of experts can affect their cumulative influence in new issue debates. My interest is in the combined work of experts, not the efforts of individual experts, which are assessed in the next chapter. The cases suggest two points. First (and not surprisingly), the potential for experts to be influential is greater in issue debates where substantive policy research is being produced and promoted than in debates where it is not. Second, the influence of expertise is greater in issue debates where the findings from research enjoy consensus in the policy research community (or at least go largely uncontested), rather than serve as a source of conflict and disagreement.

---

[82] See Rochefort and Cobb, *The Politics of Problem Definition*, pp. 10–15.

All three of the issues considered here are technically complex. This complexity made them good candidates for contributions by experts. But, of course, not all issues are complex – at least not in a technical sense. Abortion, gay rights, and euthanasia are examples of issues that produce far more moral than technical quandaries for policy makers. None is an issue over which a great number of policy experts toil; not only are the moral dimensions of these issues more complicated than the technical ones, but the moral dimensions typically trump whatever technical ones exist for resolving the issues. Other issues can lack strong moral dimensions but can require policy makers to focus far more on the political rather than the technical land mines that they embody; these issues also are seldom venues for policy research. Decisions on how to appropriate spending for new roads and bridges and decisions on which military bases to close are examples of political choices that can be politically difficult but that demand relatively little technical expertise.

Experts respond to signals from the policy community about what types of issues warrant their attention. And they organize accordingly. As I note in Chapter 1, more than 85 percent of nationally focused think tanks are specialized, with a focus on just one or two issues. These think tanks, and issue-specific university institutes as well, are not evenly distributed across issue areas but rather tend to cluster in policy areas that, on the one hand, have obtainable sources of financial support for research and, on the other hand, have some demand for the research that is produced. Quite simply, experts exist in greatest number in issue areas where there is support and demand. And, of course, experts have to be present in an issue area for there even to be the possibility of their having influence in an issue debate.

All three of my cases involve technical complexity; each has room for a role by experts. Yet clearly the importance of experts still varied tremendously in these three debates. This variation is explained in part by differences in the content of pre-existing research and knowledge as the debates were about to begin.

When telecommunications deregulation became the subject of advocacy by industry representatives, for example, the policy research community was already in general agreement about what direction reform should take. A scholarly consensus favoring competition and some measure of deregulation in the industry had developed in much of the work of economists and policy analysts during the 1980s. This consensus carried over to convince many lawmakers of the merits of that direction for reform by the time the debate began in earnest in 1993. In addition, the perceived success of airline and trucking deregulation in the 1980s, which had itself been inspired by the work of economists at think tanks and universities in the 1960s and 1970s, had made believers out of even many initial skeptics that a similar philosophy might suit the telecommunications industry.[83] Policy makers entered the debate convinced of the general point; as one congressional aide observed, "These committees had grappled with this issue for a long time, and the members had built up considerable expertise. They were ready to do something.... It really wasn't rocket science."[84] The cumulative consensus of experts in the telecommunications debate created a useful foundation as the issue moved on to the policymaking agenda.

By contrast, in health care reform, the Clinton administration put together a task force for the express purpose of involving experts in a process aimed at developing a level of consensus around reform ideas. That consensus did not exist as the debate began, and it was never reached. There were scores of evaluation studies, briefs, and books about the provision of health care that informed the work of the task force and other policy makers concerned about the issue. But despite many helpful findings, health services researchers had not rallied around a particular proposal or even a general approach to reform. Instead, proposals ranged from a government financed single-payer scheme to incremental reforms that left health coverage to private-sector insurers. Differences in proposals among health services researchers reflected as much their differences in philosophy about the appropriate role of government as any variance in how analysts read results from twenty years of health care research. While there was widespread consensus on the nature of the health care problem, there was no agreement among experts on how it could be fixed. This lack of consensus – in fact, the active disagreement among experts on health care reform – diminished their cumulative influence early in the debate.

The same was true in the tax cut debate, although to a lesser extent. Research pointed to the different incentives for spending and saving that would be created by forms of tax reduction. But this research supported a number of alternative directions for reform. From the very beginning of the debate over tax cuts, policy makers gravitated toward research that was supportive of their pre-existing ideological predilections about taxes.

---

[83] On the influence of economic research on airline and trucking deregulation, see Martha Derthick and Paul J. Quirk, *The Politics of Deregulation* (Washington, D.C.: Brookings Institution Press, 1985).
[84] Interview with congressional staff, Washington, D.C., 10 May 1999.

That research and its purveyors could be helpful in formulating proposals, but the lack of agreement among economists and policy analysts on how tax cuts could most benefit the American people – and even on whether cuts were desirable – diminished the cumulative power of research early on in the debate.

Deborah Stone observes that "problem definition is the active manipulation of images of conditions by competing political actors."[85] For experts, influence over this manipulation is made easier when they are in general agreement on the image of the problem and the direction for policy reform viewed as most desirable. Issue debates are also more easily resolved when this kind of agreement exists.[86] The lack of agreement on features of the problem and especially its solution, which extended among the ranks of policy makers, contributed to the failure in health care reform. Despite disagreement on the need for it, the tax cut was enacted by sheer force of political will on the part of the new president and by helpful, even if tenuous, majorities in both the House and Senate.

The Political Origins of Issues

The substantive weight of research findings provided experts in telecommunications some advantage over those in health care and tax relief. But once the policy debates were underway, experts were actually more active and in demand in the debate over health care reform than in either of the others. That greater activity reflects differences in the dynamics surrounding the issues' emergence among policy makers.

The health care reform debate, as well as the debate over the tax cut, emerged from the speeches and promises of presidential elections. Each issue took on a high profile from the moment presidential candidates realized the subjects had political traction. Public interest in the issues meant that many policy makers beyond the narrow range with jurisdiction to shepherd new laws through Congress were looking for guidance and advice on how to talk about them. Not just presidential candidates but lawmakers and other candidates for office who might otherwise have waited for bills to emerge through the traditional committee process instead sought to develop their own proposals. In health care reform, Senator Bob Kerrey's quick effort to develop the Health USA bill in 1991 is a good example. Kerrey had little background on health care prior to 1991;

---

[85] Deborah Stone, "Causal Stories and the Formation of Policy Agendas," *Political Science Quarterly* 104 (1989): 281–300.
[86] See Baumgartner and Jones, *Agendas and Instability in American Politics*.

he did not serve on the relevant health care committee in the Senate. His interest was in capitalizing on the issue in his run for president. On health care reform and the tax cut, every candidate needed a plan. Therefore every candidate – and many other public officials as well – became audiences for the efforts of policy experts.[87]

In the debate over telecommunications reform, by contrast, the issue from the start had a low public profile. Recognition of a need for legislation, when it occurred, came from the relevant ranking congressional committee members, who saw to it that legislation was developed and drafted. The committee chairs in the House and Senate were virtually the only ones developing reform proposals. As a result, the opportunities for experts to affect the development of legislation were minimal. Experts had few policy makers to whom they could make an appeal.

Differences in the development of the issue debates carried over to affect the demand for experts in policy deliberation. On health care, once the issue had a high profile, policy makers, even those with little prior interest in the topic, felt the need to have information with which to form and defend points of view. Policy makers received questions from constituents and journalists that were difficult to avoid. As a result, think tanks and policy experts continued to have influence by making the case for – or against – reform in ways that reflected the public interest; politicians could, in turn, attach themselves rhetorically to research and policy positions. With the general public less interested in telecommunications reform, politicians did not need to rely on experts or expertise as much to provide public justifications or support for their positions in the debate. Rank-and-file lawmakers did not feel the need to develop their own telecommunications reform bills.

The high-profile tax cut debate created demands for experts much as the health care reform debate did, but to what seemed a lesser extent. Expressions of support for or opposition to tax cuts could be made more easily without the help of research than could positions on the health care debate. The tax cut was a more straightforward ideological issue and one the public could understand. Policy makers were comfortable talking about it without referring to complicated research. Overall, demand for

---

[87] Interestingly, this finding differs with Baumgartner and Jones's observation that "The skills and resources useful in private negotiations may not be the same as those useful in public debates. Technical expertise, inside contacts, and legal skills may prove to be of no value where an emotional public media campaign is waged." Baumgartner and Jones, *Agendas and Instability in American Politics*, p. 9. Technical expertise may indeed be valuable in media campaigns, but perhaps just not in a substantive way.

policy research was less once the debate was underway than in health care reform.

Speed in Policy Making

One more important difference between the health care and tax cut debates, which contributed to the reduced demand for research in the latter, is the time it took for each topic to be considered. President Clinton began his first term with a pledge to win health care reform in his first 100 days. Instead, it took nearly 18 months before the issue debate was declared dead. By contrast, President Bush signed the tax cut legislation only 138 days into his new administration. The great speed with which the tax cut was approved – with the first portion passed in the House just 47 days after the president's inauguration – left little time for experts to construct studies or commentaries that might be immediately useful. Even if they could, there were few opportunities for them to gain a hearing. Opponents or potential proponents of the president's plan who were among the ranks of policy makers had little time to launch much of a campaign to build on or thwart the president's proposal. During President Clinton's drawn-out fight for health care reform, a wide range of alternative health care proposals was considered in House and Senate committees. During the tax cut debate, virtually the only place to offer amendments was on the floor of the House and Senate, and even there, opportunities were few, as the tax bills whizzed through both chambers.

Interest Group Dominance

The speed with which the tax cut passed in the Congress put not only policy makers who would have liked to change it at a disadvantage but also interest groups with hopes of winning favorable provisions in the tax bill. Interest groups had to work quickly to have their preferences served in the final bill. And many failed, as the president and lawmakers remained focused on the original legislation, oriented toward individuals more than corporations.

By contrast, the drawn-out nature of the health care reform debate created opportunities for the organized interests that opposed the Clinton administration plan to mobilize the public against it. The Health Insurance Association of America was the most visible of more than a dozen interest groups and trade associations that launched television advertisements, direct mailings, and the pressure tactics of face-to-face lobbying to derail the Clinton proposals. Presidential scholars have long observed that moving quickly can be critical to the success of presidential initiatives, especially at the beginning of a term in office[88]; the tax cut and the health care reform debates illustrate this point again.

As it relates to experts, the lesson from all three issue debates is that the likelihood that experts will have the chance to make a meaningful contribution to issue debates is inversely related to the power of interest groups and advocates in the debate – whatever their timing. Opportunities for experts are the most diminished when interests become involved that perceive themselves as at risk of great loss from pending decisions. In many issue debates, even those where interest groups do not start out as dominant, groups that feel threatened become a potent force as deliberation moves toward enactment. In some debates, the dominance of interest groups leaves experts little opportunity to be influential from the start.

Telecommunications reform was an example of the latter experience. With the exception of the expert-built consensus around promoting competition, experts never had much of a chance. It was a subject brought to policy makers by industries that were heavily invested in how it was resolved. Throughout its consideration, the industry representatives worked with their various allies in Congress to craft the final legislation. If there was need for technical knowledge or assistance, the expertise came from the industries affected, not from disinterested parties. As I discuss in the next chapter, think tanks and other experts were producing research on telecommunications reform right up to the moment the new law was passed, but little of it was getting to policy makers or past the industry representatives who were dictating the details of the new law. The telecommunications industries had too much to lose in the debate over reform to leave policy makers susceptible to efforts by uncontrolled sources of information. Policy makers, usually benefiting from the financial largesse of some segment of the telecommunications industry toward their campaigns, typically followed the lead of industry allies.

The early moments of the health care reform debate were different for experts. Health services researchers played an important role in policy makers' efforts to develop proposals for reform. The issue was complex; the public was concerned about the issue. And the interest groups and trade associations that would later mobilize against the Clinton administration proposal were not yet sure how they might fare under a new health care regime. Interest groups were following the issue closely, but they did not initially devote their resources to scuttling the policy process. Had the interests of the health insurance industry not come under attack, health

[88] Richard E. Neustadt, *Presidential Power and the Modern Presidents: The Politics of Leadership from Roosevelt to Reagan* (New York: Free Press, 1990).

care reform might have passed, and the debate might have remained one characterized by majoritarian politics. The influence of experts would certainly have been traceable in a new health care system. But the health care debate broke down when industries realized the great potential for loss – for them – if reform was enacted. They mobilized against the legislation, and once their mobilization was underway, not only was the legislation doomed but the prospects for contributions by experts to the debate were lost as well.

It is the common experience of all three issues that by the time policy enactment rolled around, the opportunities for contributions of policy research were minimal. Frequently, the minds of policy makers had been made up. Even more often, though, the specific issues that remained to be resolved tended to be narrow provisions that had the greatest consequences for interests heavily vested in the outcomes. These interests were loath to permit outside researchers to play a role. The general lesson seems to be that experts finish behind other sources of influence that have more resources and better contacts.

But there is something of an exception to this experience in the tax cut debate. Late in the fast-moving debate, when proponents of the tax cut were seeking to win moderate Republican votes in the Senate, a proposal for an expanded child tax credit was added to the legislation. The proposal had come from think tanks. A proposal from the Brookings Institution, promoted by the Center on Budget and Policy Priorities, for expanding the child tax credit was helpful in mending a disagreement between moderate and conservative Republicans in the Senate. Its acceptance paved the way for the tax cut's passage there. Experts, in this case, were substantively successful latecomers to the debate. They succeeded, though, because those with interests represented in the tax cut debate had little to lose from the child tax credit's inclusion, and most interests had been effectively blocked from participating in the fast-moving debate anyway. The tax cut debate generally was over an issue that had few big losers among those that were well organized to represent their interests (even if there were some who would have liked to have been bigger winners). In this case, the prospect of using the child tax credit compromise to win passage of the larger legislation made those skeptical of its merits sit on their hands.

Lessons for Experts about the Opportunities of Different Issues

I began this chapter with Wilson's typology for classifying issues by the distribution of costs and benefits. That typology was helpful for identifying three very different issues for analysis. But the prospects for experts in these issue debates ends up having less to do with the perceived costs and benefits associated with their subjects than with the variable dynamics of the policy debates over them. The opportunities for experts tend to be dictated by the nature of the cumulative knowledge base when the issue debate begins, the nature of the debate's origins, the speed with which the debate is resolved, and the level of concern and mobilization by vested interests. On topics about which researchers enjoy a near-consensus both on problems and solutions, researchers tend to play a more important early role than on topics where disagreement prevails. Issues that provoke high-profile public debates experience a greater demand for experts than those that are out of the public eye. And issues that move relatively slowly and experience little interest group opposition provide more opportunities for experts than others. In the end, the possibilities for experts to be influential in the policy process – from whatever sources, think tanks or otherwise – depend on at least these four attributes of issue debates.

So the burdens laid out here that work against success for experts seem discouragingly large. Indeed, the last of these lessons for experts is especially daunting. The preponderance of issues have groups in society with an investment in how they are settled, and many of those groups – an ever-increasing number of them – are organized to represent their interests effectively with decision makers. They can provide research and ideas, along with political advice and support, that drown out the work of think tanks and independent policy experts generally. This is a serious constraint on experts.

I began the chapter drawing on the example of the 1996 welfare reform debate. It was a debate in which policy experts had substantial influence. Policy research from think tanks and other independent experts informed the critique of the old welfare system; it informed the proposals that were shaped for a new cash assistance program. And researchers provided key influential advice on technical provisions of the final law as it moved from deliberation to enactment. Welfare reform was an issue where a consensus was developing in the research community, at least about the problems with previous policy, as the subject reached policy makers. It was an issue that enjoyed a high public profile, and it moved slowly through Congress. These conditions favored experts. But experts were so successful in informing the welfare reform debate, in the end, because there were few well-organized interests with a stake in its outcome. No major industry was in peril; no major voting constituency stood to lose. In this context, experts had almost unobstructed access to policy makers, who, in turn, had interest in what researchers were producing. Experts were by no means the dominant force in the welfare reform debates, but they had more opportunity in this debate than they do in most because those who stood to "lose" from the policy enacted were poorly represented in the policy process.

Welfare reform falls toward one end of a continuum of issue debates that runs from those with few well-organized interests facing loss to issue debates with many of these organized interests. For experts working in issues that fall toward the latter end of the continuum, hope is not lost, however. The influence of experts in debates with many organized interests will typically be most limited during the final stage of those debates, as the resolution of lucrative technical provisions in legislation is dominated by those with an investment in their outcome. But experts can still make important contributions to the early foundations of policy change in interest-dominated issue debates. The importance of the consensus among economists about telecommunications deregulation is a good example. And this early foundational role for experts is in many ways their most substantively important opportunity for guiding the content of new laws. By the latter stages of the policy process, much of the work of experts, in any policy debate, is no more than justification for views already taken.

Experts were more visible in the latter stages of the health care reform debate than in the latter stages of telecommunications reform. But their role during deliberation over health care was as fodder and ammunition for dueling policy makers (on an issue that ultimately imploded). All sides used policy briefs and press releases to bolster different sides of already well-worked arguments. This work added marginally to the politics of the issue's demise, but it brought little substance to the debate. By contrast, experts made a meaningful early substantive contribution to the telecommunications debate. As Bob Blau, vice president of Bell South, recalls:

Congress was obviously sensitive to arguments from the industry, but part of their job is also to look out for the best interests of the public, consumers, and the economy. I think there was a sense in those days that they needed to get it right. And I think there was a general feeling that competition was better than a monopoly. They listen to a variety of people, including economists, a variety of people who write about how this industry works. . . . And I think most of that heavy lifting by the academic community occurred in getting Congress to the point where they felt like they needed to do something, which is probably 75 percent of the battle.[89]

[89] Interview with Bob Blau, Bell South, Washington, D.C., 6 May 1999.

This experience in telecommunications reform leaves hope for experts who work in other issue areas where the investment of interested parties is great that they likewise might contribute to a policy consensus that will be substantively important, once consistent findings accumulate over time.

In fact, Derthick and Quirk point to another example, in the experience of experts on similar issues in the 1980s. Policy experts played a very direct, substantive role in prompting deregulation of the trucking and airline industries in that decade. Leading up to deregulation, as Derthick and Quirk observe, "Economists were convinced that much economic regulation in fundamentally competitive markets had large costs yet yielded no benefits, and their analysis reinforced the work of other disciplines that had criticized regulatory agencies as captives of the regulated industries."[90] Through the 1950s and 1960s, academic economists had converged on the argument that price, entry, and exit regulations were generally inefficient and undesirable. In the 1970s, this research was turned into specific proposals, and, as Derthick and Quirk illustrate, policy experts propelled policy makers' confidence in deregulation to the point that deregulation "became a preferred style of policy choice in the nation's capital, espoused more or less automatically, even unthinkingly, by a wide range of officeholders and their critics and used by them as a guide to position taking."[91] This same sentiment reemerged in a similar way when telecommunications reform came up for debate in the 1990s.

Experts working in issue areas with strong interest group participation have another potential advantage: Their work can be lucrative. One tactic that industries and interests use to influence the preferences of policy makers is the sponsorship of research. They hire experts at think tanks and universities to produce studies about the areas of policy that worry them. If the results of that research reflect favorably on the sponsoring organization, they are promoted among the ranks of decision makers. During the telecommunications reform debate, again, this is exactly what happened. Nearly every think tank scholar or leading academic in the field had a consulting relationship with one or another of the telecommunications companies. These relationships provided financial rewards. They also often provided very constructive indirect paths for their work

[90] Martha Derthick and Paul J. Quirk, *The Politics of Deregulation* (Washington, D.C.: The Brookings Institution, 1985), p. 238.
[91] Derthick and Quirk, *The Politics of Deregulation*, p. 35.

to those active in the policy process. The research of experts in the hands of well-placed advocates at times took on considerable weight.[92]

The opportunities to work for the affected industries, when they dominate a debate, suggest that hope remains for experts working in these areas. But the consultant-client relationship that experts often develop in these areas has its disadvantages as well. In establishing paid relationships with interested parties, experts can often impair perceptions of their credibility and that of their research. Experts, as a whole class of actors, experienced this loss of credibility in the telecommunications debate. Henry Geller, a former assistant secretary of Commerce in the Carter administration and a telecommunications industry observer, offers a view shared by many about the experts involved in the debate:

> These are all very bright people, and they really do believe, I believe, in what they did. But they were all hired. They're so bright, and they're so able. And people go to them . . . [but] you've got to take everything they say with a ton of salt. They've been retained. Now they make that clear, you know, they always say. . . . But what I'm telling you is that nobody's going to pay attention. You're a hired gun. You wouldn't pay attention to their lawyer. Oh, you'd listen to his arguments, but you wouldn't be stroking your brow saying, I've just heard great truth. You'd say, I've just heard a great advocate.[93]

So there are important tradeoffs for experts working in areas with resource-rich interests. Gaining direct access to policy makers is difficult. Building relationships with the interests can open indirect avenues for research consumption, but it can damage perceptions of the integrity of experts as well.

The challenges that experts face across issue domains in bringing their work to the attention of policy makers and making it influential operates as well on the individual level for particular experts – including think tanks – in each and every policy debate. The tension between gaining an audience for research and sacrificing integrity is especially real, collectively on some issues like telecommunications reform but even more often on an individual basis, as each expert and each expert organization seeks to build a credible reputation as well as a record for having successfully influenced policy. These challenges are the subject of the next chapter.

In the end, this chapter provides a roadmap of sorts for experts across different types of issue domains. There are features of issues and issue

---

[92] In fact, this indirect path for research is the one traditionally characterized by policy scholars. See Lindblom and Woodhouse, *The Policy-Making Process, Second Edition.*
[93] Interview with Geller, 5 May 1999.

debates that sometimes make effective policy influence easier for experts generally, and some that make influence more difficult. Even more, the features of issue debates present frequent tradeoffs for experts. Yet as much as one lesson of the chapter is that the opportunities for experts vary across issue debates, another is that this variance need not make any issue debate insurmountable to contributions from researchers. Experts can and do adapt to different circumstances, and they show a collective capacity to leave a mark on what can be even the most difficult of debates for them.

5

Policy Influence: Making Research Matter

The origins of the Heritage Foundation are famous in the halls of the now-sprawling think tank perched on Capitol Hill. While working for a Republican senator in 1971, Paul Weyrich received a careful analysis of the supersonic transport program from the American Enterprise Institute (AEI). But the brief arrived days after the Senate had voted on the issue. He and his friend Edwin Feulner inquired of a friend at AEI to learn that the brief had been intentionally delayed so as not to influence the Senate vote. Weyrich and Feulner were frustrated; the brief would have been helpful. Their frustration fueled efforts to form the Heritage Foundation, which from its beginning made informing congressional decision making central to its mission. In fairness, the skittishness at the American Enterprise Institute at the time was probably warranted: AEI had just weathered a congressional probe of its president's involvement in Senator Barry Goldwater's 1964 presidential campaign, with political activity prohibited among nonprofit organizations. But still, the product of the frustration – the formation of the Heritage Foundation – marked a turning point for think tanks. As their numbers have exploded in the years since, the efforts by think tanks to influence policy making have intensified, just as the explosion in their numbers has made achieving that influence all the more difficult.

I focus in this chapter on how, in a crowded organizational environment, the common interest of think tanks in policy influence translates into success for some think tanks and failure for others. With a knowledge that some issues are more accommodating of experts than others, I examine how particular experts succeed in drawing attention to their work during issue debates. Chapter 3 illustrated characteristics and strategies of think tanks that shape their visibility among journalists and congressional staff. In this chapter, I consider whether these factors also affect their access and actual influence among policy makers. When it was formed in 1973, the Heritage Foundation crafted strategies for informing lawmaking that its founders thought would improve on those of the American Enterprise Institute. In the context of so many and such diverse sources of expertise thirty years later, I evaluate the specific behaviors of think tanks – Heritage, AEI, and many others – at different points and among different policymaking audiences.

My focus is the three issue debates described in the previous chapter: health care, telecommunications, and tax reduction.[1] My interest is in the influence of think tanks and experts generally in these policy debates. How do experts succeed in defining the terms of issue debates? How do they succeed in informing the content of final deliberations? I define influence here as success by experts in making their work known among a set of policy makers so that it informs their thinking on or public articulation of policy relevant information. Whether this influence on individual policy makers carries over to affect final policy outcomes is of interest, but that type of influence is subject to the constraints characterized in the previous chapter – and possibly others – that are typically out of the control of experts, whatever their talents.

The work of think tanks and policy experts generally can be important to an issue beginning years before it becomes a subject of debate among policy makers, and that importance can continue right through to the period when a new policy is implemented. My focus in this chapter is restricted to perhaps the most intense portion of the policy cycle: the period that starts when an issue begins to pick up steam among decision makers and ends with either legislation's final enactment into law or its defeat. My analysis is organized around an understanding of expertise as supplied to policy makers in four forms, organized along two dimensions, as illustrated in Figure 5-1. The form that research takes varies by its purpose and scope. Research can have the purpose of informing late agenda-setting moments, when interest among policy makers is building and ideas are being translated into legislative language. This is priming research. In this form, studies provide general insight on how social, political, or economic problems might be addressed by policy makers, what

---

[1] My particular interest is in the behavior of experts in legislative policy making, of which each of the issue debates is an example. That is a defined limit of the analysis, but it is an intentional one. The greatest number of new think tanks since 1970 are principally focused on legislative policy making.

Purpose of Research	Scope of Research	
	General	*Specific*
Priming	Issues and Options Research	Proposals
Prodding	Commentary	Estimates

FIGURE 5-1. Forms of expertise in policy making

I call "issues and options research." This work summarizes the many dimensions of policy problems and the range of alternatives available to policy makers. Or research at this point can be offered in the form of specific policy proposals; rather than discussing a variety of options, research can explicitly endorse a particular course of change in policy. Priming research generally can be helpful in catapulting issues to the attention of policy makers, to the point where decision makers might take action. It can also provide guidance on what that action might be.

Research can also be prodding. Prodding research encourages policy makers either to support or oppose existing legislation or to amend its content. In its general form, this research is commentary on the desirability of particular reform proposals already under consideration. In its more specific form, this research takes the form of specific estimates of the financial or performance benefits and drawbacks of legislation. Commentary is often helpful to policy makers as they articulate points of view in ongoing issue debates. Specific estimates often provide guidance on particular provisions of pending legislation, guidance that sometimes has a substantive consequence for policy outcomes.

This typology of policy research captures the types of work that think tanks and policy experts generally produce. It is also helpful analytically as a guide for discerning the potential for particular research products to be influential. Overall, experts can improve their chances of being influential if they intentionally produce research in a form that is directly relevant to the purposes for which it is intended. They do better when they consciously consider: Is the research intended to help publicize a new issue or produce a particular policy outcome? Is the research intended to make a general case for a set of ideas or to offer a tailored analysis of specifics? These are basic questions for analysts to resolve, and their decisions can affect whether their work has the potential to be useful among policy makers. Moreover, my analysis in this chapter suggests that experts who produce work in its more specific forms – either as proposals or estimates – as issue debates move from agenda setting through deliberation to enactment have some advantage in securing substantive influence.

Besides form, four characteristics and behaviors affect the likelihood that experts might be influential among policy makers: (1) their perceived credibility, (2) their access to policy makers, (3) the timeliness of their efforts, and (4) the intensity of their marketing. In specific policy debates, those offering expertise more easily find a stage for it when they are viewed as credible by prospective audiences. Experts have an advantage if they are already known by and have ready access to policy makers. Expertise should be timely; a pointed analysis three weeks after an issue is decided is of little use. (AEI's supersonic transport analysis is a case in point.) Finally, experts are more influential when they effectively market their work so that it is available and accessible to potentially interested policy makers.

The results discussed in this chapter confirm my general conclusion that the intentional efforts of experts matter for how, when, and why their contributions are influential. Particularly to the extent that marketing is a key feature of what makes experts successful, influential experts may be far more dynamic and animated – and politically involved – than they are often portrayed to be in established explanations of policy making. It is accepted implicitly and explicitly across a range of studies that take different approaches to the policy process that the researcher or expert has little role in policy making once his or her product is released. Experts, even when their work becomes important, are themselves quiescent and detached. The research speaks for itself or, more often, other types of actors – the intended "advocates" – become its promoters and defenders. My analysis in previous chapters indicates some of the limits to this view. These limitations become even more apparent in the analysis here. Far from playing a detached role, experts can be quite active and intentional in policy debates.

A Note on Methodology

My analysis in this chapter is framed around an examination of the contributions of think tanks and other sources of expertise in the health care and telecommunications reform debates of the 1990s and the tax cut debate in 2000–1. My choice of the three cases was explained in Chapter 4. The focus of my analysis in this chapter is on the particular activities of a set of think tanks in each case with expertise in the policy area, along with a range of non–think tank experts successful in making their research noticed by policy makers. The think tanks tend to be the largest and most well-known ones working in the areas as well as some with specialized expertise in the policy areas.[2] The evidence comes from original archival research and journalistic records from each period and 135 in-depth interviews conducted with personnel from think tanks, interest groups, the media, Congress, and the executive branch. Those interviewed are listed in Appendix B, along with their affiliations.

My approach in this chapter could be a case-by-case narrative of the activities of think tanks in each policy area from the start of the debate to final enactment. Those narratives would be thorough but also long and perhaps painfully tedious. Moreover, they would be redundant. Once I account for the important differences in the aggregate opportunities for policy experts between issue areas, as done in the previous chapter, the particular strategies that think tanks and experts use to make their work influential, when opportunities for them do exist, vary little from one issue area to the next. It took a start-to-finish analysis of the think tanks along with other experts associated with each case to make this point with confidence, but given the similarities from one case to the next, I present findings from one portion of each of the three issue debates here rather than full narratives for all three.[3]

I begin with the experience of think tanks and experts generally during the late agenda-setting stages of health care reform. I then consider the experience of think tanks and experts generally during deliberation over final telecommunications reform legislation. Along with a qualitative assessment of deliberation over telecommunications reform, I examine the number of newspaper citations to and frequency of congressional testimony by the experts involved. Finally, I consider some particular experiences of think tanks and other experts in the final moments before enactment of the tax cut in 2001.

---

[2] In each case, the group of organizations includes all of the think tanks that produce research in the policy areas that were among the top half of those rated as influential in the survey of congressional staff and journalists, reported in Chapter 2. Additional think tanks are included in the analysis because of their specialized focus in the policy area and the corresponding likelihood that they might have sought to be active in reform debates. In the health care reform debate, for example, these include the Employee Benefit Research Institute, the Hastings Center, the Manhattan Institute, and the National Center for Policy Analysis.

[3] Full narratives for two of the three cases (health care and telecommunications reform) are available in my dissertation, Andrew Rich, *Think Tanks, Public Policy, and the Politics of Expertise*, Ph.D. Dissertation, Yale University, 1999, Chapters 5 and 6.

Agenda Setting on Health Care Reform

As interest in health care reform grew during the 1992 presidential election, the volume of research contributions from think tanks and elsewhere was enormous. The range of ideas represented in the research was enormous as well. Reform ideas fell into five basic categories, two with appeal to Democrats, two with appeal to Republicans, and one that had joint appeal. Democrats were attracted to (1) managed competition plans, (2) play or pay approaches, and (3) single-payer schemes. Ideas with appeal to Republicans included (1) tax incentive schemes, (2) insurance market reform and medical savings account plans, and (3) managed competition, in a different form from that preferred by Democrats. Each idea had more than one proposal associated with it, and each was served by more than one expert. Table 5-1 briefly characterizes each of the plans that was represented in legislation as well as the products of relevant think tanks early in the debate. It also illustrates how each ranks according to the criteria by which they were assessed: the type of research produced, the credibility of the source, the expert's access to decision makers, the timing of product release, and marketing strategies.

Of the think tanks examined, seven made no contributions of research as the issue grew in visibility in 1991 and 1992. Many of the think tanks were new to the health care issue at the time and were in the process of hiring their first staff with expertise on the issue (e.g., the Cato Institute, the Center on Budget and Policy Priorities, the Economic Policy Institute). For one, the RAND Corporation, producing "prodding research" fell outside of its mission. Of the remaining seven think tanks, four produced issues and options research on health care reform, and three produced concrete proposals. But even among these seven think tanks, along with the other successful sources of policy research at this stage of the debate, there were many differences in the strategies used and the influence achieved.

Alain Enthoven, the Stanford University economist who had first developed the managed competition approach during the 1970s, continued to revise and publicize his proposal through the 1980s. He co-wrote a reformulated version of his ideas in a pair of 1989 *New England Journal of Medicine* articles.[4] With rising numbers of uninsured and quickly escalating health care costs, Enthoven was keenly aware of the potential for health care to become a central policy issue in the 1990s; writing the *New*

---

[4] Alain Enthoven and Richard Kronick, "A Consumer Choice Health Plan for the 1990s," parts I and II, *New England Journal of Medicine* 320 (5 and 12 January 1989): 29–37, 94–101.

TABLE 5-1. *Agenda-Setting Research in Health Care Reform*

Agenda-Setting Research	Type of Research	Credibility	Access	Timing	Marketing
Enthoven and Jackson Hole Group (managed competition plan)	*Proposal* 5 policy memos	High Enthoven's academic credentials	High Industry reps had lobbying connections and Enthoven and Ellwood known by lawmakers	Memos released Fall 1991	Circulated by industry representatives
Garamendi-Zelman-Starr (managed competition plan)	*Proposal* 20-page policy memo	High Garamendi's elected position and development group of scholars	High Garamendi had lobbyist on Capitol Hill and connections in Democratic politics to Clinton	Memo released February 1992	Hired lobbyist; Zelman briefings in Washington
Richard Brown (single-payer plan)	*Proposal* 12-point policy memo	High Brown's academic credentials	Medium Brown known through previous writings and, more importantly, by former UCLA student G. Brown	Principles for reform within 2 weeks of meeting Kerrey	High profile in California reform and frequent meetings and memos with Kerrey staff
Ron Pollack, Families USA (play or pay plan)	*Proposal* Product of Pepper Comm.	High Judy Feder and other academics well known w/Pepper Comm.	High Feder and other authors developed the play or pay plan as part of gov't commission	Pollack's memo to Clinton after *American Prospect* article	Made visible through Pepper Commission and made accessible in *American Prospect* article

Brookings Institution (favored play or pay, but no plan)	*Issues and Options Research* Aaron's *Serious and Unstable Condition*	High Aaron and Wiener well regarded in policy community	High Well entrenched institution. Aaron especially well known and friendly among policy makers	Aaron's book released in early 1991; Wiener available to Clinton	Little promotion of research or ideas
Center on Budget and Policy Priorities	*None*	Middle Inexperienced and unknown on health care in early '90s	Low Inexperienced and unknown on health care in early '90s		
Economic Policy Institute	*None*	Middle-Low Inexperienced and unknown on health care in early '90s	Low		
Employee Benefit Research Institute (favored market-based approaches)	*Issues and Options Research* Health Care Reform	High Known for basic facts research	Medium	Produced relevant research but not timed for impact	Send all materials to subscribers and members offices on Capitol Hill; occasional Capitol Hill briefings
Hastings Center	*None*	Middle Focused on issues of medical ethics in early '90s among policy makers	Low Focused on issues of medical ethics in early '90s but little visibility		
Progressive Policy Institute (Jackson Hole managed competition plan)	*Proposal* Rosner chapter in *Mandate for Change*	Middle Inexperienced on health care until hiring Rosner in late 1992	High Connected with DLC, to which many centrist Democrats in Congress belonged & Clinton chaired	Release of *Mandate for Change* after Clinton's election in late 1992	PPI well connected with new Clinton administration and marketing book to them

(continued)

159

TABLE 5-1 *(continued)*

Agenda-Setting Research	Type of Research	Credibility	Access	Timing	Marketing
RAND Corporation	*None*	High / Produced RAND Health Insurance Experiment in 1970s and 80s. Agenda setting research not part of mission.	Medium		
Urban Institute (favored play or pay, but no plan)	*Issues and Options Research* Holahan et al.'s book	High / Moon, Steurle, Holahan each highly regarded in policy community	High / Moon, in particular, well connected with Feder and Dem policy makers	Holahan's book in early 1991; Moon available to campaigns	Little promotion of research or ideas
Senator Nickles Heritage Foundation (tax incentive plan)	*Proposal* 1989 book followed by short analyses and op-eds with specific components	High / Republican lawmakers looked to them for cues	High / Legislative relations at Heritage ensured relationships with Members and staff	Book released in 1989 and followed up on in 1991	Circulated by Heritage staff and added to by Moffit's FEHBP comparison
Senator Gramm National Ctr for Policy Analysis (medical savings account plan)	*Proposal* Abridged version of *Patient Power* for Members	Medium / Goodman not well known so little accumulated credibility	Medium / Worked in coalition with insurance companies to become known to lawmakers	Golden Rule Insurance Co. promoted plan when Coats was looking for something	Golden Rule promoted plan along with Goodman

	Publication	Reputation	Access		
Senator Chafee Individual Mandate	*Issues and Options* Series of consultations over years	Plan derived within Congress over four years preceding health care reform. Experts drawn upon during derivation process, but principally driven by Republican senatorial staff.			
American Enterprise Institute (favored tax incentives, but no plan)	*Issues and Options* Two volumes by Robert Helms; book by Pauly	High Well regarded among Republican lawmakers	Medium Helms held regular briefings with congressional staff	Volumes not timed to inform proposal generation in health care	Books released with little fanfare
Cato Institute	*None*	Middle Inexperienced and unknown on health care in early '90s	Low		
Citizens for a Sound Economy	*None*	Middle-Low Inexperienced and unknown on health care in early '90s	Low		
Manhattan Institute	*None*	Middle-Low Inexperienced and unknown on health care in early '90s	Low		

England Journal of Medicine articles was part of a strategy for making his ideas part of the debate.[5]

Shortly after writing the articles, Enthoven joined efforts with Paul Ellwood, a Minneapolis doctor and longtime health policy activist, to craft a saleable reform proposal for the health insurance industry – and potentially for the next Congress. Independently, Ellwood had long invited experts and health industry officials to his vacation home in Jackson Hole, Wyoming, for informal discussions about health care reform. Over the years, Enthoven had been a regular participant. In 1991 and 1992, Ellwood and Enthoven intensified their collaborative effort, regularly convening a group of about twenty policy experts and reform-minded health industry executives to reach agreement on, write, and advocate a comprehensive market-based reform proposal.[6]

What became known as the Jackson Hole Group formalized a reform plan based largely on Enthoven's ideas. Enthoven and Ellwood, along with Lynn Etheredge, a Washington-based health care consultant whom they brought in to help, proselytized policy makers and industry leaders with the merits of market-based reform that provided universal coverage. In the spring of 1991, Enthoven's earlier work caught the eye of Michael Weinstein, a member of the *New York Times* editorial board, who was looking for a creative health care reform proposal. Weinstein contacted Enthoven and, within weeks, was writing editorials that endorsed Enthoven's managed competition plan as "the best way out" of the health care mess facing the country.[7] Between May 1991 and December 1992, the *New York Times* published twenty-six editorials – all written by Weinstein – that endorsed managed competition or criticized alternatives to it.[8]

The editorial endorsements began after a series of lengthy telephone conversations between Weinstein and Enthoven in which Weinstein learned the details of the Jackson Hole Group's developing proposal. Once contacted by Weinstein in May 1991, Enthoven conscientiously pursued Weinstein's continued favor. As Jacob Hacker reports, "The [Jackson Hole] group encouraged Weinstein to continue pushing for managed

---

[5] Jacob Hacker interview with Alain Enthoven, by telephone, 21 December 1994, for his book, *The Road to Nowhere*.

[6] See John Hubner, "The Abandoned Father of Health Care Reform," *New York Times Magazine*, 18 July 1993.

[7] "The Health Care System Is Broken; And Here's How to Fix It," *The New York Times*, 22 July 1991, p. A14.

[8] Hacker, *Road to Nowhere*, p. 63.

competition and invited him to Jackson Hole for their next conference. Enthoven in particular kept Weinstein up-to-date on the evolution of the approach and the progress being made by the Jackson Hole Group."[9] Through their frequent conversations, Weinstein and Ellwood became good friends. They shared an educational pedigree; both received undergraduate degrees in economics from Stanford and Ph.D.s in economics from MIT. And, as Enthoven noted, "the latter is a fairly select club in the world of graduate programs in economics."[10] The articles in the *New York Times*, and eventually in other publications as well, publicized the work of the Jackson Hole Group among policy makers.[11]

The group completed a written version of their plan by early fall and began circulating it informally among policy analysts, journalists, and industry people. David Kendall, a health policy aide to Representative Mike Andrews of Texas, a centrist Democrat, was one of those who received the plan, distributed as a series of four papers. A friend of his, who by then was a lobbyist for one of the industry members of the Jackson Hole Group, gave the proposal to Kendall in September. It became the basis for a managed competition bill introduced in the House by Democratic Representatives Jim Cooper (D.-Tennessee), Mike Andrews (D.-Texas), and Charles Stenholm (D.-Texas) in 1992, soon before Congress adjourned for the election. No action was taken on the Cooper bill that fall, but, by that point, Ellwood, Enthoven, Etheredge, and the Jackson Hole Group had quite successfully created visibility for their plan and established its political attractiveness among moderates heading into the new year and the new administration.

At the same time as moderate Democrats in the House became sponsors of managed competition, the Democratic contender for the White House became enamored of the idea as well – but of a slightly different variant on it. In June 1992, the Clinton campaign assigned two new advisors to work on health care. They, in turn, pushed the campaign to embrace a version of managed competition. Atul Gawande was hired by the campaign

---

[9] Hacker, *Road to Nowhere*, p. 65.

[10] Jacob Hacker interview with Alain Enthoven, by telephone, 21 December 1994. Ellwood confirms the conversations that developed between Weinstein and Enthoven and Enthoven's influence over Weinstein. Weinstein "was quite an admirer of Alain's. You know Alain was really quite a famous theoretical economist prior to getting his hands dirty in health care, and Weinstein has a Ph.D. in economics as well and kind of knew of Alain's work." Author interview with Paul Ellwood, by telephone, 14 April 1999.

[11] For additional endorsements, see Edmund Faltermayer, "Let's Really Cure the Health System," *Fortune*, 23 March 1992, p. 46; "We're for a Universal Health Care System," *Business Week*, 7 October 1991, p. 158.

to coordinate health and social policy issues. He was a medical student on leave from Harvard University with experience working on Capitol Hill. Ira Magaziner was also moved over to the issue, after working on economic policy earlier in the campaign. Magaziner was an old friend of the Clintons' and had been a business consultant in Rhode Island before joining the campaign. Magaziner and Gawande were central to the campaign's shift in interest to managed competition.

Magaziner was not happy with the campaign's original approach on health care, and, as Jacob Hacker recounts, he

expressed his concerns... to Harvard professor Robert Reich, an old friend of Magaziner's who was advising the campaign on economic policy. In July Reich mentioned to Magaziner that he had recently read a manuscript on health care reform written by a colleague on the editorial board of *The American Prospect*, Paul Starr. A phone call between Magaziner and Starr followed in which Starr explained the key features of his approach and the rationale behind them. Magaziner asked Starr to send him a copy of the manuscript.[12]

Starr's version of managed competition had some notable differences from the Jackson Hole Group's plan, and it had distinctly different origins. Starr's ideas were adapted from a plan developed by John Garamendi and Walter Zelman for the state of California. Garamendi and Zelman were the California commissioner and deputy commissioner, respectively, for insurance. Under their plan, consumers could choose among health plans within a global health care budget that was set and administered by a statewide purchasing cooperative.[13] The plan was more regulatory and less market-oriented than the Jackson Hole proposal.

The California plan had been publicly released in February 1992, and Garamendi and Zelman had actively promoted it, in California and nationally, for a period of weeks. They sent an advance copy to Michael Weinstein of the *New York Times* and flew to New York to spend an hour talking through the proposal with him. Two days after its release, Weinstein wrote a glowing editorial endorsing the plan as one that "artfully combines regulation and competition."[14] That was followed by favorable editorials in the *Los Angeles Times* and other newspapers.[15] The

---

[12] Hacker, *Road to Nowhere*, pp. 107–8.
[13] For more on the substance of the Garamendi–Zelman plan, see John Garamendi, "Taking California Health Insurance into the 21st Century," *Journal of American Health Policy*, May–June 1992, pp. 10a–13a.
[14] "California's Medical Model," *The New York Times*, 17 February 1992, p. A16.
[15] "Health Reform, California Style: Garamendi Plan Is Making a Lot of Friends," *The Los Angeles Times*, 29 May 1992, p. B1.

editorials put the Garamendi–Zelman plan on the map. To promote it further, Garamendi made use of the Insurance Commissioner's office lobbyist to promote the plan on Capitol Hill, and he had Zelman spend much of the spring making presentations on the plan to members of Congress and their staffs.[16]

By spring 1992 the Garamendi–Zelman proposal had become relatively well known, particularly among a group of Democratic senators with strong interest in health care issues. The group included Harris Wofford of Pennsylvania, who passed a copy of the Garamendi plan along to Paul Starr, who had advised him on health care in his 1991 campaign. Starr summarized the plan in a short book proposing health care reform, a draft of which, thanks to Robert Reich, made its way to Magaziner in July 1992.[17] From July on, the die was cast; the Clinton campaign, and eventually the administration, relied on an approach that centered on managed competition – the more regulatory Garamendi–Starr–Magaziner version of it.

Following Magaziner's intervention in the summer of 1992, managed competition displaced a "play or pay" approach to health care reform, which the Clinton campaign had embraced early on. Under pressure to stake out a health care position early in the presidential campaign, Clinton had touted a play or pay approach quite popular among Washington Democrats at the time. A version of the approach had been introduced in the Senate in 1991 by Democratic Senators George Mitchell of Maine, Edward M. Kennedy of Massachusetts, Donald Riegle of Michigan, and Jay Rockefeller of West Virginia. And play or pay had been the recommendation of the congressional Bipartisan Commission on Comprehensive Health Care, known as the Pepper Commission, which completed its work in 1990.[18] While play or pay did not last long as the preference of the Clinton campaign, how the idea was originally embraced makes an interesting story.

The first version of Clinton's play or pay proposal was drafted by Ron Pollack, executive director of Families USA, in December 1991. Pollack had been involved in conversations with the Clinton campaign about health care since late summer 1991, before Clinton had even announced his candidacy. In early September, Pollack had been part of a meeting in

---

[16] Author interview with Walter Zelman, by telephone, 12 April 1999.
[17] Paul Starr, *The Logic of Health Care Reform: Transforming American Medicine for the Better* (Knoxville, Tenn.: Whittle Direct Books, 1992).
[18] Mark A. Peterson, "Momentum toward Health Care Reform in the U.S. Senate," *Journal of Health Politics, Policy, and Law* 17 (1992): 553–73.

which Clinton was considering the relative merits of single-payer versus play or pay plans. Pollack, whose group had long been a progressive voice on health care issues, was invited to the meeting after campaign officials read an article that he co-wrote for *The American Prospect* in the summer of 1991 in which he endorsed play or pay as a "politically feasible" alternative to a single-payer, government-administered health system.[19] Clinton and his aides had seen the article and invited Pollack to the initial early September meeting with Clinton on the basis of the publication and his reputation. From September through the fall, Pollack had periodic conversations with Clinton campaign officials, culminating in a four-hour conference call in December among the campaign's principal advisors during which Pollack was asked to draft a position statement on health care for the campaign.[20]

Pollack wrote the first draft of a statement on health care that Clinton might endorse. It was reworked by Bruce Reed, issues director for the campaign, and released in January 1992. The written plan was intentionally vague but outlined support for a play or pay approach. It was elaborated upon and defended in the months that followed by a group of Washington-based health policy experts, most of whom had existing preferences for it. In January 1992, Bruce Fried, a health care consultant with the D.C.-based Wexler Group and a longtime Democratic activist, put together a group of twenty experts to advise the Clinton campaign on health care issues. Many in the group had been involved with the Pepper Commission, including Judy Feder, who had been the Commission's staff director and had written its final report, which enumerated a play or pay approach. Through the first half of 1992, the group, known as the Washington Advisory Group on Health, answered questions about health care for the Clinton campaign. After the January policy statement, however, neither Clinton nor the principal managers of the campaign focused seriously on health care again until the summer, when managed competition displaced the play or pay approach for the Clinton team.

By that point, Senator Bob Kerrey of Nebraska, who had been the first to pressure Clinton to take a stand on health care, had dropped out of the race for the Democratic presidential nomination. As a candidate, he had centered his campaign on advocacy of a single-payer scheme

---

[19] Ronald Pollack and Phyllis Torda, "The Pragmatic Road Toward National Health Insurance," *The American Prospect* 6 (Summer 1991): 92–100. Author interview with Ronald Pollack, Families USA, 1 April 1999.

[20] Author Interview with Ronald Pollack, Families USA, 1 April 1999.

for health reform. Kerrey's "Health USA Act" in the Senate was drafted by UCLA Professor Richard Brown, a longtime single-payer advocate. Brown's path to assisting Kerrey followed a different trajectory from that of the experts who helped Clinton. In early 1991, Kerrey was relatively inexperienced on the health care issue, so when he decided to write legislation, his health care aide, Gretchen Brown, set up a series of seminars for him with health policy experts around the country. It was in connection with one of these events in Los Angeles that he spent a whole day with Richard Brown. At the end of that day, Brown offered to write a memo outlining principles for a health care proposal that the senator might endorse. In April 1991, several months after sending his proposal to Kerrey, Gretchen Brown contacted the UCLA professor and said that the senator wanted to turn his proposal into legislation. Over the next three months, Richard Brown made three trips to Washington and made himself available by phone and fax to develop the legislative proposal for Kerrey. After it was filed as a bill in July 1991, Richard Brown continued to advise the senator as he prepared for a presidential race, and Brown wrote several articles promoting the Health USA proposal.[21] Through the fall and winter, at his own expense, Brown made several trips to New Hampshire to advise Kerrey on campaign health care questions and wrote scores of health care talking points for him while he was on the campaign trail.

Think Tanks During Health Care Agenda Setting

Conspicuously absent from this narrative of the intellectual origins of the Clinton health care plan and Kerrey's single-payer scheme is mention of think tanks. Where were the experts at think tanks when health care reform was emerging during the campaign? What were experts at think tanks offering with regard to broad-based proposals?

Health care analysts at think tanks had clear opinions about all three approaches under debate by Democrats: managed competition, play or pay, and single-payer schemes. Some became known to candidates. But think tank experts were neither the principal nor the most effective voices for any of these broad-based reform proposals among Democrats.

The Economic Policy Institute (EPI), a liberal and generally marketing-oriented think tank formed in 1986, had ties to the Clinton campaign

[21] See E. Richard Brown, "Health USA: A National Health Program for the United States," *Journal of the American Medical Association* 267 (4): 552–61, 22 January 1992.

through Robert Reich, a campaign advisor who had been among EPI's founders and was later Clinton's Secretary of Labor. But on health care in the early 1990s, EPI was relatively quiet. Edith Rasell was EPI's health economist and had just joined EPI in 1991 as she finished her doctorate at American University.

The Brookings Institution, more than seven times the size of EPI, had several people devoted to health care. Joshua Wiener, an expert on long-term care, participated in discussions with the Clinton campaign's health advisory group about how to present the campaign's health reform ideas. His role was more to support the campaign in elaborating the chosen policy directions than to develop the fundamentals for what might become the campaign's proposal. Henry Aaron, the most well-known scholar on health care at Brookings at the time, weighed in during the agenda-setting period with a 1991 book, *Serious and Unstable Condition*, in which he reviewed the financing problems facing the health care system and explained and endorsed a play or pay approach to reform.[22] Aaron joined the chorus of Democratically connected experts in 1991 who supported play or pay. The book was intended to "explain the field in as simple terms as possible for ordinary readers, give them some economics on why this is a hard question, and end up with some policy recommendations. Mostly it was meant to convey some information." Aaron and others working in the issue area did not perceive the book as having drawn much attention, though, and, as he recalled, once Clinton was elected, "it wasn't on bookstore shelves any more."[23]

During the agenda-setting stage on health care reform in 1991 and 1992, researchers at the Urban Institute, like those at Brookings, were only moderately engaged. The Urban Institute had a unit of more than twenty-five researchers working on health care in the early 1990s. Most were working on government contracts. Only two were senior fellows. One was Marilyn Moon, an economist in health policy. Moon advised Senator Kerrey briefly on health care financing as he was developing his

---

[22] Henry Aaron, *Serious and Unstable Condition* (Washington, D.C.: Brookings Institution Press, 1991).

[23] Author interview with Henry Aaron, Brookings Institution, 11 February 1999. Joseph White, who was also at Brookings, was in the early 1990s only beginning work on health care. For most of 1991 and 1992, White, a political scientist and budget specialist by training, was working on a book about the budget appropriation process. Only in late 1992 was he approved to write his next book on differences in the delivery of health care across nations, but by this point, the health care agenda-setting stage was nearly over. White was becoming familiar with the issue as Clinton was elected to office.

single-payer plan.[24] In 1991, Moon also joined with some of her colleagues at the Urban Institute to write a short book, similar in format to Aaron's, that reviewed reform options and outlined the benefits of a play or pay approach.[25] Moon was part of the group advising the Clinton campaign on health care, but only until Magaziner was put in charge of the issue and the campaign became focused on managed competition.[26]

More active among the Democrats in agenda setting on health care was the Progressive Policy Institute (PPI), which played a role popularizing a proposal already circulating. Jeremy Rosner became the health care analyst at PPI in 1992, and he played a role in working out the details of the managed competition proposal that the moderate members of the House (Cooper, Andrews, and Stenholm) introduced that year. Rosner then summarized the ideas behind the Jackson Hole Group's version of managed competition in an accessible proposal published as a chapter in *Mandate for Change*, a book that the Progressive Policy Institute and the Democratic Leadership Council produced as a policy guide for the new Clinton administration.[27]

Besides these four, there were few other think tanks working on proposals or issues and options research for health care reform in ways that may have appealed to Democrats in the early 1990s. The differences among

[24] Author interview with Marilyn Moon, Urban Institute, 24 February 1999; Author interview with Ellen Shaffer, by telephone, 5 April 1999.

[25] John Holahan et al., *Balancing Access, Costs, and Politics: The American Context for Health System Reform* (Washington, D.C.: Urban Institute Press, 1991).

[26] Eugene Steurle was the other UI senior fellow working on health care issues in the early 1990s. He had been a deputy assistant secretary of Treasury in the Reagan administration in the late 1980s and was recruited to join UI in 1989. His main focus was on the public financing and tax effects of health care programs. He did some general work on the tax treatment of health care in the early 1990s and had some communication with members of Congress, but none that came close to resulting in legislation. Author interview with Eugene Steurle, Urban Institute, 4 May 1999.

[27] Jeremy D. Rosner, "A Progressive Plan for Affordable, Universal Health Care," *Mandate for Change*, ed. by Will Marshall and Martin Schram (New York: Berkley Books, 1993). The DLC and PPI had high hopes that the new Clinton administration would heed its recommendations since Clinton had been one of its founders. See David VonDrehle, "With Friends in High Places, Democratic Think Tank Bids for Glory," *Washington Post*, 7 December 1992, p. A17. Clinton had been among the founding members of the DLC, and Bruce Reed, who was his campaign issues director and subsequently a domestic policy advisor in the White House, had previously been the DLC's policy director. After writing the health care chapter for *Mandate for Change*, Rosner left PPI and took a foreign policy speechwriting position at the White House. See Haynes Johnson and David S. Broder, *The System* (New York: Little, Brown, 1997), pp. 21–3. Rosner's only other foray into health care came when he was called by David Gergen on the day before the president was to deliver his health care plan to Congress and asked to rewrite the president's speech.

researchers at the agenda-setting stage begin to reveal the limits for policy makers who might be looking for experts with reform proposals. The experts who did produce research exhibited wide variation in preferences and capacities. Only some were actively engaged in efforts to form proposals for policy makers, and only a portion of these were effective in making their ideas available and accessible to policy makers.

To be sure, whether Clinton, for example, embraced managed competition or play or pay had more to do with his ideological predilections and political calculations than with differences in the manner by which the plans were supplied to him. But each of the three broad frameworks that Democrats considered – managed competition, play or pay, and single payer – had origins going back to the 1960s and 1970s, and each had many potential proponents among the ranks of contemporary experts. Why certain experts surfaced as influential had much to do with their own characteristics and efforts – most notably, the form of their research; their credibility, access, and timing; and the effectiveness of their marketing.

Of the think tanks active, only the Progressive Policy Institute was espousing a clear proposal on health care reform, and its plan, in the form of Jeremy Rosner's managed competition chapter in *Mandate for Change*, was largely an adapted version of the Jackson Hole Group's proposal. Aaron's book, *Serious and Unstable Condition*, was intended for a broad audience, well beyond policy makers, and it was not written as a proposal. Only the last forty pages of the book addressed reform ideas, and it was quite general in its advocacy of a play or pay approach. The book by Marilyn Moon and her colleagues at the Urban Institute followed a similar format. As Moon described it, it was "just a little book evaluating some of the reform proposals."[28]

If raising their visibility on proposals was not the focus for think tanks on the Democratic side, the benefits of marketing health care proposals were clearly in evidence among think tanks in relation to Republican proposals. Think tank experts were both visible and influential among Republicans on health care. Two of the three original Republican alternatives reflected direct consultation with think tanks: one based on the employer tax deductibility of health insurance costs, the other premised on insurance market reform and medical savings accounts.

In 1993, Senator Don Nickles (R.-Oklahoma) and Representative Cliff Stearns (R.-Florida) introduced the Consumer Choice Health Security Act.

---

[28] Author interview with Marilyn Moon, Urban Institute, 24 February 1999.

Their bill, co-sponsored by twenty-four Republican senators, proposed providing those in need of health care with a tax credit that served as a voucher for the purchase of private insurance options.[29] Their proposal was based on a plan drafted by the Heritage Foundation. In 1989, Stuart Butler and Edmund Haislmaier of the Heritage Foundation published a book outlining a "Consumer Choice Health Plan."[30] The reasoning behind their 1989 analysis was not original. Harvard economist Martin Feldstein was among those who had been arguing for tax reform as the necessary first step in health care reform since the early 1970s, and Heritage was not the only organization advocating tax reform for health care in the 1990s.[31] But Butler and Heislmaier promoted their plan with op-eds and briefings in 1989 and 1990.[32] As Robert Moffit, who joined Heritage to replace Haislmaier in 1991, puts it, "what Butler and Haislmaier did was to crystallize this debate in plain English for a large audience."[33]

From 1989 forward, the outlines of the Heritage plan did not change. When Moffit joined the staff, he worked to make the Heritage plan seem more concrete for policy makers with an illustration that compared the plan to the Federal Employee Health Benefit Program (FEHBP).[34] The comparison was intended to counter critics, who viewed the consumer choice associated with the Heritage plan as too complex for ordinary people to negotiate. It was also aimed at making their proposal appealing to members of Congress who happened to be served by the FEHBP. Moffit recalls:

We found that if you talked to people about the idea of creating a system of consumer choice in a normal market, it was an abstraction. . . . And the *New York*

---

[29] For details on the plan, see Spencer Rich, "Health Care, Minus U.S. Controls; Nickles Bill Would End Employer-Paid Benefits," *The Washington Post*, 5 December 1993, p. A19.

[30] Stuart M. Butler and Edmund Haislmaier, *A National Health Care System for America* (Washington, D.C.: Heritage Foundation, 1989).

[31] Martin S. Feldstein, "A New Approach to National Health Insurance," *Public Interest* 23 (1971): 93–105; Martin S. Feldstein, "The Welfare Loss of Excess Health Insurance," *Journal of Political Economy* 81 (1973): 251–80; Martin S. Feldstein, *Hospital Costs and Health Insurance* (Cambridge, Mass.: Harvard University Press, 1981).

[32] See, for example, Stuart M. Butler, "Coming to Terms on Health Care," *The New York Times*, 28 January 1990; Edmund F. Haislmaier, "Canada's Health System Has Its Ills," *The Chicago Tribune*, 9 October 1991. For an example of how it was picked up by journalists, see Spencer Rich, "The Federal Page: Ideas and Findings – Making Active Shoppers of the Uninsured: Heritage Foundation Plan for Health Coverage Relies on Market," *The Washington Post*, 12 March 1992, p. A25.

[33] Author interview with Robert Moffit, Heritage Foundation, 19 February 1999.

[34] Robert E. Moffit, *Congress and the Taxpayers: A Double Standard on Health Care Reform?* (Washington, D.C.: Heritage Foundation, 1992).

Times editorialized in December of 1991 that the purchase of health insurance was something that was best left to professionals because of its complexity.[35] It was beyond the capacity of ordinary individuals.... Well, that's where I came on the scene, because the big point – the big simple point in red letters – was that there was at least one class of Americans who actually did what the *New York Times* thought couldn't be done. And that is, they actually picked and chose from different plans each year and made determinations about what kind of plans they wanted... and that was federal employees.[36]

The comparison of the Heritage proposal with the FEHBP was an effective rhetorical technique with members of the Senate. Senator Nickles, who was chairman of the Republican Policy Committee, liked the core ideas in the Heritage proposal. Heritage publications reached Nickles and his staff, though, amid a variety of conflicting reports from think tanks and others at the time. As Doug Badger, Nickles's principal health care aide at the time, remembers it, "There were a variety of groups making a number of different points." Besides being ideologically appealing, Badger recalls:

The advantage to Heritage was that they probably devoted more intellectual capital not merely to analyzing the problem but to devising a solution. And they'd gotten a very well respected econometric firm to sort of model different tax-based approaches, so that you could at least kind of understand what the relative effects would be on people at various income levels, and how they would be advantaged or disadvantaged by a reform of this nature relative to current law. So I think Heritage had gone much further than some of the other groups in having these ideas tested, studied, and submitted to independent evaluation. And I think that gave them some advantage.[37]

At the same time that Butler and Moffit made themselves and their analysis available to Nickles, they actively sought the editorial endorsement of newspapers around the country, making trips to editorial boards, much as Garamendi and Zelman had. Between 1991 and 1994, the consumer choice plan espoused by the Heritage Foundation was endorsed by ninety-five daily newspapers in thirty-four states with combined circulation of 7,337,000.[38] In mid-November 1993, the Nickles–Stearns bill was introduced in the House and Senate.

[35] See "Tax Credits for Health: Wrong Rx," *The New York Times*, 16 December 1991, p. A18.
[36] Author interview with Robert Moffit, Heritage Foundation, 19 February 1999.
[37] Author interview with Doug Badger, former aide to Senator Don Nickles, 30 March 1999.
[38] Editorial Endorsements of Heritage Consumer Choice Health Plan (Washington, D.C.: Heritage Foundation, 1995). Sample confirmed by author.

Another proposal traceable to experts at think tanks was that for medical savings accounts (Msas). Like all of the proposals under consideration in 1991–2, the idea of medical savings accounts had a lengthy history, in this case dating back to the 1960s. The idea was popularized among members of Congress in the early 1990s by a coalition of forces that included John Goodman, president of the National Center for Policy Analysis, a Dallas-based think tank. The medical savings accounts advocates proposed that consumers pay the first increment of the cost of medical care each year, perhaps $3,000, out of a personal tax-free medical IRA. At the end of each year, whatever amount not spent on health care could be kept by individuals tax-free. Any amount required for catastrophic care above $3,000 would be covered by employer-provided high-deductible insurance.

Goodman had been writing about the merits of MSAs since the mid-1980s.[39] In 1990, he joined efforts with Pat Rooney, chairman of the Indiana-based Golden Rule Insurance Company, an insurance industry executive who had become interested in the idea. The two worked together relentlessly, through publications and seminars with members of Congress, to win introduction of MSA legislation in the early 1990s, most notably, as the centerpiece of a Republican health care reform alternative crafted by Senator Phil Gramm (R.-Texas) in late 1993.[40]

The third and arguably most substantial Republican health care proposal came from John Chafee (R.-Rhode Island) in the Senate and Bill Thomas (R.-California) in the House, with support from a coalition of ideologically moderate Republicans. The Chafee–Thomas legislation mandated universal coverage through an individual, not employer, mandate; some called it a "Clinton lite" proposal, one that drew on principles of managed competition.[41] Unlike the other two Republican

[39] John Goodman and Richard W. Rahn, "Need for Reform of Medicare System," *The Wall Street Journal*, 20 March 1984, p. A32.

[40] Also helping Rooney by this stage of the process in the lobbying was the Council for Affordable Health Insurance (CAHI), which was a new trade association of small and medium-size health insurance companies that resulted from the 1990 industry/think tank meeting. See Dana Priest, "The Federal Page – A Floor at a Time...Room to Room," *The Washington Post*, 13 August 1992, p. A23; Author interview with Jack Strayer, Vice President for External Affairs, National Center for Policy Analysis, and former chief lobbyist, Council for Affordable Health Insurance, 17 February 1999. The first MSA legislation was introduced by Representative Andy Jacobs (D.-Ind.) and Senator Dan Coats (R.-Ind.) in 1992.

[41] The principal differences were the individual mandate and a reliance on voluntary versus mandatory purchasing cooperatives in the provision of health care. Author interview with Christine Ferguson, by telephone, 28 May 1999.

plans, the Chafee–Thomas bill, which originated in the Senate, had evolved over several years in a weekly seminar of senators concerned about health care issues. In the early 1990s, the seminar became a ve- hicle for Senate staff to draft a bill. Christine Ferguson, Chafee's top health care aide, began meeting on the side in 1990 with Ed Mihalski, Oregon Senator Bob Packwood's Finance Committee aide, and Sheila Burke, Senator Bob Dole's chief of staff, to work out a Republican plan based on the discussions of the seminar group. All three had substan- tial expertise on health care issues. Their bosses introduced a bill in 1991 forming a foundation for the Chafee bill introduced at the end of 1993.

Experts in health policy were involved in the Chafee plan's develop- ment throughout the early 1990s, but none was closely involved with its drafting or provided the principal intellectual foundations for it, akin to the experiences with the Nickles and Gramm plans.[42] Enthoven, Ellwood, and Butler had all been consulted at various points during its evolution, but the Senate's staff combined expertise was enough to work out the specifics of the proposal. Still, Chafee's aide, Christine Ferguson, makes the point that they "involved a cross section of people who were con- sidered experts in health care, but who could also speak to Senators in layman's terms, which is another talent that a lot of people who have expertise in health care don't necessarily have. It's important to be able to combine those two things together, which is why I think the pool ends up being limited."[43]

As with the Democrats, some think tanks with the potential for influ- encing Republican lawmakers had little influence during agenda setting. These included the American Enterprise Institute, the Cato Institute, and the Manhattan Institute. Like the Heritage Foundation, the American En- terprise Institute (AEI) had long published research arguing for the elimi- nation of the employer tax deduction for health care costs. Robert Helms was AEI's director of health policy research in the early 1990s after hav- ing served in the Department of Health and Human Services during the Reagan administration. Having just returned to AEI, he did not anticipate Clinton's election or his making health care a top priority.[44] Even if he

---

[42] Author interview with Christine Ferguson, by telephone, 28 May 1999.
[43] Author interview with Christine Ferguson, by telephone, 28 May 1999.
[44] Author interview with Robert Helms, American Enterprise Institute, 23 February 1999.

had, however, Helms says it is unlikely he would have more aggressively advocated a tax reform proposal.[45] In 1991, Helms spent his time organizing two academic conferences on health care issues, which produced two 300-page edited volumes about the range of options facing the health care delivery system.[46]

Independent of Helms, four AEI-affiliated scholars based elsewhere published a short book on health care reform with AEI in 1992, which proposed tax reform as the central feature of health reform.[47] The AEI book was actually a follow-up to an article that appeared in the journal *Health Affairs* in 1991 and that drew brief attention within the Bush administration.[48] Largely in response to the Wofford election, the Bush administration at the end of 1991 furiously sought to craft a health care reform plan. At the end of 1991, Mark Pauly, a professor at the University of Pennsylvania's Wharton School and the principal author of the *Health Affairs* and AEI studies, was invited for a meeting with Richard Darman and Deborah Steelman, Bush's OMB director and his health policy advisor, to explain his ideas. But beyond the one meeting, Pauly did little to cultivate a further relationship with the Bush administration, and his ideas were not much reflected in the final Bush plan.[49]

Aside from this one contact, Pauly and AEI received little attention for their tax reform proposal – despite the high credibility of its authors and institutional sponsor and the effective timing of its release as a proposal.[50] The plan was similar in content to the Heritage proposal. But the difference, as Pauly recalls, was that Heritage "kept going with it. And they got [Senator] Nickles to turn it into a proposal. AEI, that isn't really

---

[45] As Helms puts it, "We put the things out there and stand back from them a little bit." Author interview with Helms, 23 February 1999.

[46] Robert B. Helms, *American Health Policy: Critical Issues for Reform* (Washington, D.C.: The AEI Press, 1993); Robert B. Helms, *Health Policy Reform: Competition and Controls* (Washington, D.C.: The AEI Press, 1993).

[47] Mark V. Pauly, et al., *Responsible National Health Insurance* (Washington, D.C.: The AEI Press, 1992).

[48] Mark V. Pauly, "A Plan for Responsible National Health Insurance," *Health Affairs*, Spring 1991, pp. 5–25.

[49] As Pauly recalls, "What finally came out [of the Bush administration], I think had only a family resemblance to our original proposal." Author interview with Mark Pauly, University of Pennsylvania, by telephone, 26 March 1999.

[50] For example, in 1992 Mark Pauly's proposal received one reference in the *Washington Post*; Stuart Butler of the Heritage Foundation had eight for his quite similar proposal.

their style, and I don't have anybody behind me."[51] AEI and Pauly did not aggressively market their ideas to a policymaking audience.[52]

The Cato Institute and the Manhattan Institute were not visible during the agenda-setting stage on health care reform either. Cato had no staff person assigned to health care in 1991 and 1992. Cato hired Michael Tanner to direct its health care studies in October 1993. During 1991 and 1992, while in principle the Institute supported a free market alternative on health care, its only agenda-setting contribution was sponsorship of the publication of a book by NCPA's John Goodman. Cato printed abridged copies of his book for distribution to policy makers. The Manhattan Institute had neither a health care analyst nor any emphasis on the issue in 1991 and 1992.

Lessons from Agenda Setting on Health Care

The first lesson from the experiences of experts in the agenda-setting moments of health care reform is that their explicit efforts to make research influential improve the chances that it will be. The groups that were successful in having their ideas translated into legislation by Democrats each had proposals clearly intended for a policymaking audience – likewise for Republicans, even though the efforts of Republican lawmakers to craft plans were geared more to obstruct President Clinton's plan than to realistically win enactment of their own. Successful proposals were written in memo style, intended to be read by policy makers rather than published for an academic or general audience.

In addition, the experts who were influential were generally credible. Part of Alain Enthoven's appeal as an aggressive advocate for managed competition in 1991 and 1992 was that he had a long-established, highly

---

[51] Author interview with Mark Pauly, Wharton School of Business, University of Pennsylvania, 26 March 1999.

[52] Pauly makes the point that marketing research was neither his style nor that of the American Enterprise Institute. He points out,

> I think there are some think tanks who, basically, their main product is to influence legislation.... There's that kind, and I don't want to be negative at all.... Then there's places like AEI and Brookings, which are kind of more – even though they kind of get politically characterized – are in the way they operate, much less partisan. The partisanship, if there is some, shows itself by who they select rather than by what they tell them to do. And they will produce things that will cover a wide range of ideas, and they don't all agree. And usually there isn't some specific proposal that comes out of one of those places.

> Author interview with Pauly, 26 March 1999.

credible reputation both as an academic and as a government official. As Enthoven points out, "My ideas, before all of this, had been published widely in the *New England Journal of Medicine*. They had been put into proposed legislation. . . . If you talk to people [who knew me], they'd tell you that I was a pretty influential figure in the Kennedy and Johnson administrations. I received the President's Medal for Distinguished General Civilian Service from President Kennedy."[53] His public service and academic writings enhanced his reputation – and marketing capacity – when he resumed his advocacy of managed competition in the early 1990s. As the *New York Times*'s Michael Weinstein points out, "I knew Alain Enthoven's name. Obviously most of us who were professional economists knew at least his name, if not intimately his work."[54]

For Garamendi and Zelman, credibility came from Garamendi's elected position as overseer of the insurance industry in California. In addition, Zelman had pulled together a group of highly regarded academics and consultants to help him piece together their plan, and he recalls, "When we started promoting our plan, it helped, I think, to have had an advisory group of experts. And it particularly helped that some of them were willing to help promote it, which gave us some more credibility among policy makers."[55]

The legitimacy of the Garamendi–Zelman plan was further validated by the quick endorsement it received in the *New York Times*, *USA Today*, and other newspapers. For both Garamendi and the Jackson Hole Group, media visibility became a further source of credibility. The visibility of these experts and ideas in trusted news sources helped to make them of interest to policy makers. On this point, one veteran congressional staffer noted, "whether a study makes a big splash in the *New York Times*

[53] Hacker interview with Alain Enthoven, 21 December 1994.
[54] Jacob Hacker interview with Michael Weinstein, 8 September 1993. A congressional staffer makes a similar point. He notes, "I suppose if the Jackson Hole Group were not around, these ideas may not have been as well publicized and as well-formed. I think that's what the Jackson Hole Group did; it took ideas that were already there, really developed them into a workable concept, and the fact that there were so many prominent players involved in the Jackson Hole Group gave it a little credence." Jacob Hacker interview with Senate staff member.
[55] Author interview with Walter Zelman, by telephone, 12 April 1999. In a previous interview, Zelman commented, "I thought we needed a group not so much to get expertise. It was a matter of making whatever we came out with credible and giving [Garamendi] standing on health insurance and health care. . . . The notion was, in order to give whatever recommendations we had some force, to make them credible, we had to put together the trappings of a real team." Jacob Hacker interview with Walter Zelman, 20 October 1994.

or the *Wall Street Journal* makes a big difference. That is what attracts [congressional] attention."[56]

Media visibility was also a channel of access for policy experts. It was because of the exposure his ideas received in the *American Prospect* that Ron Pollack was invited to meet with Bill Clinton during the early stages of the campaign when Clinton was searching for a saleable idea on health care. The Jackson Hole group benefited from the access to lawmakers enjoyed by their industry members, one of whom first brought the idea to the attention of David Kendall in Representative Andrews's office.

Timing was also important in making the work of certain experts relevant. The advocates who succeeded in being influential appeared to have fresh and ready proposals at exactly the time policy makers were ready for them. All of the "effective" experts among Democrats were quick to respond when interest was first shown by various policy makers. By contrast, Henry Aaron laments of his book, "it was too early in terms of the Clinton plan. Once the Clinton plan came, this was an old book."[57] At the opposite extreme, Jeremy Rosner's chapter in *Mandate for Change* offered a succinct summary of the free market managed competition proposal, but it came out too late to be influential in agenda setting. It was only after the 1992 election that Rosner's chapter was released; Rosner became a convert to the managed competition approach at the same time as the members of Congress who introduced it – Representatives Cooper, Andrews, and Stenholm – and after the Clinton administration had already been drawn to the idea via a different path.

Finally, active marketing appears to have made a difference for which experts with health care proposals were effectively heard. California was not the only state developing a reform plan of its own in 1991 and 1992. Minnesota and Washington were among others that were also debating

---

[56] Author interview with House congressional staffer, 5 March 1999. Another congressional staffer made a similar point in relation to how managed competition became popular. He said,

> I think it's not insignificant that the *New York Times* endorsed managed competition a long time ago. And it got people like my boss thinking about it. I can remember him first really taking a good look at managed competition when the *New York Times* came out with a series of editorials pressing the concept. He said, "I need to know more about this." Not so much because he thought it was such an intriguing idea, but because, he said, "If the *New York Times* endorses it, then people are going to start talking about it. So I have to be able to talk about it."

Jacob Hacker interview with congressional staff.

[57] Author interview with Henry Aaron, Brookings Institution, 11 February 1999.

and implementing reforms at the time.[58] But Garamendi and Zelman set out to make their ideas nationally known. In January 1991, before their plan was even released, John Garamendi took the opportunity to speak to Clinton for forty-five minutes on his ideas for reform during a Clinton campaign swing through California.[59] And Garamendi's subsequent aggressive advocacy of the plan with the *New York Times* and other newspapers as well as on Capitol Hill helped secure its visibility among policy makers. The plan was well timed and effectively marketed. As Zelman recalls, "The week after we put out our proposal, the Catholic Health Association put out its proposal, and it was very, very similar. Now we had better PR than they did. We had much, much better PR. But when I saw that plan, I said, 'God, I'm glad we just out-publicized them or they would have been where we are.'"[60]

Similarly, Richard Brown was aggressive in sharing his single-payer proposal with Senator Kerrey after their initial meeting. Brown made frequent visits to Washington, D.C., and New Hampshire at his own expense in order to remain an effective advisor to Kerrey through 1991. As Kerrey's former health care policy aide, Gretchen Brown, recalls, "Rick had a more definite proposal in mind than some of the others at the time.... He wanted to be involved, and it seemed like a good thing. He was assertive about wanting to be involved in everything, and it helped because I didn't have any staff."[61]

Marketing ideas, beyond simply publishing them as proposals, improved the chances for experts aiming to make their health care ideas influential. Why were the think tanks that would be inclined to produce Democratic proposals not more relevant in this context? Besides generally not presenting their ideas as proposals, they did not actively market them. Henry Aaron, for example, had high levels of credibility and access in Washington, as did the Brookings Institution, and, despite his own view, his 1991 book was not so early that it could not have affected at

---

[58] "State Health Care Reform Initiatives, 1993," Employee Benefit Research Institute, Vol. 14 (3), September 1993.

[59] Author interview with Walter Zelman, 12 April 1999.

[60] Jacob Hacker interview with Walter Zelman, 20 October 1994. Speaking of Walter Zelman, one congressional staffer recalled, "Walter Zelman had a big effect, one, because he had come up with this proposal and, two, because he was this timeless advocate in Washington. He was at every luncheon that I went to for about a year." Jacob Hacker interview with congressional staff.

[61] Author interview with Gretchen Brown, formerly staff to Senator Bob Kerrey, 5 April 1999.

least the early health care agenda-setting stage. But Aaron did little to promote the book or its ideas. He remarks:

That's a foreign mindset to [Brookings]. I think that the way everybody here approaches the work that they do is that there's a problem out there. What are the ways of dealing with it? What are their strengths and weaknesses, and talk about both of them. But any particular policy initiative, to become a devotee of that policy initiative and spend time and resources pushing that, it's boring, and since what you want is good staff who want to do interesting new work, they're not going to want to do that. There'd be nobody in the organization to cause you to want to do it.[62]

By contrast, think tanks were more effective – and successful – marketers with some of the Republican proposals. On why Heritage had an advantage over AEI on the tax reform proposal, Doug Badger, principal health care aide to Senator Nickles in the early 1990s, recalls, "I talked to Bob Helms [at the American Enterprise Institute] a little bit, and they clearly like the [Mark] Pauly approach. I mean that would be pretty obvious to anybody... but Heritage devoted a lot more resources to refining the proposal than the others did, so I think they became most useful in the debate."[63] Much the same was true of John Goodman from NCPA with Senator Gramm's office. John Cerisano, Gramm's health care aide at the time, recalls that Goodman made himself "very available" for consultation, traveling to Washington for staff meetings about developing the legislation.[64] Overall, the combination of credibility, access, timing, and especially marketing was important for experts seeking to make their ideas influential in the late agenda-setting stages of health care reform.

Policy Deliberation on Telecommunications

The contributions of think tanks and experts generally remained enormous as deliberation over President Clinton's health care proposal took on steam in late 1993, but that issue debate was headed for disaster as health care reform was declared dead less than a year later. By contrast, telecommunications reform was headed for enactment, but as the issue debate began to accelerate, telecommunications reform was headed for many fewer opportunities for think tanks and policy experts generally

---

[62] Author interview with Henry Aaron, Brookings Institution, 11 February 1999.
[63] Author interview with Doug Badger, formerly with Senator Don Nickles's office, 30 March 1999.
[64] Author interview with John Cerisano, formerly with Senator Phil Gramm's office, 18 March 1999.

than in health care reform. Nevertheless, the strategies that think tanks and other experts used in deliberation over telecommunication were similar to those used in health care reform as well as in the tax cut debate.

The first round of legislative deliberation over telecommunications reform began in the House in 1994. With two complementary telecommunications bills ready for discussion in the Commerce Committee, the committee's chairman organized a series of ten hearings held over a two-week period in January and February. Think tanks and researchers generally were almost completely missing from them. As illustrated in the first column of Table 5-2, of sixty-nine witnesses, none came from think tanks and only five were research experts of any kind. Of the remaining sixty-four, eight came from government, and fifty-two came from interest groups and corporate offices of the industries concerned. The committees approved the legislation in the middle of March, and the House passed both bills by overwhelming margins on June 28, 1994.[65] Compromise could not be reached in the Senate, and on Friday, September 23, 1994, Commerce Committee Chairman Ernest Hollings (D.-South Carolina) announced that there would be no telecommunications reform bill passed in the Senate that year. He blamed Senator Dole, the minority leader, along with the Baby Bells, for the impasse.

Throughout the first deliberation over policy change, most non-industry experts refrained from providing estimates and commentary. Of the thirteen think tanks examined in relation to telecommunications reform, only one was active during the first round of policy deliberation: the Heritage Foundation. It was joined by Citizens for a Sound Economy (CSE), a hybrid research-based interest group. In the summer and fall of 1994, both became aggressive opponents of Chairman Hollings's Senate bill. James Gattuso was the economist working on telecommunications at CSE in 1993. He joined the organization in 1993 after three years at the Heritage Foundation and, previous to that, two years working at the FCC. As an organization, CSE fails to qualify as a think tank because it has a distinct but attached 501(c) 4 branch that engages in direct advocacy. CSE employees can bill their hours to either the 501(c) 3 or (c) 4, depending on whether they are doing research or direct advocacy.

In the 1994 telecommunications debate, its hybrid status led CSE to make two contributions. First, as the Senate Commerce Committee was

---

[65] On committee passage, see "Bill Advances in House on Telecom," *The New York Times*, 17 March 1994, p. D2. The Brooks–Dingell bill (HR3626) passed 423–5, and the Markey–Fields bill (HR3636) passed 423–4. See "House Passed Telecommunications Legislation by Big Margins," *Communications Daily*, 29 June 1994, p. 1.

TABLE 5-2. *Congressional Testimony in Telecommunications Reform*

	House 1994	Senate 1994	House 1995	Senate 1995
Government Experts and Officials				
Member of Congress	0.0%	1.4%	0.0%	10.0%
Congressional Budget Office	0.0%	0.0%	0.0%	0.0%
General Accounting Office	0.0%	0.0%	0.0%	0.0%
Department of Commerce	2.9%	2.9%	2.0%	10.0%
Department of Justice	2.9%	1.4%	2.0%	10.0%
Federal Communications Commission	2.9%	1.4%	2.0%	0.0%
State/Local Government Officials	2.9%	11.4%	8.2%	10.0%
Subtotal	11.6% (8)	18.6% (13)	14.3% (7)	40.0% (3)
Experts and Researchers				
Conservative Think Tanks	0.0%	0.0%	0.0%	10.0%
Centrist/No Identifiable Ideology Think Tanks	0.0%	0.0%	0.0%	0.0%
Liberal Think Tanks	0.0%	0.0%	0.0%	0.0%
University Faculty	2.9%	2.9%	0.0%	10.0%
Private Consultants	1.4%	0.0%	0.0%	0.0%
Other experts	2.9%	0.0%	0.0%	0.0%
Subtotal	7.2% (5)	2.9% (2)	0.0% (0)	20.0% (2)
Telecommunications Industry				
Baby Bells/RBOCs	23.2%	17.1%	10.2%	20.0%
Long Distance	11.6%	8.6%	12.2%	10.0%
Cable	5.8%	2.9%	4.1%	10.0%
Broadcasters	5.8%	5.7%	12.2%	0.0%
Newspaper Publishers	5.8%	2.9%	2.0%	0.0%
Burglar Alarm Companies	2.9%	1.4%	2.0%	0.0%
Cellular Companies	0.0%	1.4%	8.2%	0.0%
Internet/computer companies	7.2%	7.1%	4.1%	0.0%
Subtotal	62.3% (43)	47.1% (33)	55.1% (27)	40.0% (4)
Other Interested Parties				
Public interest/consumer groups	8.7%	7.1%	6.1%	0.0%
Labor unions	4.3%	0.0%	2.0%	0.0%
Subtotal	13.0% (9)	7.1% (5)	8.2% (4)	0.0% (0)
Other	5.8% (4)	24.3% (17)	22.4% (11)	0.0% (0)
TOTAL	100% (69)	100% (70)	100% (49)	100% (10)

finishing its debate, CSE constructed a chart for Senator John McCain (R.-Arizona), an opponent of the Hollings bill, that illustrated the complexity of the pending legislation. Gattuso and his CSE colleague Beverly McKittrick had gone to McCain once it was apparent that he opposed the Hollings bill and offered to make the chart for visual appeal. They based it on a chart that had just gained substantial media attention in the health care policy debate, illustrating the complexity of the health care system proposed by President Clinton. The CSE chart did little to sway votes on the committee, but it gained notice by journalists and among Republican Senate colleagues not on the committee, who may have otherwise passively waited for the bill to reach the Senate floor.[66]

CSE also acted in relation to the universal service provisions in the bill. In August, Gattuso and McKittrick began distributing buttons that read "No Phones for Fish. Vote No on S1822." The obscure reference to fish related to a provision of the universal service section of the Hollings bill in which phone service to aquariums was among that subsidized by other consumers. Despite their cleverness, the button campaign had little bearing on the debate. Not long after it was launched, the Hollings bill was declared dead for 1994.

The Heritage Foundation played a somewhat more conventional think tank role in the first round of deliberation on telecommunications, albeit one that reflected tremendous marketing efforts. Adam Thierer had been hired at Heritage in 1992, after a year at the Adam Smith Institute in London while finishing college. He began as a general research analyst but moved by 1993 to specialize in telecommunications and utility regulation, for which Heritage had no previous programs. Without an advanced degree, Thierer was not making original contributions of research to the telecommunications debate. But unlike his more experienced colleagues at other think tanks, Thierer moved quickly to establish relationships with congressional staff – particularly Republican congressional staff – and to make himself available and helpful in pursuing their goals. In 1992 and early 1993, Thierer recalls,

I was taking affirmative steps to go over and meet with various staffers on the respective Commerce Committees, particularly the Senate Commerce Committee, and with the lead staffer on these issues in Senator Dole's office. . . . We meet with them one by one, and say here's our paper. Here's our proposal. I just want to

---

[66] "Packwood and McCain Opposed: Senate Commerce Panel Passes Telecommunications Bill," *Communications Daily*, 12 August 1994, p. 1.

talk to you for about five minutes. You give them a quick sell. And you say, if you have any questions or anything you need help on, feel free to give us a call.[67]

The first paper Thierer wrote on telecommunications reform was released as a *Heritage Issue Bulletin* on June 3, 1994. It outlined in twenty-four pages – unusually long by Heritage standards – the key issues involved in telecommunications reform and the appropriate steps, in general terms, for deregulating the sector.[68] It was followed in three weeks by an op-ed in the *Wall Street Journal* in which Thierer endorsed an amendment offered by Senators John Breaux (D.-Louisiana) and Bob Packwood (R.-Oregon) that would have provided fuller and quicker deregulation of the telecommunications sector than the Senate bill favored. The op-ed was followed a month later, at the end of August, with a seven-page *Heritage Backgrounder* in which Thierer enumerated the merits of a draft alternative to the Hollings bill written by Senator Dole's staff.[69]

Thierer's endorsements of the Breaux–Packwood amendment and then the Dole draft were well-timed and intentionally marketed attempts to provide commentary helpful to killing the Hollings bill in 1994. Whether influential or not, the backgrounder on the Dole draft was particularly appreciated by Dole's staff. In early August, David Wilson, Dole's staff member on telecommunications issues, had shown a copy of the Dole draft to Thierer. Wilson asked Thierer "to check this stuff out, and, if you feel comfortable with it, write something positive about it." Wilson notes, "We wanted to use [Heritage's] credibility to also reach out to others. . . . One of the reasons for that is that, if you want to get the Republicans into line, Heritage is where they usually look."[70] In the end, Thierer's contribution was no more than peripheral support as Dole used his powers as minority leader to leverage an end to the telecommunications debate in 1994.

With Republicans in control of the next Congress, the 1995 iteration of bill drafting involved little more think tank or general expert participation than had been the case in 1993–4. The only bill drafter in either the

---

[67] Interview with Adam Thierer, Walker Fellow, Heritage Foundation, Washington, D.C., 26 April 1999.
[68] Adam D. Thierer, "A Guide to Telecommunications Deregulation Legislation," *Heritage Issue Bulletin* #191, June 3, 1994.
[69] Adam D. Thierer, "Free Markets for Telecom: No Halfway House on Deregulation," *The Wall Street Journal*, June 23, 1994, p. A14; Adam D. Thierer, "Senator Dole's Welcome Proposal for Telecommunication Freedom," *Heritage Backgrounder Update* #233, August 24, 1994.
[70] Interview with David Wilson, 6 May 1999.

House or Senate for whom think tanks were of some consequence was Donald McClellan. McClellan was the more ideological of the two Senate Commerce Committee co-counsels, a true believer in deregulation who worked for Senator Larry Pressler (R.-South Dakota), the new chairman of the Commerce Committee. He called frequently on Thierer, Gattuso, and Peter Huber, a more senior scholar in the telecommunications field affiliated with the Manhattan Institute, for help in developing his intellectual understanding of the reform issues, particularly as he negotiated with his Democratic counterparts. As he recalls, "They gave intellectual rigor and foundation to the atmosphere that had been created by the election... [and] they were good at offering specific suggestions – sometimes specific legislative language; sometimes more historical context to sort out how to be looking at these issues."[71] The committee negotiations in both the Senate and the House moved quickly in 1995. The Senate Commerce Committee approved a bill on March 23, 1995; the House Commerce Committee passed a bill in mid-May.

With the Senate committee process over, McClellan took note of an additional organized effort by think tanks expressly directed at the telecommunications reform debate. It came from the Progress and Freedom Foundation. In 1993, George Keyworth, previously at the Hudson Institute, teamed with Jeff Eisenach, former executive director of GOPAC, House Speaker Newt Gingrich's political action committee, to form the Progress and Freedom Foundation (PFF), a think tank focused on "the digital revolution" and its implications for public policy. With Eisenach's close ties to the new speaker, PFF seemed to be in a unique position to influence the direction of policy when the Republicans took control of Congress. And it was. In January, soon after the new Congress was sworn in, Eisenach and several of his PFF colleagues had a dinner with Gingrich; Representative Tom Bliley (R.-Virginia), the new chairman of the House Commerce Committee; and Jack Fields (R.-Texas), chairman of the House Commerce telecommunications subcommittee. Gingrich made it clear to Bliley and Fields that he viewed PFF as worth listening to.

It had the ear of policy makers, but Eisenach recognized that the Progress and Freedom Foundation did not have in-house telecommunications scholars. Keyworth was chairman of the Foundation but was not writing much in that area. So Eisenach resolved to convene a working group that would form recommendations for the new Congress. What became known as the FCC Working Group brought together many of the

---

[71] Interview with McClellan, 18 May 1999.

best-known people in the think tank community who favored telecommunications deregulation. Peter Huber from the Manhattan Institute, Robert Crandall from the Brookings Institution, and Greg Sidak from the American Enterprise Institute participated, as did Peter Pitsch, a new scholar at PFF, along with Gattuso and Thierer. Rounding out the group were Tom Hazlett, an economist at the University of California–Davis and nonresident fellow at AEI; Ken Robinson, a former FCC attorney and frequent consultant to the Baby Bells; and four PFF staff, including Eisenach and Keyworth.[72] The incentive for participating on the part of the various scholars was the chance to make recommendations that the speaker and his leadership team might take seriously.

Meeting every couple of weeks through March and April, the group formed a consensus relatively quickly. In a well-attended, C-SPAN–broadcast press conference on May 30, 1995, the group made three broad proposals for (1) replacing the FCC with a much smaller and less powerful executive branch Office of Communications, (2) privatizing the broadcast spectrum, removing the government from its auction and allocation, and (3) turning the universal service obligation over to the states to mandate and administer. Reaction to the proposals was immediate but not wholly favorable.[73] The group's recommendations were seen as politically untenable, and the FCC abolishment, in particular, was seen as far beyond the scope of what policy makers could address. Even the journalists who attended the briefing seemed a bit contemptuous of recommendations that seemed unrealistic. In briefings with House leadership and committee members in the weeks preceding and following the press conference, reactions were similar. Moreover, and importantly, despite their relatively quick work, the recommendations came too late to affect committee deliberations over telecommunications reform in either the House or the Senate.

Without having a direct impact on the specific content of reform, the PFF recommendations, by some accounts, did have a residual effect in the debate. As Senate staffer McClellan recalls, "When this hit, it was immediately prior to Senate floor consideration, and my view is that it gave us a second shot or a second burst of energy for the free-market deregulatory effort."[74] In the face of political pressures to limit the scope

---

[72] Interview with Eisenach, 22 April 1999; interview with Bill Myers, Progress and Freedom Foundation, 29 April 1999.
[73] *The Telecom Revolution: An American Revolution* (Washington, D.C.: Progress and Freedom Foundation, 1995).
[74] Interview with McClellan, 18 May 1999.

and extent of reform in the telecommunications bill, McClellan found the PFF report personally encouraging.

Among most of those involved, though, the report was more cause for annoyance than inspiration. As one House staffer recalls:

> They [PFF] were in the *Wall Street Journal* expressing their views. It wasn't helpful for moving a bill forward. But I think that was their role. They were trying to move it more in one direction. . . . I even think they're correct on a lot of this stuff. But being correct isn't always tantamount to actually getting something done on the Hill. You know there's this political process you have to go through. It's not a vacuum up there. And that was frustrating with them, because they pounded so hard and they really did beat us up in the *Wall Street Journal* all the time, which is kind of annoying because we were supposed to – we were actually trying to do a little bit of deregulation here, and to be told constantly that we weren't doing enough, I don't know whether it helped or hurt.[75]

By most accounts, by the time the report was released, Speaker Gingrich, its most likely advocate, was distracted by other issues. None of the recommendations of the PFF FCC Working Group were incorporated into the Telecommunications Act. Intended as a proposal, the group's report became a contribution of commentary instead because it was so late in the debate.

By 1995, PFF was far from alone in contributing such commentary. Independently, Thierer, Gattuso, and Erik Olbeter, a new actor on the scene at the Economic Strategy Institute, were making contributions. Thierer was directing his effort toward coaxing Pressler and the Senate to move their legislation in a more deregulatory direction before taking it up on the Senate floor. On May 5, Thierer released a critical assessment of the Pressler bill. As an attention-getting gimmick, Thierer packaged the *Issue Bulletin* as a report card on the bill. He gave the bill a grade of C-. Even before it was released, on rumor of the grade, Thierer began hearing from Republican Senate staff. As he recalls:

> I started getting invites from the folks around the Pressler camp and the [Senator Trent] Lott [R.-Mississippi] camp. And at one point, Senator Lott's staffer on the issue brought me into the room and basically said, Adam, we don't want you to grade this this way. We want you to change the grades. So there were actually attempts being made by members of Congress and their staff to have a conservative policy group change their positions and their grades even before the papers came out, because they heard I was going to do something like this.[76]

---

[75] Interview with congressional staff, Washington, D.C., 10 May 1999.
[76] Interview with Thierer, 26 April 1999.

When it was released, Thierer's report card became ammunition for those dissatisfied with the Senate legislation, most notably Senators Dole and McCain.

Dole and his staff had been patient with Pressler as he negotiated with Hollings to accommodate Democratic preferences. David Wilson, Dole's staff person, had sat in on the discussions leading up to the committee-approved bill, but, at Dole's insistence, he had refrained from trying to dictate the terms on which agreement should be made with Hollings. The Heritage report, though, was just one of many sources of pressure during May that led Dole to work with Pressler on amendments to the bill as it headed for the Senate floor. Beyond the report card, Wilson called on Thierer directly to advise him on what might be included in the "Dole amendment." Industry groups were tremendously involved as well in working with Wilson, but Thierer was a frequent source of ideas and he "was very good about bringing forward others." As Wilson recalls, "I would say I need a person on X, Y, or Z, and he would go out and find them."[77] Through this process, Peter Huber and Peter Pitsch met with Wilson as well in 1995.

In addition to the Dole amendment, which passed on the Senate floor, McCain was inclined to introduce an assortment of deregulatory amendments. McCain had not been satisfied with the Pressler bill since the start of the process in 1995. His staff worked closely with Gattuso and McKittrick from CSE as well as with Thierer in drafting deregulatory amendments, almost all of which were defeated on the Senate floor. Through May, Mark Buse, McCain's staff person, was faxing draft language back and forth with both Gattuso and Thierer. Thierer was even offered a chance to work for McCain part-time in 1995 but declined in favor of staying at Heritage.

Three additional sources of expertise were of some note during this period: an economics consulting firm doing work for the Baby Bells, a former Nixon administration official and self-described futurist, and the Congressional Budget Office. By the mid-1990s, it had long been the practice for the telephone companies – both long distance and local – to pay private consulting firms to produce studies favorable to their positions in ongoing policy debates. There was an assortment of firms from which to choose that were producing studies during the telecommunications debate. Most studies, treated as proprietary by the firms that financed them, never saw the light of day. One notable exception was a February

[77] Interview with Wilson, 6 May 1999.

1995 study by the Massachusetts-based WEFA Group that estimated $550 billion in cost savings and 3.4 million new jobs over ten years if the telecommunications industries were fully deregulated.[78]

The study was financed by the U.S. Telephone Association, a coalition of the Baby Bells. At the Baby Bells' insistence, MIT economist Jerry Hausman and U.C. Berkeley economist Robert Harris were pulled in as consultants to the study. Soon after its release and promotion by the Baby Bells, the entire study was entered into the *Congressional Record* by Representative David Bonior (D.-Michigan), a Baby Bell ally.[79] It became a frequent point of reference for pro-deregulatory lawmakers in floor debate.

Also frequently referred to was George Gilder, a former Nixon speechwriter, lecturer at Harvard's Kennedy School of Government, and consultant to high-tech firms. His writings on technology were frequently cited in the 1980s by President Reagan, and, in the 1990s, he was a particular favorite of Republicans in the debate over telecommunications reform. In 1990, Gilder published a book, *Life After Television*, in which he argued that within the next two decades, there would be a convergence of technology prompting the rise of the "teleputer" through which people might pursue unstructured two-way communication.[80] In 1995, Gilder became a frequent visitor to Capitol Hill to informally advise members. David Wilson remembers a dinner organized by one of the Baby Bells in which there were "basically just a few of us. And it was just a real opportunity to sit there and sort of pick his brain about where he saw things going and what was on the horizon and things we might want to take into consideration as we moved forward on a bill."[81]

Gilder also served once in another capacity, as a witness at a Senate hearing about telecommunications reform. In the right-hand columns of Table 5-2, introduced earlier, the general affiliations of those who participated in congressional hearings during 1994 or 1995 are illustrated. Gilder was one of the "other experts" in 1995. Generally speaking, far fewer witnesses testified about telecommunications reform than was the case in health care reform, and, among them, industry representatives were the favorite source of testimony – at least 40 percent of all cases. Only one think tank expert testified during the whole debate: Peter Huber

[78] The WEFA Group, *Economic Impact of Deregulating U.S. Communications Industries* (Burlington, Mass.: The WEFA Group, 1995).
[79] *Communications Daily*, 27 March 1995, p. 6.
[80] George Gilder, *Life After Television, Revised Edition* (New York: W.W. Norton, 1994).
[81] Interview with Wilson, 6 May 1999.

TABLE 5-3. *References to Experts in Floor Debate on*
Telecommunications Reform

Organization	Number of Mentions
Liberal	
Center for National Policy	0
Economic Policy Institute	0
Centrist or No Identifiable Ideology	
Brookings Institution	0
Economic Strategy Institute	1
RAND Corporation	0
Conservative	
American Enterprise Institute	1
Cato Institute	0
Citizens for a Sound Economy	4
Heritage Foundation	5
Hudson Institute	0
Manhattan Institute	2
Progress and Freedom Foundation	0
Government	
Congressional Budget Office	15
General Accounting Office	6
Congressional Research Service	1
Federal Communications Commission	2
Office of Technology Assessment	2
Other Experts/Researchers	
George Gilder	8
American Psychological Assoc	3
Consumer Federal of America	2
WEFA Group	7

of the Manhattan Institute, who testified once before the Senate Judiciary
Committee in 1995.

Table 5-3 records results of a coding of references to experts and expertise during floor debate in both the House and Senate on telecommunications reform. As with congressional testimony, nongovernmental
experts and expertise were hardly cited on the floor, the exceptions being
the Heritage Foundation and Citizens for Sound Economy, which received
5 and 4 mentions, respectively. Think tanks and policy experts generally
also received little attention in news accounts of reform. But then again,
telecommunications reform received relatively sparse attention in general
compared with the health care reform and tax cut debates. Table 5-4
records the frequency with which the think tanks under consideration

TABLE 5-4. *References in* Washington Post *to Telecommunications Reform*

Organization	1993	1994	1995	Total Citations
Liberal				
Center for National Policy	0	0	0	0
Economic Policy Institute	0	0	0	0
Centrist or No Identifiable Ideology				
Brookings Institution	0	3	2	5
Economic Strategy Institute	0	0	0	0
RAND Corporation	0	0	0	0
Conservative				
American Enterprise Institute	0	0	1	1
Cato Institute	0	1	3	4
Citizens for a Sound Economy	0	0	0	0
Heritage Foundation	0	0	1	1
Hudson Institute	0	0	0	0
Manhattan Institute	0	0	0	0
Progress and Freedom Foundation	–	0	2	2
Government				
Congressional Budget Office	3	6	1	10
General Accounting Office	2	4	1	7
Congressional Research Service	0	0	1	1
Federal Communications Commission	3	2	10	15
Other Experts/Researchers				
WEFA Group	0	0	0	0
Interested Parties				
United States Telephone Association	1	1	0	2
AT&T	1	9	28	38
Bell Atlantic	3	15	31	49
Bell South	0	1	0	1
Sprint	0	1	5	0
Total Number of Articles on Telecom	43	71	75	189

were mentioned in *Washington Post* articles about telecommunications reform in 1993, 1994, and 1995. Think tanks, combined, received only 13 mentions in a total of 189 articles about reform. The expert agency that received the most references was inside the government: the Congressional Budget Office (CBO).

The CBO was also the most-cited source in Senate and House floor consideration of telecommunications bills. After raising faint concerns about the Hollings bill's universal service provisions in 1994, Republican Senate Commerce Committee staff tried to rewrite the legislation in 1995 to forestall CBO estimates of universal service transfers as a tax. But in their eagerness to move the Senate bill through committee quickly, they bypassed the normal process of getting CBO estimates on the bill prior to committee passage. In early May, as the Commerce Committee anticipated bringing its bill to the floor, the CBO released a draft report in which the universal service requirement was estimated to constitute a $7 billion tax.[82] The CBO estimates became the basis of commentary by Adam Thierer, among others, who made the case for dropping the universal service provision or devolving it to the states, an argument he had made before.[83] Through technical changes in the bill's language, the CBO's concerns were mollified, and the bill could move to the floor for consideration. But the CBO was unavoidable and influential as a source of estimates in the debate.

Senate floor consideration of the Pressler telecommunications bill began in the second week of June. On the core issues of Bell entry into long distance and manufacturing, the Dole amendment moved the bill in a more deregulatory direction. McCain's amendments were mostly defeated.[84] After a week of debate, the amended bill passed the Senate by a vote of 81–8.

With passage of the Senate bill, the flow of commentary and estimates from experts continued. The Economic Strategy Institute (ESI), a relatively small, "pro-competitive," internationally focused think tank, released three short studies in June and July 1995. Erik Olbeter was ESI's new telecommunications policy analyst that year. He had actually started at ESI as an intern in 1993 while finishing his masters degree in statistics at Georgetown. Olbeter, only twenty-five years old in 1995, took a different view from that of many of the think tank experts who had spoken out on telecommunications reform already in the debate. In his three briefing papers, Olbeter argued for maintaining restrictions on the Baby Bells until they demonstrated real competition in their markets.[85] The reports were

---

[82] "CBO Draft Opinion on Telecommunications Bill," *Communications Daily*, 5 May 1995, p. 2.

[83] Adam D. Thierer, "How to Solve the CBO's Telecom Tax Problem," Executive Memorandum #414, May 23, 1995.

[84] A number of side issues gained public attention during the course of debate, some far more than the core competition issues in the bills. Most notably, Senator James Exon (R.-Neb.) introduced a controversial amendment banning pornography from the Internet. The amendment passed and was part of the final legislation (although overturned in part by the Supreme Court in 1997). Experts played no role in the provision's development. Interview with Chris McLean, Senator Exon's office, Washington, D.C., 12 May 1999.

[85] Lawrence Chimerine, Erik R. Olbeter, and Robert B. Cohen, "Eliminating Monopolies and Barriers: How to Make the U.S. Telecommunications Services Industry Truly Competitive," Economic Strategy Institute, June 1995; Lawrence Chimerine, Erik R. Olbeter, and Robert B. Cohen, "Ensuring Competition in the Local Exchange," Economic Strategy

released in press conferences and follow-up briefings on Capitol Hill in August 1995. But by all accounts, Olbeter and the ESI reports were little noticed in the House where, by the beginning of August, the leadership was ready to move the bill to the floor.

Following its passage in committee, the House Commerce Committee bill had gone through a vetting process by the House leadership. In their institutional reforms upon taking over the majority, Republicans had set up an extra-committee Republican task force process, through which many pieces of legislation had to pass on their way to the floor.[86] As had happened in the Senate, the House leadership viewed the legislation as too regulatory. With the urging of the Baby Bells, the leadership compelled Rep. Bliley to offer an amendment when the bill came to the floor, relieving the Baby Bells of certain competitive restrictions for entering long distance and bringing it closer in line to the amended bill that the Senate had passed.[87] After nine-and-a-half hours of debate that began close to midnight on August 3, the full House passed an amended telecommunications reform bill by a vote of 305–117.

Following passage in both Houses, only the conference committee remained. But reconciling differences between the House and Senate versions and, more important, contending with increasingly mobilized competing interests was no small task. The contentious conference process began in late October, and, with only one day off through Christmas, the staffs of the conferees, particularly committee staff, worked with legislative counsel to find a bill acceptable to both chambers. Side issues, like wiring classrooms and regulating the Internet, were as hard fought as core telephone and cable concerns. By comparison with the spring and summer,

---

Institute, July 1995; Lawrence Chimerine and Erik R. Olbeter, "Lessons from Abroad: Deregulation Efforts in New Zealand and the United Kingdom," Economic Strategy Institute, July 1995. Chimerine was an intern for Olbeter.

[86] On the task force process, see C. Lawrence Evans and Walter J. Oleszak, *Congress Under Fire: Reform Politics and the Republican Majority* (Boston: Houghton Mifflin, 1997), pp. 132–3.

[87] Kirk Victor, "How Bliley's Bell Was Rung," *National Journal*, 22 July 1995, p. 1892–3. With the pending deregulatory shift in both bills, Vice President Gore became more active in the debate in the summer of 1995, after playing a surprisingly low-profile role through much of the process to that point. Although Gore delayed the process a bit, it's notable that he did not have substantial influence over the legislation for much of the debate. As *National Journal* reported in April 1995, "Gore is surely unhappy at the growing perception that for all his pronouncements on the importance of the information superhighway, he's had little noticeable impact on the legislative process. . . ." Kirk Victor, "Will the Real Chairman Stand Up," *National Journal*, 18 April 1995, p. 892.

commentary and estimates by experts were infrequent and little noticed. During the conference, debates were technical and industry-dominated.[88] On February 1, 1996, the conference report was approved by both chambers of Congress, making way for the president's signature, in a signing ceremony on February 8.

Lessons from Deliberation in Telecommunications Reform

During the deliberative stages of telecommunications reform, two organizations that made substantial, somewhat successful efforts to offer commentary to lawmakers were the Heritage Foundation and Citizens for a Sound Economy. They packaged their research in accessible formats, timed and marketed it aggressively, and benefited from tremendous access to lawmakers – or at least their staffs.

Adam Thierer at Heritage had made a point at the earliest stages of the policy debate to introduce himself to relevant congressional telecommunications staff. In one case, Thierer contacted a new telecommunications aide to Senator Packwood before the aide even moved from Oregon to Washington, offering to orient him to the issue during his first days on Capitol Hill. With a 501(c)4 organizational arm, Gattuso and McKittrick at CSE used similar, sometimes even more aggressive tactics to ensure access to lawmakers' offices. As Gattuso points out, "We approached all the offices. At CSE – especially at CSE, which is more of an activist group than a pure think tank – we just make regular visits to everyone on the committees: people we knew would be against us; people who were friends; people who were on the fence."[89]

Thierer, Gattuso, and McKittrick had another advantage in establishing relationships and access to congressional staff: They were young. Thierer was in his mid-twenties; Gattuso and McKittrick were only a little older. The personal and committee staff to members of Congress tended to be around the same age. Many of the other experts – Huber, Crandall, and Sidak included – were in their forties and fifties. Thierer, Gattuso, and McKittrick had the opportunity to become not just advisors but trusted

---

[88] Senator Dole nearly scuttled the process at the beginning of January 1996, objecting to a provision that gave broadcast spectrum away to television networks to support their launch of high-definition television. The question of spectrum allocation was ultimately removed from the bill, however.

[89] Interview with James Gattuso, Citizens for a Sound Economy, Washington, D.C., 30 April 1999.

friends to the congressional aides. Thierer recalls:

I think one of the reasons that I was so successful and that Beverly McKittrick, who was at CSE, was so successful is that we were both about the same age as the majority of the staffers covering the issue and the reporters following it. And it was a very strange clan because here was a group of mostly kids – I mean if you call 20-somethings kids – who hung out together on the weekends. You'd see them in a bar as much as you'd see them in Congress, and I developed a real relationship with a lot of these people.[90]

Senate Commerce Committee counsel Donald McClellan had similar recollections in response to a question about whom he looked to for expertise, "I think of Adam Thierer at the Heritage Foundation and James Gattuso at Citizens for a Sound Economy, where they're younger. They're more of staff age. And so they had social relationships and friendships with me and with others on the staff."[91]

As much as gaining access represented a concerted effort by Thierer, Gattuso, and McKittrick, coordinating the timing and marketing of their products was a priority as well. Thierer came out with his report card on Pressler's bill just as the Senate was about to consider it on the floor. His op-eds were timed to be released when lawmakers were meeting on the issues addressed in them. Thierer had an advantage in negotiating the timing of his products in that his close contact with staff meant that he knew the day-to-day status of negotiations. As one industry lobbyist who often found herself in opposition to Thierer's conclusions lamented, "Adam Thierer is a good writer and a very hard worker. And he is fast. It was hard to balance his drumbeat with another think tank's steady drumbeat."[92]

And marketing was a central feature of Thierer's strategy. Heritage products – and Thierer's were no exception – tend as a rule to be relatively short issue briefs and backgrounders. Beyond these publicly available reports, Thierer also made a point of repackaging his conclusions and recommendations into even shorter formats when they could be helpful. He observes:

Sometimes I boiled it down to one to two page memos to Senate staffers that I would title "re: long distance entry issues." Here are five quick principles. Here are five quick answers for how to do this. And then I'd go meet with these people

[90] Interview with Thierer, 26 April 1999.
[91] Interview with Donald McClellan, Washington, D.C., 18 May 1999.
[92] Interview with industry representative, Washington, D.C., 19 May 1999.

individually. Hey, consider us an extension of your own staff. However we can help, let us know. Give us a call. Whatever we can do, we'd be happy to do that.[93]

In contrast with Thierer, Erik Olbeter, the new telecommunications scholar at ESI in 1993, established little access to congressional staff and made little effort to market his views, which actually represented a clear alternative to Thierer's positions. As Olbeter recalls, "ESI has never really been involved in Congress. At that time we didn't do anything with Congress.... I don't think I talked to a congressional staffer or lobbyist at any time during that period. Well, you know, I was what? 25? I mean, I didn't know anybody. We just didn't touch it."[94]

The influence of commentary in policy debates is far more difficult to assess than the role of proposals in agenda setting. In the case of telecommunications reform, the dominance of industry in the debate was hard to supplant or disentangle from expert commentary. But recalling my definition of influence – that the experts and their ideas become known among a set of policy makers and inform their thinking on or public articulation of policy-relevant information – Heritage and CSE in the deliberative stages of the debate appear to have had some effect. In Senate debate over the telecommunications debate, McCain made reference to Thierer's report card grade on the original Pressler bill, Thierer's criticism of the bill's universal service provision, and his call for FCC reform.[95] McCain also went so far as to enter into the *Congressional Record* lengthy letters from both Heritage and CSE in which flaws of the bill were enumerated.[96] Heritage and CSE may have played no more than a supporting role for McCain's already formed views on the bill, but it was a role nonetheless, one carved out by their aggressive efforts.

Policy Enactment on the Tax Cut

Deliberation over the tax cut moved more quickly than the debate over health care and telecommunications reform. It also involved fewer opportunities for experts to make contributions. Table 5-5 illustrates the number of references to think tanks and other sources of research in floor debate on the matter. But within what was generally a difficult issue debate for experts, research played an important and substantive role in at

---

[93] Interview with Thierer, 26 April 1999.
[94] Interview with Erik Olbeter, Economic Strategy Institute, 23 April 1999.
[95] *Congressional Record*, Thursday, June 8, 1995, pp. 7954–5.
[96] *Congressional Record*, Thursday, June 8, 1995, pp. 7956–7.

TABLE 5-5. *References to Experts in Floor Debate on the Tax Cut*

Organization	Number of Mentions
Liberal	
Center for Law and Social Policy	0
Center on Budget and Policy Priorities	3
Economic Policy Institute	0
Centrist or No Identifiable Ideology	
Brookings Institution	0
National Bureau of Economic Research	1
Urban Institute	0
Conservative	
American Enterprise Institute	0
Cato Institute	0
Citizens for a Sound Economy	0
Heritage Foundation	4
Hudson Institute	0
Inst for Rsch on the Economics of Taxation	0
Tax Foundation	0
Government	
Congressional Budget Office	20
General Accounting Office	1
Congressional Research Service	1
Joint Committee on Taxation	17
Other Experts and Advocates	
Children's Defense Fund	0
Citizens for Tax Justice	4
David Ellwood	0
Stephen Moore	2
Joel Slemrod/Office of Tax Policy Rsch	0

least one way in the final moments before enactment. The right research fell into the right hands at the right moment. The product was a provision added to the tax cut legislation that won over the last holdouts needed for its victory. This sort of last-minute opportunity is not typically available to experts, but the episode is further evidence of how research – properly timed, packaged, and marketed – can on occasion be influential right up to the final moments of policy enactment.

Senate Democrats and moderate Republicans watched with surprise and some frustration as the tax cut flew through the House, along mostly party-line votes. Senator Lott, now the majority leader, knew the same could never happen in the Senate, as did his ninety-nine colleagues. In a Senate split 50–50 and committees split evenly as well, it was going to take compromise to craft something that could earn fifty-one votes.[97] The task in the Senate was made more difficult by the presence of a stronger core of moderate Republicans than in the House. The pivotal figures in Senate negotiations were five moderate Republicans: Lincoln Chafee (R.-Rhode Island), Susan Collins (R.-Maine), James Jeffords (R.-Vermont), Olympia Snowe (R.-Maine), and Arlen Specter (R.-Pennsylvania). All had expressed reservations about the size of the president's tax cut proposals early on. They favored debt reduction, and each expressed concern as well about the high proportion of benefits in the tax relief package targeted at those in the top income brackets. Of the five moderates, Snowe and Jeffords had seats on the Finance Committee, which would write the Senate version of the tax cut. They therefore had the greatest leverage over how the tax cut might be reshaped. Snowe, in particular, came to play a key role in adapting the tax cut proposal in ways that would ultimately win her moderate colleagues' support.

The substantive focus of what became a major source of compromise in the Senate was the provision for expanding the child tax credit. Tax policy before the tax cut was enacted permitted parents with incomes up to $110,000 to deduct $500 from their taxes owed for every child in their family. During the campaign, President Bush had pledged to double the child tax credit from $500 to $1,000 for each child at the end of ten years. His proposal on the child tax credit was the fourth piece of his larger tax cut, behind cuts in marginal tax rates, the marriage penalty, and the estate tax.[98] The child tax credit proposal was widely supported as family-friendly and middle class–oriented. It was easily passed as part of the House version of the tax cut, and Senate leaders, including moderates, looked kindly on it.

But Senate moderates wanted to do more. As they examined alternatives for redistributing some of the benefits of the tax cut down the income ladder, they ultimately settled on the child tax credit. Senator Snowe, who was the chief proponent of a proposal to expand it beyond the president's plan, came to the idea with the help of some well-timed and marketed ideas from a coalition that included the Center on Budget and Policy Priorities, the Brookings Institution, and the Annie E. Casey Foundation.

---

[97] By the early decision to consider the tax cut under the restrictive rules of the budget resolution, proponents of the tax cut avoided the need for a filibuster-proof sixty-vote margin of victory. Filibusters were not allowed for legislation considered under the budget resolution.

[98] Richard W. Stevenson, "Bush to Propose Broad Tax Cut in Iowa Speech," *The New York Times*, 1 December 1999, p. A1. See also George W. Bush, "A Tax Cut with a Purpose," *USA Today*, 2 August 2000, p. 16A.

The idea involved extending the child tax credit expansion already endorsed by the president to those making as little as $10,000. Under the existing proposal, the child tax credit was available only to those with incomes large enough that they had tax burdens of $500 or $1,000, which could be refunded. Under the alternative that Snowe came to endorse, the credit would be available to families with smaller tax burdens, in the form of subsidies paid out to them up to a percentage of their earned income over $10,000.[99]

This child tax credit idea was developed in research by Isabel Sawhill and Adam Thomas at the Brookings Institution, who by spring 2001 had spent much of the previous year developing and applying a computer model for working out the effects of a variety of possible policy changes on the bottom one-third of income-earning families. With debate over a tax cut a near certainty after Bush's election, and given his stated support for expanding the child tax credit during the campaign, Sawhill and Thomas saw an opportunity late in 2000 to develop as part of their research what might be a politically palatable proposal for expanding the child tax credit's benefits for those with low incomes. Sawhill and Thomas recognized that they could break the child tax credit piece out of their larger research project and turn it into a proposal. They joined a select group of researchers and advocates for discussions about tax proposals in 2000, organized by the Annie E. Casey Foundation. At the same moment, as Bush's claim to the presidency was becoming a certainty, Robert Greenstein, executive director of the Center on Budget and Policy Priorities, was having discussions at the Center about ideas that might be useful in cajoling tax cutters to provide more benefits for low- and middle-income Americans in whatever they passed. He too was a part of the Annie E. Casey Foundation discussions in 2000.

Through December 2000 and into the new year, Greenstein and representatives of the Annie E. Casey Foundation put together several additional meetings of researchers working on proposals relevant to the child tax credit. The group heard from Sawhill and Thomas, who had developed their proposal into a *Brookings Policy Brief* by January 2001, as well as several others with more far-reaching ideas for expanding tax benefits for low-income families.[100] Greenstein and some of the others involved

---

[99] Glenn Kessler and Juliet Eilperin, "Hill Negotiators Reach Tax Cut Deal," *The New York Times*, 27 May 2001, p. A5.

[100] Isabel Sawhill and Adam Thomas, "A Tax Proposal for Working Families with Children," *Brookings Policy Brief, Welfare Reform and Beyond*, January 2001. Other major, more far-reaching proposals came from Robert Cherry and Max Sawicky at the Economic Policy Institute and from David Ellwood and Jeffrey Liebman at Harvard

in the discussions may have liked the more far-reaching ideas, but they settled on the Sawhill–Thomas proposal as the most realistic for appealing to moderate lawmakers. Greenstein put the considerable marketing resources of the Center on Budget and Policy Priorities behind promoting the child tax credit idea, and he struck the interest of Senator Snowe just as she was looking for a proposal to offer.

Snowe became the champion of an expanded child tax credit in collaboration with her Democratic colleagues John Kerry of Massachusetts and Blanche Lincoln of Arkansas. Her advocacy for it began as it started to appear that her first line of attack in the tax cut debate – a "trigger" that would have prevented the tax cut from being implemented if debt reduction targets were not met – lacked adequate support inside or outside the Senate.[101] Greenstein and his colleagues played a key role in raising the idea with Snowe and her staff. Isabel Sawhill at Brookings had briefed a bipartisan group of Senate Finance Committee staff early in 2001 on her child credit idea. But in late April and early May, as the Senate Finance Committee was crafting its proposal, Sawhill recalls,

> Greenstein and his group began advocating for our proposal or something very much like it. We were not engaged in advocating our own proposal. I mean if someone called, we would talk to them, obviously, enthusiastically, but we are not in the business here of doing any kind of lobbying or anything, so it was really up to the more advocacy-oriented groups to take this stuff and run with it if they wanted to, and the key people who ran with our stuff were Greenstein and his staff.[102]

The Senate Finance Committee was developing the parameters for its version of the tax cut in late April and early May, as members awaited completion of the final budget resolution. By the first week of May, Snowe had won the support of several of her Republican Finance Committee colleagues for the child tax credit expansion. When the committee's tax cut plan was publicly released on May 11, the expanded child tax credit was included.

Several conservative Republicans in the Senate and the House vociferously opposed the expanded provision. They viewed the refundable

University. See Robert Cherry and Max B. Sawicky, "Giving Tax Credit Where Credit Is Due," Economic Policy Institute Briefing Paper, 2000; and David T. Ellwood and Jeffrey B. Liebman, "The Middle Class Parent Penalty: Child Benefits in the U.S. Tax Code," Kennedy School and NBER Working Paper, July 2000.

[101] The trigger was voted down as an amendment in the Senate by a final vote of 50–49. See Karen Masterson, "Tax Showdown Looms in D.C.," *The Houston Chronicle*, 22 May 2001, p. A1.

[102] Author interview with Isabel Sawhill, Brookings Institution, 24 September 2001.

portion of the credit as a new subsidy that had no place in a bill intended for tax reduction. Nevertheless, the support of Snowe and her moderate colleagues was essential for winning passage of the tax cut. The expanded child tax credit stayed in the bill through conference, and on June 7, 2001, it became law.

Concluding Thoughts

The path taken by the child tax credit expansion was unusual. It was unusual because the debate moved so quickly that it accommodated new policy proposals right up to the moment of final enactment. In most debates, when last-minute substantive adjustments are made, they are not based on new proposals. Amendments are derived from research that has been waiting in the wings for many months, if not years.

This episode was also unusual because in spring 2001 the Senate was divided evenly, 50–50, between Republicans and Democrats. In this environment, the ideas of the moderate Republicans could not be ignored. In fact, they were crucial right up to the moment of final passage. The Republicans' weak hold on the Senate along with the political importance of the legislation for President Bush made the moments before final enactment in the Senate more critical than those for most major legislation, where positions are not as fluid so late.[103]

Yet for all that was unusual about the final moments of the tax cut debate, the lessons from the experience of the child tax credit expansion are remarkably similar to those from agenda setting on health care reform and deliberation over telecommunications legislation. As in those debates, the intentional efforts of experts were critical to making research visible and influential among policy makers. In their last-ditch efforts to modify the tax cut, Senator Snowe and her staff could have pursued many types of adjustments. They were drawn to the child tax credit proposal because it was actively marketed to them with credible research backing it up. It helped that one of its principal marketers was Robert Greenstein, who as executive director of the Center on Budget and Policy Priorities, had a sterling reputation for the quality of his work and the depths of his commitments to low- and moderate-income Americans. The involvement of analysts from the Brookings Institution, viewed as broadly credible, helped as well.

---

[103] The fluidity ended with passage of the tax cut, but it also contributed to mistakes during the tax cut debate that led to Vermont Senator James Jeffords's decision to leave the Republican party immediately following the tax cut's passage, transferring control of the chamber to the Democrats.

In fact, all of the key components for experts to be successful were present in this episode. The experts had research in its proper form, marketed in a timely manner; its purveyors were viewed as highly credible and also had broad access to the appropriate decision makers. With any of this missing – whether or not it represented a good idea backed up with quality research – the expanded child tax credit may never have happened.

Most remarkable as a lesson from this episode, however – and with this point I conclude – is that the contributions of research in the final moments of the tax cut debate took on something more than the typical importance of research at this point, when according to models of the policy process research is typically support and ammunition for those with already formed views. Research and researchers in this instance played a *substantively* important role. What made that possible?

The distinctive features of the policy debate offer one explanation. The debate's quick speed and high stakes for the president made Republican leaders welcoming of substantive ideas right up to the end, if they could help in brokering a winnable bill. On the other hand, the experience of the child tax credit is in no sense an anomaly; the episode confirms that research can play a substantive role occasionally right up to policy enactment. Its best chances for doing so are when its producers follow the precepts already outlined for marketing, credibility, access, and timing. Even more, it helps when the research contains substantial specificity. Detailed estimates of how particular legislative provisions alter services or extend budget commitments can lead to minor or even major adjustments to legislation. The Brookings Institution's computer model for calculating the costs and benefits of the child tax credit was helpful in the tax cut debate. Researchers supplied policy makers with information that they could not otherwise have had. The estimates of the Congressional Budget Office (CBO), a source inside of government, are often important in the last moments before votes on legislation. CBO has models for estimating the costs of new commitments.[104] CBO estimates were substantively important in both health care and telecommunications reform.

---

[104] In many instances, its estimates are binding. The CBO's legally prescribed role in the health care legislative debate made it influential. As Sheila Burke, Dole's chief of staff, points out, "Essentially, at the end of the day, we had to live by CBO estimates." At one point, late in the process, the House even temporarily stopped debate on health care reform to await the CBO's assessment of a compromise proposal. Author interview with Sheila Burke, chief of staff to Senator Bob Dole (R.-Kans.), in person, 7 May 1999. See also Dana Priest, "Congressional Scorer of Health Care Bills Finds Itself at Hub of Frenzied Reform Competition," *The Washington Post*, 16 August 1994, p. A8.

The challenge for researchers with this knowledge that their work can be substantively important late in the game is that estimates are far more difficult to produce, especially under time pressures, than more general commentary. Commentary is much more easily produced. And highly polemical commentary is much more easily publicized. The effects of this research, when it becomes important, are typically not in its substance but in how it can be used as support and ammunition by lawmakers. The problem for think tanks, other experts, and American policy making generally is that it is this latter kind of research that is increasingly produced in great abundance by the many new experts involved in the policy process. And its new producers are some of the most aggressive in seeking public attention for their work. This is a problem insofar as it changes – by compromising – the environment for experts and expertise generally in policy making.

6

Think Tanks, Experts, and American Politics

By the end of the twentieth century, think tanks were ubiquitous in American policy making. From fewer than 70 in 1969, the number of think tanks had expanded to more than 300 by the late 1990s. Whereas in the 1960s, only the Center for Strategic and International Studies had a name that began with "center," by the late 1990s, 28 think tanks used that word in their name, ranging from the Center for Defense Information to the Center for Defense of Free Enterprise, from the Center for Equal Opportunity to the Center for New Black Leadership, from the Center for Democracy and Technology to the Center for Military Readiness.

As their numbers grew, think tanks came to vary substantially in size and specialties. Many new think tanks identified with political ideologies – broadly conservative, liberal, or centrist. Many relied on aggressive, marketing-oriented strategies to promote their products and points of view. Think tank staff often became active and visible participants in deeply partisan and divisive political debates.

Yet in their growing numbers and increased activism, there is little indication that the overall impact of think tanks as sources of expertise is expanding. Think tank influence does not appear to have grown in proportion to the growth in think tank numbers. The role of think tanks in the policy process often has become one focused more on providing skewed commentary than neutral analysis. With these efforts, think tank influence is diminished, and the reputation of think tanks and experts generally among some policymaking audiences is damaged. This is a curious result for a group of organizations that seem to have much to offer American policy making. How are the experiences of think tanks accounted for, and what are their implications for the practice of American politics? What are their lessons for scholarly accounts of the policy process?

The Evolution of Think Tanks as Political Institutions

The trend for think tanks to become both more often ideological and more aggressively marketing-oriented is rooted in ideological and institutional changes in American politics. The first think tanks, which formed during the Progressive Era, embodied the promise of neutral expertise. Through the first half of the twentieth century, new think tanks largely sought to identify government solutions to public problems through the detached analysis of experts. Think tank scholars wrote on topics relevant to policy makers but typically maintained a distance from the political bargaining in the final stages of the policymaking process. This analytic detachment was a behavior to which researchers held fast and upon which they prided themselves. It was a behavior that fostered an effective relationship between experts and policy makers. Between 1910 and 1960, think tank experts often influenced how government operated. The Brookings Institution informed the creation of the Bureau of the Budget at the beginning of the century. The RAND Corporation developed applications of systems analysis for the Department of Defense at midcentury. In these cases, the influence of think tanks was significant, and their research served political purposes. But the policy process did not typically compel experts to become directly involved in high-profile partisan battles. Experts were mobilized by policy makers to prescribe possibilities for change.

Beginning in the 1960s, the political environment changed, and the forms of and expectations for think tanks evolved substantially. Until the 1960s, large private foundations like the Rockefeller and Ford Foundations, in combination with the government, had been the principal sources of support for think tanks; these were patrons that appreciated, even encouraged, the detached and neutral efforts of think tanks. In the last decades of the twentieth century, however, these traditional sources of support were partially displaced by individuals, corporations, and smaller, more ideological foundations. These new patrons often preferred think tanks that promoted consistent points of view through highly visible, sometimes partisan activities. Moreover, in a political environment increasingly dominated by anti-government conservatives who posed an effective challenge to the statist status quo, the leaders of ideologically consistent, particularly conservative think tanks found an increasingly engaged, attentive, and receptive audience among policy makers.

As the number of think tanks grew rapidly between the mid-1960s and the mid-1990s, the proportion of organizations with identifiable ideologies grew from less than one-quarter to more than half. Conservative think tanks came to outnumber liberal organizations by a ratio of two to one. Along with this growth, neutrality – even attempted neutrality – was lost as a reliable characteristic of think tanks. The activities of think tanks no longer reflected an ancillary and passive role in the policymaking process. New, especially ideological think tanks, beginning with the Heritage Foundation, became more aggressively marketing-oriented.

Locating its offices on Capitol Hill, the Heritage Foundation hired separate full-time House and Senate liaisons. From its start, its research products were intentionally designed to be shorter and more accessible than the products of its think tank forbearers. Heritage *Backgrounders* had to pass the briefcase test: Members of Congress had to be able to pull *Backgrounders* from their briefcases and read them completely in the fifteen minutes it takes to ride from Reagan National Airport to Capitol Hill. Drawing on congressional liaisons, short publication formats, and a large communications staff, Heritage aggressively promoted its policy positions to policy makers and journalists.

Since the founding of the Heritage Foundation in 1973, efforts to format and promote expertise to gain immediate visibility and influence have become a regular strategy of more and more think tanks. The increased prevalence of such political marketing reflects, in part, the shift in funding sources among think tanks. It also stems from the more ideologically contentious environment in which they operate. This marketing orientation is sustained – and encouraged – by growing pressures that result from a more heavily populated and increasingly competitive environment for experts generally and from the proliferation of new media outlets that regularly lavish attention on well-marketed research and expert pundits.[1]

The good news for think tanks is that in this environment, their intentional efforts make a tremendous difference in whether or not their research becomes visible and influential among policy makers. The likelihood that think tank expertise will be influential is increased for those

---

[1] Reflecting on the shift to shorter, more marketable products at the National Center for Policy Analysis, John Goodman, its president, observes that, "We wanted studies that could be put out in a short amount of time. We wanted them very readable.... So we put out a product that not only can get out more quickly, but it is a product that has a lot of visual appeal. It was a product designed to be skimmed. And this is important. If you pick up an NCPA product in our office, you can skim it. You can look at the call-outs, look at the graphics, pick up a few bullet points." Author interview with John Goodman, National Center for Policy Analysis, 10 February 1999.

think tanks with established political access, perceived credibility, and timely research made available in a form generally relevant to the policy process. And experts who actively market their research improve its chances of being influential. Think tanks can often gain a competitive advantage by strategically placing op-eds in the *Washington Post* or by holding well-timed sets of meetings with congressional staff.

The intentional efforts of experts can matter greatly for whether or not their research is recognized, and in an environment where marketing matters, think tanks have a certain advantage. They are efficiently tooled organizations. Most think tanks operate on budgets of less than $5 million annually. Despite their small size, they easily attract more political visibility and policy influence than other types of organizations with experts, such as universities and research centers, many of which do not or cannot restrict their focus to policymaking issues. As Joel Fleishman, who served for many years as a board member to foundations and think tanks, observes, "The policy relevance of the think tank is just much more secure than that of the academic institutions, where faculty members are notorious for being more concerned about methodology than about policy."[2] As Richard Posner illustrates, the pressures of academia also force scholars to become highly specialized, making it difficult for them to become schooled in the subjects and patterns of public decision making.[3]

For think tanks, their success as marketers of expertise reflects a capacity to make marketing a part of their organizational behavior rather than the responsibility of individual experts. Given a principal focus on influencing public policy, think tanks frequently can and do follow the Heritage Foundation's model, having entire departments that serve as a liaison with Capitol Hill and the news media, creating opportunities for experts to actively promote their ideas – and have them promoted on their behalf. Other research-oriented organizations, like universities, are

[2] Author interview with Joel Fleishman, Atlantic Philanthropic, 1 February 1999. Norman Ornstein, resident scholar at the American Enterprise Institute, concurs: "People at the universities didn't know very much about the political arrangements and had a hard time communicating with [members of Congress]." Author interview with Norman Ornstein, American Enterprise Institute, 23 July 1996. Marilyn Moon, a senior fellow at the Urban Institute, makes a different point that illustrates an additional advantage for think tanks: "I think the big difference between academics and think tanks that have a policy bent is that academics have no sense of time frame. They have no sense of the value of time. So if you talk to somebody at universities, they'll say, gee, that is a very interesting idea. Maybe I'll do that study next year. There is no sense that by next year a different issue will be on the table and this will be passé." Author interview with Marilyn Moon, Urban Institute, 24 February 1999.

[3] Richard A. Posner, *Public Intellectuals: A Study of Decline* (Cambridge, Mass.: Harvard University Press, 2001), pp. 1–13.

unlikely to provide such a service for experts because informing policy makers is not central to their missions. In virtually every instance, think tanks are a more efficient vehicle for generating attention for research than universities.[4] Dollar for dollar, think tanks attract greater attention than most any other organizational source of expertise. Think tanks are well positioned to communicate directly with policy makers. They have become a visible, commonplace, and accepted (even expected) part of the political architecture of policy making.

To be sure, the opportunities for think tanks vary across issues and issue debates. Think tanks are more active in some areas of policy than others, and they have to be active in order to have influence. There are characteristics of issue debates as well that affect the cumulative chances for think tanks and policy experts generally to play a meaningful role, ranging from the speed with which an issue is considered to the level of involvement by lobbyists and interest groups.

The opportunities vary, but overall the institutional profile of think tanks at the beginning of the twenty-first century looks quite different from that of half a century before. Experts behave quite differently from the detached, long-range–oriented researchers of previous decades. Present-day experts, particularly those at think tanks, are often aggressive advocates in the hard-fought battles of the policy process.[5] The role of experts has changed, and the good news for think tanks is that marketing along with other intentional behaviors by experts matters for the degree of exposure their research attracts in policy making. So long as these behaviors matter, think tanks have something of an advantage with policy makers. Think tanks can be sleekly styled marketing machines.

Experts, Policy Making, and Political Science

The emergence of think tanks as "sleekly styled marketing machines" should give political scientists reason to pause. The advantages that think

---

[4] In Richard Posner's count of media citations to 607 leading public intellectuals between 1995 and 2000, many of the most often cited were based at think tanks (e.g., William Bennett, Empower America, 9,070; Herbert Stein, American Enterprise Institute, 3,093; Thomas Mann, Brookings Institution, 2,043). Many of the other most often cited in his study were journalists and government officials. The media citations of people based at think tanks at least rivaled the citations of those based at universities, where the number of people with the possibility of being cited is obviously much greater. Posner, *Public Intellectuals*, pp. 210–11.

[5] John W. Kingdon, *Agendas, Alternatives, and Public Policies, Second Edition* (New York: HarperCollins College Publishers, 1995), p. 228.

tanks enjoy reflect features of their behavior that are far different from those identified in most scholarly accounts of the role of experts in the policy process. Experts played what was ostensibly a detached role in policy making through much of the twentieth century. They are still understood to play that detached role in most accounts of the policy process. A firewall separating experts from advocates and analysis from politics is an explicit feature of accounts of policy making by scholars like Merriam, Lasswell, and Kingdon, and it is at least implicit in most existing models of the policy process.[6] But from the first half of the century when Merriam was involved in forming the Social Science Research Council and the middle of the century when Lasswell held fast to the belief that "it is not necessary for the scientist to sacrifice objectivity in the execution of a project," belief that the social sciences can (or should) reveal neutral and definitive answers has declined in policymaking circles.[7] And far from focusing in a detached way "on matters like technical detail, cost–benefit analyses, gathering data, conducting studies, and honing proposals," as Kingdon, for example, describes them, experts – especially think tanks – are a frequent presence alongside interest groups and lobbyists in the political process.

The firewall is gone, and the change in the role and behavior of experts in recent decades suggests need for a fundamental revision in how scholars treat them in accounts of policy making. Relegating experts to the sidelines in these accounts or ignoring them all together, which is all too common among political scientists, misses their active role. And that active role can have consequences for policy making. Research and expertise is not just made useful to policy makers by others – the advocates or entrepreneurs. It is often made relevant – in fact, most effectively made relevant – by experts themselves. The independent efforts of experts can make their work visible and influential with policy makers or with non-expert advocates or entrepreneurs who might use it. And the failure of some experts to match the intentional efforts of other experts to secure this visibility or influence can disadvantage their work in the policy process.

---

[6] Even in models of the policy process that take seriously the role of *expertise*, the role of the *expert* is typically either ignored or described as ancillary and detached. See Paul A. Sabatier, *Theories of the Policy Process* (Boulder, Colo.: Westview Press, 1999). For an exception, see Hank C. Jenkins-Smith, *Democratic Politics and Policy Analysis* (Pacific Grove, Calif.: Brooks/Cole Publishing Company, 1990), pp. 83–199. See also Laurence E. Lynn Jr., *Knowledge and Policy: The Uncertain Connection* (Washington, D.C.: National Academy of Sciences, 1978).

[7] See Harold D. Lasswell, "The Policy Orientation," in *The Policy Sciences*, ed. by Daniel Lerner and Harold D. Lasswell (Stanford, Calif.: Stanford University Press, 1951), p. 11.

For some in the scholarly world, acknowledging these developments may be troubling or even threatening. The distance between experts and politics was not just a descriptive point about the policy process made by scholars, especially during the first two-thirds of the century; it was a normative one as well. Merriam and Lasswell were not just accounting for the role of social scientists in the political world; they were arguing for a conception of what that role should be. Their view and the view of many up through the 1970s and 1980s was that the social science expert was most effective as a detached analyst, producing research that would serve a common and neutral view of the public interest.[8] When debates erupted among (usually liberal) social scientists about the possibilities for researchers to become politically active, arguments that favored preserving the social scientist as "neutral analyst" usually prevailed.[9] But the very idea of a "neutral analyst" has been openly discredited by the behavior of experts in think tanks. Out of the developments among think tanks – and largely thanks to their efforts – research is often produced from many sources that represent many different sides of every issue. What these experts produce is often far from a neutral or objective analysis of what serves the public interest. And experts are quite politically active. Few policy makers believe that experts are neutral or detached. The evidence suggests that political scientists should not hold that belief either.

The Practical Politics of Think Tanks

Experts are political actors, and think tanks are among the most active and efficient expert political institutions. Think tanks have certain advantages for making their work influential, advantages that enhance the political role of experts. But these advantages have a significant unintended and eventually self-defeating consequence. In practice, think tanks all too often squander their potential influence by focusing resources and efforts on producing commentary about immediately pending policy decisions. Ideological think tanks pursue an interest in making their points of view known among policy makers and the general public. They hold public meetings or release policy briefs rating pending legislation; acting as agents of ideologies rather than as independent analysts, they want

---

[8] For a discussion of this view of the social sciences and movement away from it, see John B. Judis, *The Paradox of American Democracy* (New York: Pantheon Books, 2000).

[9] These debates came in many forms. See, for example, Alvin W. Gouldner, *The Future of Intellectuals and the Rise of the New Class* (New York: The Seabury Press, 1979); Ivan Illich, *Celebration of Awareness* (Garden City, N.Y.: Doubleday, 1970).

to fight for a particular vision of public policy, not simply inform policy debates with research. Moreover, in a pressure-filled environment, where the funders and supporters of think tanks want to see visibility as an immediate sign of success, think tanks feel pressure to generate attention, which is most available when issues are about to be decided. When issues are under final deliberation, they can draw the attention of most policy makers – as well as journalists, who might feature and publicize think tank work. The attention the work receives at these moments serves an organizational maintenance role for think tanks. The attention validates the investments patrons make in a think tank's work. The new generation of think tank patrons – corporations, individuals, and ideological foundations – likes to see think tanks mentioned in the news; it represents a return on their investment. So the visibility that commentary generates can play a worthwhile role for think tanks. As Jeff Faux, founder and president of the Economic Policy Institute, observes, "In order to have a presence – and therefore to continue to affect the policy process with ideas – you need to be relevant and visible. So we do spend time trying to affect and provide information that illuminates the current debate over legislation."[10]

But as Faux and others readily acknowledge, think tank commentary in these moments most often serves as ammunition for policy makers who need public justification for their already preferred policy choices. This form of media-friendly research is not the most substantively useful product that think tanks can produce. Rather, specific estimates of the financial costs of new initiatives or the program benefits of legislation are much more often substantively influential during the final stages of policy debates. The cost estimates that the Congressional Budget Office produces about new legislation routinely lead to the successful amending of legislation or the thwarting of policy change altogether. The CBO has an advantage insofar as its estimates are binding on members of Congress; that is, within the constraints of the congressional budget process, members of Congress must treat CBO estimates as accurate. But specific estimates produced by think tanks and other experts based outside of government can be substantively influential as well. Brookings Institution estimates of the costs and benefits of an expanded child tax credit were helpful to Senator Olympia Snowe (R.-Maine) late in the debate over the tax cut. She used the estimates to finalize the substantive dimensions of her proposed child tax credit and to illuminate the effects of the expanded credit

---

[10] Author interview with Jeff Faux, Economic Policy Institute, 18 July 1996.

for her Senate Finance Committee colleagues. Likewise, micro-simulated estimates of health care proposals produced by the consulting firm Lewin-VHI during the health care reform debate proved valuable for its clients who could win substantive changes in various proposals based on Lewin's estimates of their costs and consequences.

Estimates are frequently of greater substantive value than commentary late in policy debates. But estimates are less often produced by think tanks. They are seldom produced because estimates are expensive and time consuming to generate and because their results can be unpredictable. These are all significant disincentives for think tanks to make them the focus of their attention.

The Brookings Institution was capable of producing estimates of the child tax credit during the final stages of the tax cut debate only because Isabel Sawhill and Adam Thomas, the scholars working on the subject there, had spent the previous year developing a computer model and gathering data that would permit it. Their preparation of the model and data was for a larger project, and it turned out to be fortunate for Sawhill and Thomas that they had the model in place when the estimates could be helpful. Developing the model on short notice would have been nearly impossible.

During the health care reform debate, congressional committee staff complained that too few organizations were equipped to provide micro-simulations of the projected effects of different health care reform plans. Lewin-VHI was one of the few that could, but it had taken Lewin a decade to develop its micro-simulation capacity. With little lead time, most think tanks and other organizations could not produce the types of models necessary to estimate the effects of health care plans accurately. Moreover, few of the organizations had the resources to devote to the task. If it takes years – and substantial staff time – to develop computer models and data sources in order to produce reliable estimates, the cost of the endeavor is prohibitive for most think tanks, especially those most reliant on the new sources of patronage. Corporations, individuals, and small ideological foundations have little interest in waiting years to see a return on their investment.[11]

---

[11] On this point, James Piereson, executive director of the conservative John M. Olin Foundation, observes about the foundation's mission, "I think our role has been to promote ideas. The tax laws don't permit you to lobby or anything like that. So what we try to do is to get behind some people or some institutions that can have some influence in promoting a set of ideas." Author interview with James Piereson, John M. Olin Foundation, 2 February 1999. That description is quite different from the goals of some of the first

Producing estimates is additionally desirable for many think tanks because estimates are unpredictable. Computer models can produce unwanted results. If your interest as a think tank leader is in making the case for or against proposed policy changes, computing complex estimates of pending legislation might not be your preferred strategy. If results do not turn out as you had hoped, you are faced with the problem of choosing among thorny options. You can release the results and thereby damage the chances that your preferred policy change will occur; you can change the computer model, manipulate the data, and re-run the analysis to produce different results. Or you can withhold the estimates altogether. These are costly options, some of which carry potential damage to your reputation. If an organization has the option instead of producing inexpensive, reliable, and highly marketable commentary, its leaders might make that choice every time.

Think tanks and policy experts generally can also produce research intended for other points in the policy process, especially the early stages of an issue's development. Research that explores the foundational features of a growing problem and possibilities for addressing it with public policy can create a substantive context for future policy change. This issues and options research can accumulate over time in a policy area to convince decision makers of a preferred course of action. The accumulation of issues and options research by economists in the 1960s and 1970s is credited with creating conditions for airline and trucking deregulation in the late 1970s and 1980s.[12] Another body of research going back to the 1970s is noted for making the case for privatizing Social Security, which has generated enthusiasm for such schemes in Congress in recent years.[13] This work does not have an immediate effect on policy debates, but it can play a critical and substantive role in the long run.

foundations that invested in think tanks. Interestingly, however, even the Ford Foundation, which was one of these first supporters when the goal of support was to produce ostensibly neutral analysis, has become anxious to see a return on its support, both in terms of content and visibility of think tank products. As Michael Lipsky, a Ford Foundation program officer, puts it, "The Ford Foundation is a values-based, values-driven organization. It's not likely to support on a regular basis – on an institutional level – an organization whose policy commitments are more difficult to discern." Author interview with Michael Lipsky, Ford Foundation, 2 February 1999.

[12] Martha Derthick and Paul J. Quirk, *The Politics of Deregulation* (Washington, D.C.: The Brookings Institution, 1985).

[13] Steven M. Teles, "The Dialectics of Trust: Ideas, Finance, and Pensions Privatization in the U.S. and U.K." Paper presented at the Conference on the Varieties of Welfare Capitalism in Europe, North America, and Japan, Max Planck Institute, Cologne, Germany, 11–13 June 1998.

Experts can have a meaningful impact on how new problems are defined. Rochefort and Cobb point out that problem definition involves a process that includes constructing a causal story about the nature of a new dilemma – its severity, incidence, novelty, and proximity to those attentive to it.[14] The story created around any given issue can take many directions. Policy makers ultimately seek to manipulate the story to suit their political goals. But experts offer early guidance on the dimensions of new problems, often laying the substantive foundations for how new stories evolve into the subjects of issue debates.

In both the case of transportation deregulation and that of Social Security privatization, issues and options research was transformed into concrete proposals by think tanks. In relation to transportation deregulation, proposals came from the American Enterprise Institute and the Brookings Institution, which in a series of conferences and papers in the 1970s and early 1980s laid out details of what might be involved in deregulating the airline and trucking industries. With Social Security reform, the Cato Institute has been an ever-present voice for specific privatization schemes. Proposals that reach interested policy makers as they prepare action on an issue can provide substantive help to them. In some instances, well-substantiated proposals can cajole policy makers to take action that they would not take otherwise.

The point here is that estimates, issues and options research, and proposals can all play a more substantive role in policy making than can commentary. Yet commentary is all too often – and increasingly – the product of think tanks. Commentary is never the only product of any think tank; think tanks are all typically involved in producing some variety of all four types of research. Even the most ideological and even the most marketing-oriented among them produce some research intended to generate interest in and inform the debate over new issues.[15] But far more effort is devoted by think tanks, especially some think tanks (and increasingly many think tanks), to producing and marketing commentary than used to be the case. And these efforts do not yield the substantive influence that other work by think tanks can, when it is successful. Even when commentary is well timed, well tailored, and well received by policy makers, the role it plays is typically nonsubstantive, and the role of the

---

[14] See David A. Rochefort and Roger W. Cobb, *The Politics of Problem Definition: Shaping the Policy Agenda* (Lawrence: University Press of Kansas, 1994), pp. 15–27.

[15] The Cato Institute's twenty-year effort to popularize the idea of Social Security privatization is an example. The Heritage Foundation's efforts to build support for a Missile Defense System is another.

researcher at this point is nonsubstantive as well. The research and the researcher are providing cover and justification for the views of already supportive policy makers.

Moreover, commentary from think tanks, even when it is well packaged, well marketed, and well received, serves as little match for the commentary and contributions of interest groups and others who are heavily invested in the outcomes of legislative debates. When think tanks become involved in producing commentary, they abandon the most distinctive niche for experts in the policy process, the point in the process when the contributions of researchers are least contested by other types of actors. Instead, in efforts to attract attention for work that at best serves little substantive role anyway, think tanks compete with the scores of non-expert actors involved in policy debates, especially interest groups and lobbyists, that almost invariably have more resources and power than they do. In the competition between interest groups and think tanks to make views influential at latter stages of policy debates, interest groups almost always win out. As a result of the efforts of so many think tanks to make producing commentary a high priority, think tanks have not achieved the substantive influence in U.S. policy making that their increased numbers might suggest they could. As Henry Aaron, a longtime economist at the Brookings Institution, observes of the change, "On any given subject that is important or at all controversial, the lay reader is routinely confronted with experts saying conflicting things. And therefore, the reader is at a loss. And it tends to undercut the capacity of any of the studies to have a major influence on policy. People wield their social science research studies like short swords and shields in the ideological wars."[16] The consequence is that at precisely the moment when think tanks and experts generally have become politically active enough to warrant new scholarly attention, the nature of their activity often undermines their influence.

---

[16] Author interview with Henry Aaron, Brookings Institution, 11 February 1999. Herb Berkowitz, Vice President for Communications at the Heritage Foundation, acknowledged a similar limitation to the influence of think tanks as a result of the ideological orientation of groups like Heritage. Speaking of Heritage, he notes, "I think it probably hurts us sometimes on the Hill [that we are known to be conservative] because there are fewer truly open-minded individuals on Capitol Hill than I think the American people would like to think there are. And I think that unfortunately, we publish a lot of work that an open-minded, fair-minded, moderate or liberal member of Congress would probably agree with, but they probably don't look at it very carefully because it comes from the 'conservative' Heritage Foundation." Author interview with Herb Berkowitz, Heritage Foundation, 22 July 1996.

The Reputation of Experts

The focus by think tanks on producing commentary has had another consequence: It has damaged the collective reputation of think tanks and policy experts generally among some policymaking audiences. At the beginning of the twenty-first century, research is frequently evaluated more in terms of its ideological content and accessibility to audiences than by the quality of its content. In interviews with longtime congressional staff, many of the best known think tanks were assessed only in terms of their ideological and marketing proclivities.[17] The appeal of each and its predicted or reported influence were infrequently dictated by methods of research, which were hardly acknowledged, or the replicability of results. Rather, the Heritage Foundation was viewed as consistently helpful to those who are most conservative, the American Enterprise Institute to less strident conservatives, and the Brookings Institution to moderates and liberals. Institutions and their experts are identified, assessed, and used according to their views rather than according to their capacities for rigor or accuracy.

Congressional staff and policy makers generally, particularly experienced policy makers, are capable of assessing the quality of research, but they appear to be more inclined to evaluate it in terms of its ideological content and accessibility. Its production as commentary heightens this inclination. The shorter formats of research reports and policy briefs that are composed of commentary rarely provide space for descriptions of the methodology or data-collection techniques used in research. Congressional staff and policy makers have little with which to judge much of this research, except whether it accords with their existing preferences.

By the end of the twentieth century, even those think tanks that, by their organization and mission, sought to maintain a balance or neutrality in their research were regularly perceived by policy makers and funders as ideologically aligned in some way. At the beginning of the

---

[17] Think tanks are often identified by their ideological predilections among academics as well, although individual researchers at some of the best-known think tanks are known for their work by academics as well. But as Leslie Lenkowsky, former president of the Hudson Institute, points out, "We are among the so-called conservative think tanks, probably among the least conservative and always have been. But nonetheless we constantly get labeled. It does affect you. It does affect what you can do. For example, one of my problems in Indiana [where Hudson is based] is attracting high-level staff to Hudson from universities." Author interview with Leslie Lenkowsky, Hudson Institute, 11 July 1996.

twenty-first century, experts and expertise generally are not imbued with the same promise nor held in near the regard that they were in the first decades of the previous century by those involved in lawmaking. The partisanship and ideological divisiveness that characterize much of the behavior of Congress and those in Washington, D.C., generally, carry over to the general environment for experts and expertise. Experts – and not just think tanks – have contributed to this environment. Joining the trend, in recent years many researchers, including academics, have begun producing commentary and deliberately marketing it in polemical terms in ideological venues. Kent Weaver observes of the 1996 welfare reform debate that scholars often chose to publish their ideas leading up to the debate in traditionally biased publications like the *American Prospect* and the *Public Interest*. He notes, "While these publications may have helped to diffuse knowledge about policy research more broadly, it is also possible that they had a less salutary effect: because many of these outlets had ideological images, researchers who published in them may have undercut their perceived legitimacy as objective scholars with policymakers on the other side of the growing welfare ideological divide."[18]

There is a real tradeoff for think tanks and experts generally in the developments of recent decades. By responding to a political environment in which ideology and marketing often override basic credibility as the criteria by which experts are judged, some think tanks contribute to lowering the standards for expertise. Experts at some, particularly newer, think tanks are less frequently scholars who produce original research, whether marketed or not, than previously was the case. Experts at many think tanks frequently have M.A.s or B.A.s rather than Ph.Ds. These are the organizations that focus primarily on producing commentary rather than on making their own original contributions of research. This change in staffing at some think tanks along with their tendency to value marketing commentary over doing original research has blurred the distinctions between experts and advocates. The participation in this trend by academics and other researchers only makes the problem worse. Beyond fulfilling a different, more aggressive, less detached role in policy making than that described by Kingdon and others in previous work, the attributes and conduct that have historically distinguished experts from advocates are disappearing. Experts act as advocates; advocates pass as experts. But

---

[18] R. Kent Weaver, "The Role of Policy Research in Welfare Debates, 1993–1996," Presented at Inequality Summer Institute 1999, 24 June 1999, p. 38.

in this environment, as Herbert Stein laments, "the role of experts is diminished."[19]

Expert-Saturated Politics and the Future of Think Tanks

There is no end in sight to the proliferation of think tanks. Particularly at the state level, where almost fifty new think tanks formed in the 1990s alone, the emergence of new organizations seems likely to continue. As the number of think tanks continues to grow, the trend toward specialization is likely to continue as well. The expert-saturated political environment and the preferences of funders give specialized think tanks an advantage. But the imbalance between conservative and liberal think tanks seems likely to diminish. In the 1990s, liberal ideology, joined by new centrist thinking, began to rebound from the depths of its unpopularity in the late 1970s and early 1980s. Building on this environment, more liberally oriented think tanks may have a better chance of emerging in greater numbers. The New America Foundation, formed in 1999, is one example. While expressly not liberal, it aims to develop ideas with appeal among "New Democrats" and to provide a home and base of support for "third way" – basically centrist – intellectuals in Washington, D.C. Lead writers from *The New Republic* were among its first fellows, and its initial support came from foundations and individuals that include Silicon Valley CEOs.[20] Also in 1999, Demos, a new progressive think tank, was formed in New York City, intent on bringing "everyone into the life of American democracy and [achieving] a broadly shared prosperity characterized by greater opportunity and less disparity." It emerged out of efforts by the Nathan Cummings Foundation, among others, and its size and stature was growing by 2003.

Two widely publicized reports funded by the Nathan Cummings Foundation and released by the National Committee for Responsive Philanthropy in 1997 and 1999 contributed to an environment in which these new organizations might succeed. The reports sought to shed light on the funding and organizational disparities between conservatives and

[19] Author interview with Herbert Stein, American Enterprise Institute, 24 September 1997.
[20] Richard Morin and Claudia Deane, "Dude, Let's Talk Policy," *The Washington Post*, 11 May 1999, p. A19. In 2002, the New America Foundation agreed to publish ten books a year about policy and current events with the commercial publisher Basic Books, an indication of its growing size and stature. Richard Morin and Claudia Deane, "Out of Silicon Valley and Looking Homeward," *The Washington Post*, 14 May 2002, p. A19.

liberals in the "marketplace of ideas."[21] Targeted at those who might provide patronage to more liberal-leaning think tanks, the reports ignited interest among potential benefactors in at least considering expanded support to liberal centers for ideas and experts.[22] Additional, even more heavily publicized treatises that documented – and expressed worries about – the power and strength of conservative think tanks published in the early 2000s fueled additional interest in a counter-effort among liberals.[23]

If liberals do begin to overcome their organizational and resource-based deficiencies, they will have to decide how marketing-oriented they want to be. Classifications of think tanks as marketing-oriented or non–marketing-oriented, while useful for the purposes of analysis, do not fully reveal the differences among those within each category of organization. The conservative Heritage Foundation set the standard for marketing by think tanks beginning in the 1970s, and many new think tanks have followed its model, expressly devoting resources to promotional efforts. In the Heritage formulation, marketing is more than a recognition by experts that they should themselves package and promote research for policy makers. It is an *organizational* commitment to support the promotion of research and ideas.[24]

---

[21] Sally Covington, *Moving a Public Policy Agenda: The Strategic Philanthropy of Conservative Foundations* (Washington, D.C.: National Committee for Responsive Philanthropy, 1997); Daniel Callahan, *$1 Billion for Ideas: Conservative Think Tanks in the 1990s* (Washington, D.C.: National Committee for Responsive Philanthropy, 1999). See also Jean Stefancic and Richard Delgado, *No Mercy: How Conservative Think Tanks and Foundations Changed America's Social Agenda* (Philadelphia: Temple University Press, 1996), for a similarly critical – but more academic – analysis produced during these years.

[22] After years of declining support, the Ford Foundation was, in fact, among those considering increasing its funding of think tanks.

[23] See David Brock, *Blinded by the Right* (New York: Crown Publishers, 2002), which refers to the activities of the Heritage Foundation, in particular, in his revealing account of life as a conservative writer. See also Trudy Lieberman, *Slanting the Story: The Forces That Shape the News* (New York: New Press, 2000).

[24] One of the most recent developments involves the formation of hybrid organizations that explicitly combine research and advocacy. Citizens for a Sound Economy (CSE) is an example. CSE combines a 501(c)3 research arm with a 501(c)4 advocacy apparatus. Another is the Family Research Council, a 501(c)4 organization formed by Gary Bauer in 1983. These groups are even more aggressively marketing-oriented than think tanks, but they are still perceived as think tanks by many in policymaking circles. Yet they rely not just on overt lobbying in Washington but also on substantial constituencies based around the country. In assessing why Citizens for a Sound Economy has influence in Washington, James Gattuso, a former staff member at CSE, observes, "A lot of it is the fact that if you have 250,000 people who are constituents of Congress [supporting the organization], they listen to that. You talk to the people who elect them, and that never fails to get their attention." Author interview with James Gattuso, Citizens for a Sound Economy, 30 April 1999.

As an organizational matter, liberal think tanks along with think tanks of centrist or no identifiable ideology have traditionally shown a greater reluctance to fully commit organizational resources to marketing. This resistance by liberal think tanks and think tanks of centrist or no identifiable ideology stems in part from the very ideologies that guide them. In interviews, some have suggested that, as an ideological matter, conservatives may be more comfortable than liberals with launching organizations that have a more corporate, as opposed to academic, structure, organizations that devote more resources and staff lines to communications and marketing.

Whatever the case, whether liberal think tanks become more marketing-oriented or whether they increase in number to rival conservative organizations, I question whether it matters as much for policy making as some activists believe. The premise of the worry among liberal activists in recent years – the ones writing books and reports railing against conservative think tanks – is that it matters how many think tanks exist because think tanks are substantively influential in American policy making; the disparity in organizational numbers must be overcome so that the important gap in think tank influence can be overcome as well. Activists have worried about the role of think tanks, while scholars of the policy process have ignored them.

But while think tanks are influential, they are not nearly so much as they could be, at least in their capacity as expert organizations. The bigger worry for liberals, conservatives, and scholars alike should be the trend for think tanks – and increasingly experts of all kinds – to produce research that is little more than polemical commentary. This work diminishes the potential for its producers to have substantive influence with policy makers. Even more, this work, especially in its most ideological and most aggressively marketed forms, damages the reputation of experts generally among policy makers. The distinction between experts and advocates is tenuous. As we head into the future, the weakness of that distinction presents a fundamental challenge for think tanks, experts, and those who rely on them. The weakness threatens the quality of policy produced; for if trusted research and analysis is not available, what becomes the foundation for informed policy decisions? The alternatives – money, interests, lobbyists – are worrisome. This is precisely what troubled scholars like Merriam and Lasswell. We have moved further away from the world that they advocated.

Appendix A

Details on the Characteristics, Perceptions, and Visibility of Think Tanks

This appendix provides additional information on the methodology used in calculating the number of think tanks active in American policy making by the mid-1990s, as well as details about the characteristics, perceptions, and visibility of think tanks.

Counting Think Tanks

My estimate of the number of think tanks operating in American politics in the 1990s, as reported in Chapter 1, is based on an examination of a variety of sources and background materials. I draw on references from directories, books, and scholarly articles about think tanks as well as newspaper and magazine clippings to arrive at a count of 306 organizations. The single most comprehensive source of think tank listings, and the one upon which I depend most, is Hellebust's *Think Tank Directory.*[1] In sorting through Hellebust's entries, I excluded from my database organizations that are not independent or not oriented toward affecting public policy debates. After I narrowed Hellebust's list of organizations, 302 institutions qualified as think tanks according to my definition. I included an additional four think tanks in the database based on references made in a variety of other sources. The four organizations added were Campaign for America's Future, a liberal/progressive think tank founded in 1996; Institute for Energy Research, a conservative, Texas-based think tank founded in 1989; Institute for Gay and Lesbian Strategic Studies, a

---

[1] Lynn Hellebust, ed., *Think Tank Directory: A Guide to Nonprofit Public Policy Research Organizations* (Topeka, Kans.: Government Research Service, 1996).

scholarly, liberal-oriented research organization started in 1994; and, the German Marshall Fund, a research and grantmaking institution founded in 1972. The first three may have been overlooked by Hellebust because they are new and relatively small. The German Marshall Fund may have been considered a foundation rather than a think tank by Hellebust. Whatever the case, the German Marshall Fund qualifies as a think tank by my definition.[2] References from all of the sources consulted combine to create a record of 306 independent, public policy–oriented think tanks operating in American politics in 1996.

Relying on only one source – *The Think Tank Directory*, in most cases – may seem risky as a method for creating a count of think tanks (even if each reference is substantiated by cross-checking annual reports and mission statements). Figure A-1 re-creates Figure 1-1 with a lower line that illustrates the pattern for only those think tanks that are cited in at least two references. Whereas my sources combine to reveal 306 organizations cited at least *once*, only 125 of these think tanks are cited by at least *two* sources. The cross-checking of think tank citations with mission statements and annual reports provides good reason to be confident in the larger count of 306 organizations, and I depend on this full database in the book. Nonetheless, it is interesting to note that even after limiting the database to the smaller group of double-cited organizations, the pattern of emergence of think tanks is the same, with the bulk of think tanks operating in the 1990s founded in the past three decades.

As an explanation of the lower count, it is worth noting that many of the supplementary sources that I consulted were published in the early 1990s; therefore, they exclude organizations founded during that decade. This may account for the flattening slope of the lower line in Figure A-1

---

[2] The fact that I added only four organizations is actually a testament to the comprehensiveness of Hellebust's directory. The other sources consulted include Robert L. Hollings, *Nonprofit Public Policy Research Organizations: A Sourcebook on Think Tanks in Government* (New York: Garland Publishers, 1993); Eleanor Evans Kitfield, *The Capitol Source* (Washington, D.C.: National Journal, 1995); James G. McGann, *The Competition for Dollars, Scholars and Influence in the Public Policy Research Industry* (New York: University Press of America, 1995); Joseph G. Peschek, *Policy-Planning Organizations: Elite Agendas and America's Rightward Turn* (Philadelphia: Temple University Press, 1987); James A. Smith, *The Idea Brokers* (New York: The Free Press, 1991); Diane Stone, *Capturing the Political Imagination: Think Tanks and the Policy Process* (Portland, Ore.: Frank Carr, 1996); Donald E. Abelson, "From Policy Research to Political Advocacy: The Changing Role of Think Tanks in American Politics," *Canadian Review of American Studies* 25 (1996): 93–126; and, Laura Brown Chisolm, "Sinking the Think Tanks Upstream: The Use and Misuse of Tax Exemption Law to Address the Use and Misuse of Tax-exempt Organizations by Politicians," *University of Pittsburgh Law Review* 1990.

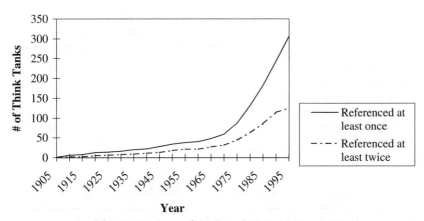

FIGURE A-1. Proliferation pattern of think tanks existing in 1990s

between 1990 and 1995. This may also help to account for the finding that fewer than half of the organizations in Hellebust are listed in other sources. The lack of double citation may also stem in part from the lack of attempt by these supplemental sources to compile a comprehensive list of think tanks. Many of the sources go no further than listing the forty or fifty most prominent think tanks.

Calculating Budget Resources

The 306 think tanks included in my study are categorized into six groups according to the size of their 1995 or 1996 budgets, those with budgets of (1) less than $250,000, (2) $250,001–$500,000, (3) $500,001–$1,000,000, (4) $1,000,001–$5,000,000, (5) $5,000,001–$10,000,000, (6) more than $10,000,000. Think tank budget information was compiled from an examination of the IRS form 990 for think tanks and from classifications made in Hellebust's *Think Tank Directory*. The distribution of state focused and nationally focused think tanks in these various budget categories is recorded in Table A-1. These data were presented in a more simplified form in Chapter 1.

Details on the Largest Think Tanks

In an effort to add organizational "faces" to all of the descriptive figures about the 306 think tanks, Table A-2 lists the 15 largest think tanks broken down by ideological clusters. Twelve of the 15 are in the centrist or "no

TABLE A-1. *State and nationally focused think tanks by budget size*

	State-focused	Nationally focused
Less than $250,000	41.5% (44)	15.0% (30)
$250,001–$500,000	31.1% (33)	17.5% (35)
$500,001–$1,000,000	14.2% (15)	20.0% (40)
$1,000,001–$5,000,000	10.3% (11)	31.5% (63)
$5,000,001–$10,000,000	2.8% (3)	6.0% (12)
More than $10,000,000	0.0% (0)	10.0% (20)

TABLE A-2. *Fifteen largest think tanks grouped by ideological cluster*

Liberal	Centrist / No Identifiable ideology	Conservative
	RAND Corporation ($115,156,938)	
	Population Council ($56,852,426)	
	Urban Institute ($37,550,453)	
		Heritage Foundation ($25,055,050)
	Aspen Institute ($19,000,000)	
	American Institute for Research ($18,450,655)	
	Brookings Institution ($17,269,872)	
	Council on Foreign Relations ($16,930,225)	
	Manpower Demonst Rsch Corp. ($15,879,576)	
		Hoover Institution ($15,477,000)
	Ctr. for Strategic and Int'l Studies ($14,687,697)	
	Urban Land Institute ($14,284,880)	
	Pacific Inst for Rsch and Eval ($13,799,290)	
		American Enterprise Institute ($12,633,796)
	Carnegie Endowment for Int'l Peace ($10,920,679)	

Source: FY 1995 total expenditures, gathered from IRS forms 990 and annual reports.

identifiable ideology" cluster. The other three are conservative. Table A-3 lists the 10 largest think tanks in each ideological cluster, indicating also their research scope, age, and location. All of the think tanks listed in Table A-3 are nationally focused organizations. None of the organizations in the liberal cluster have annual budgets over $6 million, and, whereas most of the top 10 organizations in the conservative and centrist or "no identifiably ideology" clusters are "full service," 9 of the 10 largest liberal think tanks have limited, specialized research agendas.

Methodology for Survey of Congressional Staff and Journalists

My reporting on the perceptions of think tanks among congressional staff and journalists in Chapter 3 comes from a telephone survey of 125 congressional staff and journalists that I conducted in the summer of 1997. The survey was conducted jointly with Burson-Marsteller between July 11, 1997, and September 26, 1997. While the survey spanned more than two months, the majority of surveys – 85 percent – were administered during the first three weeks of September. The survey includes responses from 71 congressional staff, split between committee and personal staff, Republicans and Democrats, and 54 Washington, D.C.–based journalists, split between journalists with national-circulation publications and those with regional papers from around the country. In terms of congressional staff respondents, the partisan makeup of those surveyed closely mirrors the partisan composition of the 105th Congress. Among both House and Senate respondents, 56 percent surveyed were Republicans and 44 percent Democrats. These proportions are within 3 percent of the partisan totals in each chamber (53 percent Republicans in the House, 55 percent Republicans in the Senate).

All congressional respondents were legislative staff; office managers, scheduling secretaries, and receptionists were not interviewed. Congressional staff included in the survey had legislative knowledge and responsibility in at least one of three policy areas: the environment, health care, or international trade. Interviews with personal legislative staff were with either administrative assistants/chiefs of staff, legislative directors, or legislative assistants. The last of these three categories made up the largest proportion of personal staff respondents. In terms of committee staff, we interviewed staff directors, staff economists, legal counsels, or professional staff with one of twelve committees: six in the House and six in the Senate. The committees were selected based on their jurisdiction

TABLE A-3. *Ten largest think tanks in each ideological cluster*

	1995 Budget	Year Founded	Location	Research scope
Centrist / No Identifiable Ideology Cluster				
RAND Corporation	$115,156,938	1946	Santa Monica, CA	defense, domestic, & int'l, mostly gov't contracts
Population Council	$56,852,426	1952	New York City	reproductive health, domestic & int'l
Urban Institute	$37,550,453	1968	Washington, D.C.	domestic & int'l, mostly gov't contracts
Aspen Institute	$19,000,000	1950	Washington, D.C.	domestic & int'l policy
American Institute for Research	$18,450,655	1946	Washington, D.C.	domestic, mostly gov't contracts
Brookings Institution	$17,269,872	1916	Washington, D.C.	economic, social, political, and int'l policy
Council on Foreign Relations	$16,930,225	1921	New York City	foreign policy and int'l relations
Manpower Demonstration Research Corporation	$15,879,576	1974	New York City	domestic, nat'l and local, mostly gov't contracts
Center for Strategic and International Studies	$14,687,697	1962	Washington, D.C.	foreign policy and int'l relations
Urban Land Institute	$14,284,880	1936	Washington, D.C.	land use & development
Conservative Cluster				
Heritage Foundation	$25,055,050	1973	Washington, D.C.	economic, social, political, and int'l policy
Hoover Institution	$15,477,000	1919	Stanford, CA	economic, social, and int'l policy
American Enterprise Institute	$12,633,796	1943	Washington, D.C.	economic, social, political, and int'l policy
Hudson Institute	$9,312,850	1961	Indianapolis, IN	economic, social, political, and int'l policy
Free Congress Foundation	$7,707,180	1977	Washington, D.C.	domestic social and political policy

Name	Amount	Year	Location	Focus
Cato Institute	$7,077,749	1977	Washington, D.C.	economic, social, political, and int'l policy
American Legislative Exchange Council	$4,612,074	1973	Washington, D.C.	state policy
Rutherford Institute	$4,357,098	1982	Charlottesville, VA	civil liberties litigation and research
Reason Foundation	$3,416,412	1978	Los Angeles, CA	domestic economic and social policy
National Center for Policy Analysis	$3,029,444	1983	Dallas, TX	economic, social, and int'l policy
Liberal Cluster				
Joint Center for Political and Economic Studies	$5,781,687	1970	Washington, D.C.	economic & social policy, particularly affecting blacks
Center on Budget and Policy Priorities	$4,196,225	1981	Washington, D.C.	domestic policy, particularly on lower-income Americans
Economic Policy Institute	$2,808,030	1986	Washington, D.C.	domestic economic & social policy
Center for Reproductive Law and Policy	$2,782,686	1992	New York City	reproductive rights and health, domestic & int'l
International Center for Research on Women	$2,631,827	1976	Washington, D.C.	int'l health & environmental policy affecting women
Rocky Mountain Institute	$2,252,198	1982	Snowmass, CO	energy and environmental policy
Center for Policy Alternatives	$2,083,385	1975	Washington, D.C.	state policy
Worldwatch Institute	$2,070,926	1974	Washington, D.C.	environmental policy
Inform, Inc.	$1,796,156	1974	New York City	energy and environmental policy
Center for Defense Information	$1,629,387	1972	Washington, D.C.	defense policy

over environmental, health care, or international trade issues. For the House, these committees included Appropriations, Budget, Commerce, International Relations, Resources, and Ways and Means. For the Senate, these included Appropriations, Banking, Budget, Environment and Public Works, Finance, and Labor and Human Resources.

Two-thirds (thirty-six interviewees) of the journalists interviewed were bureau chiefs or political or congressional reporters for local and regional newspapers. One-third (eighteen interviewees) were reporters with what I call "elite publications." Elite publications have in common a high circulation among decision makers and their staff on Capitol Hill. The specific publications from which elite publication respondents were drawn fall into four categories (1) newspapers (*Christian Science Monitor, Los Angeles Times, New York Times, Wall Street Journal, Washington Post, Washington Times, USA Today*), (2) national magazines (*BusinessWeek, Newsweek, Time, U.S. News & World Report*), (3) Washington, D.C.–focused publications (*Congressional Quarterly Weekly Report, National Journal, Roll Call*), and (4) wire services (Associated Press, Reuters, United Press International). Respondents from the elite publications included bureau chiefs, congressional correspondents, political correspondents, columnists, and, in a few instances, specific policy reporters (e.g., health care correspondents).

Among those with whom contact was made, surveys were successfully completed with 58 percent of the congressional staff and 69 percent of the journalists. Names and phone numbers of interviewees for both the congressional and journalist samples were randomly drawn within stratified sample groups from the summer 1997 editions of the *Congressional Yellow Book* and the *Media Yellow Book* (Washington, D.C.: Washington Monitor, 1997).

Two versions of the survey were administered with matching lists of think tanks to ease combining results for analysis. Three questions in the survey asked respondents to evaluate a list of specific think tanks in relation to their influence, credibility, and ideologies. In order to collect data for twenty-seven think tanks – too many organizations to ask about with each respondent – we split the sample, varying the survey only in terms of which think tanks were included in these four particular questions. Two different versions of the survey were administered. In each version of the survey, respondents were asked to evaluate nineteen organizations on 1–5 scales in relation to their influence, credibility, and ideologies. The two versions of the survey were administered on a rotating basis.

Seven of the think tanks were included in both versions of the survey – the American Enterprise Institute, the Brookings Institution, the Cato Institute, the Economic Policy Institute, the Heritage Foundation, the Hudson Institute, and the RAND Corporation. In order to examine the rankings of each of the twenty-seven think tanks in relation to the others, I took the mean of each respondent's rating of the seven think tanks in common to both versions of the survey and calculated how ratings for each organization deviated from this mean. This process standardizes the ratings from the 1–5 scale. Aside from the questions in which specific think tanks were scaled and ranked, questions on the two surveys were identical.

Results from Survey of Congressional Staff and Journalists

As part of the survey, respondents were asked to rate the influence of twenty-seven think tanks in terms of their influence "on policymaking in Washington." These results are described in Chapter 3. Results on the ratings for all twenty-seven think tanks for all respondents are provided in Table A-4. Results are translated from the 1–5 scales used by respondents into deviations above and below the mean scaling of the seven organizations common to both versions of the survey. The deviation scores range from 0.59 to –1.12. The Heritage Foundation has the highest mean "influence score." The Brookings Institution rates second, followed by the Cato Institute and the American Enterprise Institute.

Interestingly, the relative influence of various organizations was perceived differently by different groups of respondents. The Heritage Foundation scores highest among Republican congressional staff and journalists. The Brookings Institution scores higher than Heritage among Democratic congressional staff. Besides Heritage and Brookings, the ranking of other think tanks varies substantially as well from one group of respondents to another. Table A-5 captures these differences by respondent groups, with listings of the top four think tanks rated as influential by each respondent group.

The specific think tanks included in the survey were selected to represent the diversity in the full count of 200 nationally focused think tanks operating in 1996 in relation to ideology, although identifiably conservative and liberal organizations are somewhat overrepresented in the group. The specific institutions included were hand-picked to include most of the largest and best-known institutions. I was constrained in selecting them by the preferences of Burson Marsteller, the public relations firm that

TABLE A-4. *Think Tank Influence Scores in 1997*

Think Tank	Ideology Cluster	Score	% n
Heritage Foundation	Conservative	0.59	92%
Brookings Institution	No Ident/Centrist	0.37	91%
American Enterprise Institute	Conservative	0.16	88%
Cato Institute	Conservative	−0.04	92%
Ctr on Budget and Policy Priorities	Liberal	−0.12	81%
RAND Corporation	No Ident/Centrist	−0.24	81%
Ctr for Strategic & Int'l Studies	No Ident/Centrist	−0.26	72%
Progressive Policy Institute	No Ident/Centrist	−0.36	78%
Economic Policy Institute	Liberal	−0.42	68%
Hoover Institution	Conservative	−0.42	81%
Urban Institute	No Ident/Centrist	−0.48	83%
Council on Foreign Relations	No Ident/Centrist	−0.54	67%
Center for National Policy	Liberal	−0.60	57%
Nat'l Bureau of Econ Research	No Ident/Centrist	−0.64	54%
Hudson Institute	Conservative	−0.65	78%
Institute for Int'l Economics	No Ident/Centrist	−0.65	48%
Carnegie Endowment for Int'l Peace	No Ident/Centrist	−0.67	73%
Reason Foundation	Conservative	−0.77	40%
Competitive Enterprise Institute	Conservative	−0.78	52%
Resources for the Future	No Ident/Centrist	−0.81	38%
Joint Ctr for Political & Econ Studies	Liberal	−0.86	51%
Manhattan Institute	Conservative	−0.89	53%
Worldwatch Institute	Liberal	−0.93	53%
Institute for Policy Studies	Liberal	−0.98	60%
Economic Strategy Institute	No Ident/Centrist	−1.02	43%
World Resources Institute	Liberal	−1.09	35%
Progress & Freedom Foundation	Conservative	−1.12	56%

paid for the survey. They had a particular interest in including certain organizations – particularly larger and ideological organizations – in the survey. Even accounting for their preferences, however, there was a rough ideological balance in the final group of organizations. The selection of well-known institutions made some sense in the end; even among the "well-known" organizations, there were many institutions with which a great number of respondents were simply not familiar. Because the twenty-seven think tanks were not randomly selected, I do not aggregate or generalize from ratings of them. The results are nevertheless interesting in relation to the specific organizations – given that they are most of the largest and best-known think tanks, and the findings are similar to additional results reported in other portions of the book.

TABLE A-5. *Top Four Think Tanks Rated for Influence in 1997 by Respondent Group*

Republican Congressional Staff	Democratic Congressional Staff
1. Heritage Foundation (C)	1. Brookings Institution (NI)
2. Cato Institute(C)	2. Heritage Foundation (C)
3. American Enterprise Institute (C)	3. American Enterprise Institute (C)
4. Brookings Institution (NI)	4. Progressive Policy Institute (NI)

Journalists with Elite Publications	Journalists with Local Papers
1. Heritage Foundation (C)	1. Heritage Foundation (C)
2. Brookings Institution (NI)	2. Brookings Institution (NI)
3. Center on Budget and Policy Priorities (L)	3. American Enterprise Institute (C)
4. Cato Institute (C)	4. Center on Budget and Policy Priorities (L)

(C) – Conservative cluster think tank
(L) – Liberal cluster think tank
(NI) – Centrist or No Identifiable Ideology cluster think tank

Response rates for each think tank vary considerably. The relative perceptions of each think tank were likely affected by each organization's size and the scope of its research program. Some are better known than others because they produce work in a broader range of issue areas and because they are bigger. The Heritage Foundation and the Brookings Institution are both large organizations, with fiscal year 1996 budgets of $28.7 million and $21.9 million, respectively. Each organization is "full-service," with a broad range of research interests. A more specialized think tank, like the Worldwatch Institute, for example, which specializes in environmental issues, is unlikely to be rated as having as great influence overall by journalists and congressional staff unfamiliar with its area of research – but it doesn't seek as high an overall level of influence either. These cautionary notes suggest the limits within which these results should be understood. The percentage of respondents who provide a rating for each think tanks is recorded in Table A-4.

Coding for the Analysis of Media and Congressional Visibility

The analysis of the media and congressional visibility of think tanks in Chapter 3 required coding the sixty-six think tanks considered in the study for their marketing strategies and ideologies. Dummy variables were created to account for think tank marketing strategies (marketing-oriented think tanks are coded "1"; non–marketing-oriented think tanks are coded "0") and for think tank ideology (think tanks fitting into clusters as conservative and liberal, with organizations of no identifiable ideology as the excluded case). There is also a dummy variable for contract research think tanks. One important note: The variables representing think tanks of different marketing strategies and those representing their different ideologies are relatively uncorrelated with one another. The correlation coefficients range from 0.125 (between the conservative and marketing-oriented think tank variables) to 0.465 (between the liberal and marketing-oriented think tank variables).

I also use a dummy variable to detect the effects of organizational location on think tank visibility, coded "1" for organizations with a Washington, D.C., headquarters and "0" for organizations based elsewhere, and a dummy variable to detect differences in use based on age, coded "1" for think tanks founded after 1970 and "0" for think tanks founded in 1970 or before.[31] I coded age as a dummy variable for pre- and post-1970 think tanks because 1970 was roughly the breaking point after which new think tanks were founded at such a rapid pace. All equations were run with age coded as simply the number of years organizations had been in existence and as a dummy variable with the breaking point as the median age of think tanks in the sample, rather than 1970. The results are the same for all measures of age. The pre- and post-1970 variable used in the final analysis seems the most substantively defensible as when age differences might be most likely to be detected.

I also include a variable for think tank research scope, coded "1" for "full-service" think tanks (that perform research in numerous policy domains) and "0" for organizations focused on only one or a few policy areas. As described in Chapter 3, there are corresponding budget interaction terms for each of these variables.

Appendix B

List of In-Depth Interviews

What follows is a list of the 135 people with whom I conducted in-depth interviews. Interviews ranged in length from one half hour to three hours. The typical interview was between one and one-and-a-half hours. In most cases, the affiliation listed is the one that the interviewee had at the time of the interview. Most of the interviews were conducted in person. Several were conducted by telephone. Interviews were conducted between May 1996 and July 2003.

Interviewee	Title	Affiliation
Henry Aaron	senior fellow	Brookings Institution
Mike Adams	*Perspectives* editor	*Baltimore Sun*
George Akerlof	senior fellow	Brookings Institution
Doug Badger	health care aide	Senator Don Nickles (R.-Oklahoma)
Herb Berkowitz	vice president for public relations	Heritage Foundation
John Berry	business correspondent	*Washington Post*
Linda Bilheimer	health care analyst	Congressional Budget Office
Bill Bixby	executive director	Concord Coalition
Bob Blau	vice president for federal affairs	Bell South
Rick Boucher	Member of Congress	House of Representatives
Karlyn Bowman	resident fellow	American Enterprise Institute
Art Brodsky	correspondent	*Communications Daily*

(continued)

(continued)

Interviewee	Title	Affiliation
Gretchen Brown	health care aide	Senator Bob Kerrey (D.-Nebraska)
Richard Brown	professor	UCLA
Sheila Burke	chief of staff	Senator Bob Dole (R.-Kansas)
Daniel Callahan	founder	Hastings Center
David Callahan	research director	Demos
Dan Carney	correspondent	*Congressional Quarterly*
John Cerisano	health care aide	Senator Phil Gramm (R.-Texas)
Mark Cooper	research director	Consumer Federation of America
Robert Crandall	senior fellow	Brookings Institution
Edward Crane	president	Cato Institute
William Custer	research director	Employee Benefit Research Institute
Alan Daley	director of industrial relations	Bell Atlantic
Michele Davis	communications director	Citizens for a Sound Economy
William Dickens	senior fellow	Brookings Institution
Tom Duesterberg	vice president	Hudson Institute
Jeff Eisenach	president	Progress and Freedom Foundation
Paul Ellwood	director	Interstudy–Jackson Hole Group
Lynn Etheredge	consultant	Jackson Hole Group
Jeff Faux	president	Economic Policy Institute
Judy Feder	director of health care policy	Clinton presidential transition
Christine Ferguson	health care aide	Senator John Chafee (R.-Rhode Island)
Edwin Feulner	president	Heritage Foundation
Richard Fink	president	Koch Family Foundations
Joel Fleishman	executive director	Atlantic Philanthropic
Beth Fuchs	health care researcher	Congressional Research Service
Harold Furchtgott-Roth	senior economist	House Commerce Committee (R)
William Gale	senior fellow	Brookings Institution
James Gattuso	analyst	Citizens for a Sound Economy
Henry Geller	associate	Media Access Project
John Goodman	president	Nat'l Center for Policy Analysis
William Gorham	president	Urban Institute
Bill Gradison	president	Health Insurance Association of America

Interviewee	Title	Affiliation
Robert Greenstein	executive director	Center on Budget and Policy Priorities
Ted Greenwood	program officer	Sloan Foundation
Richard Haass	director, foreign policy studies	Brookings Institution
Hance Haney	telecommunications aide	Senator Bob Packwood (R.-Oregon)
Heidi Hartmann	president	Institute for Women's Policy Research
Thomas Hazlett	visiting scholar	American Enterprise Institute
Robert Helms	resident fellow	American Enterprise Institute
Link Hoewing	vice president for federal affairs	Bell Atlantic
Reed Hundt	former chairman	Federal Communications Commission
Louis Jacobson	correspondent	*National Journal*
Julie James	health care aide	Senator Bob Packwood (R.-Oregon)
Herbert Kaufman	senior fellow emeritus	Brookings Institution
David Kendall	health care aide	Rep. Mike Andrews (D.-Texas)
George Keyworth	chairman	Progress and Freedom Foundation
Katie King	telecommunications counsel	Senate Commerce Committee (R)
Ed Kutler	assistant to the Speaker	Rep. Newt Gingrich (R.-Georgia)
Michael Laracy	program officer	The Annie E. Casey Foundation
Iris Lav	deputy director	Center on Budget and Policy Priorities
Tex Lazar	executive director	Empower America
David Leach	telecommunications counsel	House Commerce Committee (D)
Leslie Lenkowsky	president	Hudson Institute
Michael Lipsky	program officer	Ford Foundation
Robert Litan	director of economic studies	Brookings Institution
Bruce MacLaury	former president	Brookings Institution
Richard Magat	former officer	Ford Foundation
Will Marshall	president	Progressive Policy Institute
Chris McLean	telecommunications aide	Senator James Exon (D.-Nebraska)

(continued)

(continued)

Interviewee	Title	Affiliation
Donald McClellan	telecommunications counsel	Senate Commerce Committee (R)
Beverly McKittrick	analyst and lobbyist	Citizens for a Sound Economy
Brian McManus	lobbyist	Golden Rule Insurance Company
Mike McNamee	correspondent	*Business Week*
David Miller	program officer	Nathan Cummings Foundation
Robert Moffit	resident fellow	Heritage Foundation
Marilyn Moon	senior fellow	Urban Institute
David Moore	telecommunications analyst	Congressional Budget Office
Bailey Morris-Eck	vice president for communications	Brookings Institution
Robert Morrison	senior director	Family Research Council
Charles Murray	resident scholar	American Enterprise Institute
Bill Myers	senior associate	Progress and Freedom Foundation
Richard Nathan	director	Rockefeller Institute
Tricia Neuman	health care analyst	House Ways & Means Committee (D)
David Nexon	health care analyst	Senate Labor Committee (D)
Len Nichols	health care analyst	Office of Management and Budget
Cathy Nolan	telecommunications counsel	House Commerce Committee (R)
Erik Olbeter	telecommunications analyst	Economic Strategy Institute
Norman Ornstein	resident scholar	American Enterprise Institute
Mark Pauly	professor	University of Pennsylvania
Robert Pear	correspondent	*New York Times*
James Piereson	executive director	John Olin Foundation
Peter Pitsch	consultant	Hudson/Progress & Freedom Fund
Ron Pollack	executive director	Families USA
Kathy Porter	research director	Center on Budget and Policy Priorities
Dana Priest	correspondent	*Washington Post*
Edie Rasell	fellow	Economic Policy Institute
Robert Rector	Senior Research Fellow	Heritage Foundation
Michael Regan	telecommunications counsel	House Commerce Committee (R)

Interviewee	Title	Affiliation
Robert Reischauer	director	Congressional Budget Office
Ken Robinson	consultant	Bell South
Marshall Robinson	former vice president	Ford Foundation
Jeremy Rosner	fellow	Progressive Policy Institute
John Rother	director of legislative affairs	AARP
Dallas Salisbury	president	Employee Benefit Research Institute
Isabel Sawhill	senior fellow	Brookings Institution
Max Sawicky	economist	Economic Policy Institute
William Scanlon	administrator	General Accounting Office
Andy Schwartzman	executive director	Media Access Project
Ellen Shaffer	health care aide	Senator Paul Wellstone (D.-Minnesota)
John Shiels	health care analyst	The Lewin Group
Michael Shuman	co-director	Institute for Policy Studies
Greg Simon	domestic policy advisor	Vice President Al Gore
Solveig Singleton	director of information studies	Cato Institute
Barbara Smith	health care aide	Rep. Jim McDermott (D.-Washington)
Sharon Soderstrom	legislative director	Senator Dan Coats (R.-Indiana)
Herbert Stein	resident scholar	American Enterprise Institute
Gilbert Steiner	senior fellow emeritus	Brookings Institution
Eugene Steurle	senior fellow	Urban Institute
Jack Strayer	chief lobbyist	Council for Affordable Health Insurance
David Super	general counsel	Center on Budget and Policy Priorities
Mike Tanner	director, health and welfare studies	Cato Institute
Adam Thierer	fellow	Heritage Foundation
Osceola Thomas	vice president for federal affairs	AT&T
Gerard Waldron	telecommunications aide	Rep. Edward Markey (D.-Massachusetts)
Kathleen Wallman	advisor	White House Counsel's Office
Joseph White	fellow	Brookings Institution
Josh Wiener	senior fellow	Brookings Institution

(continued)

(continued)

Interviewee	Title	Affiliation
Chris Williams	health care aide	Senator George Mitchell (D.-Maine)
David Wilson	telecommunications aide	Senator Bob Dole (R.-Kansas)
John Windhausen	telecommunications counsel	Senate Commerce Committee (D)
Susan Woodward	senior fellow	Brookings Institution
Bernie Wunder	attorney	Wunder, Diefenderfer
Walter Zelman	deputy insurance commissioner	State of California

Works Cited

Aaron, Henry. *Politics and the Professors: The Great Society in Perspective.* Washington, D.C.: Brookings Institution Press, 1978.

Serious and Unstable Condition. Washington, D.C.: Brookings Institution Press, 1991.

The Problem That Won't Go Away. Washington, D.C.: Brookings Institution Press, 1996.

Abelson, Donald E. "From Policy Research to Political Advocacy: The Changing Role of Think Tanks in American Politics." *Canadian Review of American Studies* 25 (1995): 93–126.

American Think Tanks and Their Role in U.S. Foreign Policy. New York: St. Martin's Press, 1996.

Do Think Tanks Matter? Assessing the Impact of Public Policy Institutes. Montreal: McGill–Queen's University Press, 2002.

Abramowitz, Michael. "Pushing Bush to a Market-led Health Solution: Enthoven Sees Competition as Best Antidote for Rising Costs." *Washington Post*, 26 January 1992.

Adams, Gina, Kathleen Snyder, and Jodi R. Sandfort. "Navigating the Child Care Subsidy System: Policies and Practices That Affect Access and Retention." *Urban Institute's Assessing the New Federalism Project*, April 2002.

Allen, William H. *Efficient Democracy.* New York: Macmillan, 1907.

Barnes, James A. "Making the Case for Tax Cuts." *National Journal*, 16 September 2000, pp. 2902–3.

Bartlett, Bruce R. "There's Room for McCain on the Right." *Los Angeles Times*, 9 February 2000, p. B7.

Baumann, David. "Budget Resolution Belatedly Approved." *National Journal*, 12 May 2001, p. 1420.

Baumgartner, Frank R., and Bryan D. Jones. *Agendas and Instability in American Politics.* Chicago: University of Chicago Press, 1993.

Baumgartner, Frank R., and Beth L. Leech. *Basic Interests: The Importance of Groups in Politics and in Political Science*. Princeton, N.J.: Princeton University Press, 1998.

Berry, Jeffrey M. *Lobbying for the People: The Political Behavior of Public Interest Groups*. Princeton, N.J.: Princeton University Press, 1977.

The Interest Group Society, Third Edition. New York: Longman, 1997.

The New Liberalism: The Rising Power of Citizen Groups. Washington, D.C.: Brookings Institution Press, 1999.

"Bids Industry Plan for Post-War Jobs." *The New York Times*, 13 February 1943, p. 20.

"Bill Advances in House on Telecom." *New York Times*, 17 March 1994, p. D2.

Bimber, Bruce. *The Politics of Expertise in Congress: The Rise and Fall of the Office of Technology Assessment*. Albany: State University of New York Press, 1996.

Bjerre-Poulsen, Niels. "The Heritage Foundation: A Second Generation Think Tank." *Journal of Policy History* 3 (1991): 152–72.

Blumenthal, Sidney. *The Rise of the Counter-Establishment*. New York: Harper & Row, 1986.

"The Left Stuff: IPS and the Left-wing Thinkers." *Washington Post*, 30 July 1986, pp. D1–D3.

Brock, David. *Blinded by the Right*. New York: Crown, 2002.

Brookings Institution Annual Report. Washington, D.C.: Brookings Institution, 1986.

Brown, E. Richard. "Health USA: A National Health Program for the United States." *Journal of the American Medical Association* 267 (1992): 552–61.

Browning, Graeme. "Search for Tomorrow: A Conversation with Vice President Gore about the 'Information Superhighway.'" *National Journal*, 20 March 1993, pp. 676–7.

Bush, George W. "A Tax Cut with a Purpose." *USA Today*, 2 August 2000, p. 16A.

Butler, Stuart M. "Coming to Terms on Health Care." *New York Times*, 28 January 1990.

Butler, Stuart M., and Edmund Haislmaier. *A National Health Care System for America*. Washington, D.C.: Heritage Foundation, 1989.

"California's Medical Model," *New York Times*, 17 February 1992, p. A16.

Callahan, David. *$1 Billion for Ideas: Conservative Think Tanks in the 1990s*. Washington, D.C.: National Committee for Responsive Philanthropy, 1999.

Carney, Dan. "Telecommunications: Indecency Provision Attacked as Clinton Signs Bill." *Congressional Quarterly Weekly Report*, 10 February 1996, p. 359.

"CBO Draft Opinion on Telecommunications Bill," *Communications Daily*, 5 May 1995, p. 2.

Cherry, Robert, and Max B. Sawicky. "Giving Tax Credit Where Credit Is Due." *Economic Policy Institute Briefing Paper*. 2000.

Chimerine, Lawrence, and Erik R. Olbeter. "Lessons from Abroad: Deregulation Efforts in New Zealand and the United Kingdom." *Economic Strategy Institute Report*. July 1995.

Chimerine, Lawrence, Erik R. Olbeter, and Robert B. Cohen. "Eliminating Monopolies and Barriers: How to Make the U.S. Telecommunications

Services Industry Truly Competitive." *Economic Strategy Institute Report.* June 1995.

"Ensuring Competition in the Local Exchange." *Economic Strategy Institute Report.* July 1995.

Chisolm, Laura Brown. "Sinking the Think Tanks Upstream: The Use and Misuse of Tax Exemption Law to Address the Use and Misuse of Tax-exempt Organizations by Politicians." *University of Pittsburgh Law Review* 51 (1990): 577–640.

Chong, Dennis. *Collective Action and the Civil Rights Movement.* Chicago: University of Chicago Press, 1991.

Coleman, James S. *Policy Research in the Social Sciences.* Morristown, N.J.: General Learning Press, 1972.

Communications Daily, 27 March 1995, p. 6.

Congressional Quarterly Almanac. 104th Congress. 2nd Session. Vol. LII. Washington, D.C.: CQ Press, 1997, pp. H8–11, S3.

Congressional Record, 8 June 1995, pp. 7954–5.

Congressional Record, 8 June 1995, pp. 7956–7.

Cook, Timothy E. *Governing with the News: The News Media as a Political Institution.* Chicago: University of Chicago Press, 1998.

Cooper, Kenneth J. "Focusing More on Cost than Compassion: In Health Care Debate, Democratic Rivals Generally See Link between Greater Access and Control." *Washington Post,* 6 February 1992, p. A16.

Covington, Sally. *Moving a Public Policy Agenda: The Strategic Philanthropy of Conservative Foundations.* Washington, D.C.: National Committee for Responsive Philanthropy, 1997.

Critchlow, Donald T. *The Brookings Institution, 1916–1952: Expertise and the Public Interest in a Democratic Society.* DeKalb: Northern Illinois University Press, 1985.

Crittenden, Ann. "The Economic Wind's Blowing Toward the Right – for Now." *New York Times,* 16 July 1978, p. C1.

DeLeon, Peter. "The Stages Approach to the Policy Process: What Has It Done? Where Is It Going?" In *Theories of the Policy Process,* edited by Paul A. Sabatier. Boulder, Colo.: Westview Press, 1999.

Dentzer, Susan. "Arrest Him, He Stole My Flat Tax!" *U.S. News & World Report,* 12 February 1996, p. 56.

Derthick, Martha, and Paul J. Quirk. *The Politics of Deregulation.* Washington, D.C.: The Brookings Institution, 1985.

Dickson, Paul. *Think Tanks.* New York: Atheneum, 1971.

Edwards, Lee. *The Power of Ideas.* Ottawa, Ill.: Jameson Books, Inc., 1997.

Ellwood, David T. *Poor Support: Poverty in the American Family.* New York: Basic Books, 1998.

Ellwood, David T., and Jeffrey B. Liebman. "The Middle Class Parent Penalty: Child Benefits in the U.S. Tax Code." Kennedy School and NBER Working Paper. July 2000.

"Endorses Brooks–Dingell: Gore Endorses Lifting MFJ Restrictions." *Communications Daily,* 12 January 1994, p.1.

Enthoven, Alain C. *Health Plan.* Reading, Mass.: Addison-Wesley, 1980.

Enthoven, Alain C., and Richard Kronick. "A Consumer Choice Health Plan for the 1990s," parts I and II. *New England Journal of Medicine* 320 (1989): 29–37, 94–101.

Evans, C. Lawrence, and Walter J. Oleszak. *Congress Under Fire: Reform Politics and the Republican Majority.* New York: Houghton Mifflin, 1997.

Fagan, Patrick. "Marriage: Next Step for Welfare Reform." *Heritage Foundation Press Release,* 11 April 2002.

Faltermayer, Edmund. "Let's Really Cure the Health System." *Fortune,* 23 March 1992, p. 46.

Feldstein, Martin S. *"A New Approach to National Health Insurance."* *Public Interest* 23 (1971): 93–105.

"The Welfare Loss of Excess Health Insurance." *Journal of Political Economy* 81 (1973): 251–80.

Hospital Costs and Health Insurance. Cambridge, Mass.: Harvard University Press, 1981.

Feulner, Edwin J., Jr. "Ideas, Think Tanks and Governments." *The Heritage Lectures.* Number 51, 1985.

"Fingers Pointing Everywhere: Hollings and Dole Promise Action on Telecommunications Next Year." *Communications Daily,* 26 September 1994, p. 1.

Fisher, Joseph. *Committee on Finance Hearing about the Tax Reform Act of 1969* (H.R. 13270). 7 October 1969.

"For Efficient Government." *The New York Times,* 14 March 1916, p. 6.

Fosdick, Raymond B. *The Story of the Rockefeller Foundation.* New York: Harper and Brothers Publishers, 1952.

Fremstad, Shawn, and Wendell Primus. "Strengthening Families: Ideas for TANF Reauthorization." *Center on Budget and Policy Priorities.* 22 January 2002.

Friedman, Milton. *Capitalism and Freedom.* Chicago: University of Chicago Press, 1962.

Friedman, Milton, and Anna Jacobson Schwartz. *A Monetary History of the United States, 1869–1960.* Princeton, N.J.: Princeton University Press, 1963.

Gans, Herbert J. *Deciding What's News.* New York: Vintage, 1980.

Garamendi, John. "Taking California Health Insurance into the 21st Century." *Journal of American Health Policy,* May–June 1992, pp. 10a–13a.

Gellner, Winard. "The Politics of Policy 'Political Think Tanks' and Their Markets in the U.S. Institutional Environment." *Presidential Studies Quarterly* 25 (1995): 497–510.

Gilder, George. *Life After Television, Revised Edition.* New York: W. W. Norton and Company, 1994.

Glied, Sherry. *Chronic Condition: Why Health Reform Fails.* Cambridge, Mass.: Harvard University Press, 1998.

Gold, Howard J. *Hollow Mandates: American Public Opinion and the Conservative Shift.* Boulder, Colo.: Westview Press, 1992.

Goodman, John, and Richard W. Rahn. "Need for Reform of Medicare System." *Wall Street Journal,* 20 March 1984, p. A32.

Gordon, Kermit. Statement before *Committee on Finance Hearing about the Tax Reform Act of 1969* (H.R. 13270). 7 October 1969.

Gosselin, Peter G. "Tax Cuts Seen as Spoiler in Boom Times." *Los Angeles Times,* 26 August 2000, p. A1.

Gouldner, Alvin W. *The Future of Intellectuals and the Rise of the New Class.* New York: The Seabury Press, 1979.

Graber, Doris A. *Mass Media and American Politics.* Washington, D.C.: Congressional Quarterly Press, 1993.

Hacker, Jacob S. *The Road to Nowhere: The Genesis of President Clinton's Plan for Health Security.* Princeton, N.J.: Princeton University Press, 1997.

Haislmaier, Edmund F. "Canada's Health System Has Its Ills." *Chicago Tribune,* 9 October 1991.

Hall, Peter A. *The Political Power of Economic Ideas: Keynesianism across Nations.* Princeton, N.J.: Princeton University Press, 1989.

"The Movement from Keynesianism to Monetarism: Institutional Analysis and British Economic Policy in the 1970s." In *Structuring Politics: Historical Institutionalism in Comparative Analysis,* edited by Sven Steinmo, et al., 90–113. New York: Cambridge University Press, 1992.

Hall, Peter Dobkin. *Inventing the Non-Profit Sector and Other Essays on Philanthropy, Voluntarism, and Non-Profit Organizations.* Baltimore: The Johns Hopkins University Press, 1992.

Hammack, David C., and Stanton Wheeler. *Social Science in the Making: Essays on the Russell Sage Foundation, 1907–1972.* New York: Russell Sage Foundation, 1994.

"The Health Care System Is Broken; And Here's How to Fix It." *New York Times,* 22 July 1991, p. A14.

"Health Reform, California Style: Garamendi Plan Is Making a Lot of Friends." *Los Angeles Times,* 29 May 1992, p. B1.

Hellebust, Lynn, ed. *Think Tank Directory: A Guide to Nonprofit Public Policy Research Organizations.* Topeka, Kans.: Government Research Service, 1996.

Helms, Robert B. *American Health Policy: Critical Issues for Reform.* Washington, D.C.: The AEI Press, 1993.

Health Policy Reform: Competition and Controls. Washington, D.C.: The AEI Press, 1993.

The Heritage Foundation 1994 Annual Report. Washington, D.C.: The Heritage Foundation, 1995.

Herzog, Arthur. "Report on a 'Think Factory.'" *The New York Times Magazine.* 10 November 1963, pp. 30–46.

Himmelstein, Jerome L. *To the Right: The Transformation of American Conservatism.* Berkeley: University of California Press, 1990.

Hodgson, Godfrey. *The World Turned Right Side Up.* Boston: Houghton Mifflin, 1996.

Holahan, John, et al. *Balancing Access, Costs, and Politics: The American Context for Health System Reform.* Washington, D.C.: Urban Institute Press, 1991.

Hollings, Robert L. *Nonprofit Public Policy Research Organizations: A Sourcebook on Think Tanks in Government.* New York: Garland Publishers, 1993.

"House Commerce Panel Passes Telecom Bill." *Communications Daily,* 26 May 1995, p.1.

"House Passed Telecommunications Legislation by Big Margins." *Communications Daily*, 29 June 1994, p. 1.

Hubner, John. "The Abandoned Father of Health Care Reform." *The New York Times Magazine*, 18 July 1993.

Illich, Ivan D. *Celebration of Awareness*. Garden City, NY: Doubleday, 1970.

Jenkins-Smith, Hank C. *Democratic Politics and Policy Analysis*. Pacific Grove, Calif.: Brooks/Cole Publishing, 1990.

Jenkins-Smith, Hank C., and Paul Sabatier. "The Dynamics of Policy-Oriented Learning." In *Policy Change and Learning: An Advocacy Coalition Approach*, edited by Paul A. Sabatier and Hank C. Jenkins-Smith. Boulder, Colo.: Westview Press, 1993.

Johnson, Haynes, and David S. Broder. *The System*. New York: Little, Brown, 1997.

Judis, John B. *The Paradox of American Democracy*. New York: Pantheon Books, 2000.

Kahn, Herman. *On Thermonuclear War*. Princeton, N.J.: Princeton University Press, 1960.

Kahn, Jonathan. *Budgeting Democracy: State Building and Citizenship in America, 1890–1928*. Ithaca, N.Y.: Cornell University Press, 1997.

Kerrey, Robert. "Why America Will Adopt Comprehensive Health Care Reform." *The American Prospect* 6 (Summer 1991): 81–92.

Kessler, Glenn, and Juliet Eilperin. "Tax Cut Is Given Hurdle to Clear." *The Washington Post*, 8 March 2001, p. A1.

"Pressure Rises for Tax Deal." *The Washington Post*, 25 May 2001, p. A1.

"Hill Negotiators Reach Tax Cut Deal." *The New York Times*, 27 May 2001, p. A5.

Kingdon, John W. *Agendas, Alternatives, and Public Policies*, Second Edition. New York: HarperCollins College Publishers, 1995.

Kitfield, Eleanor Evans. *The Capitol Source*. Washington, D.C.: National Journal, 1995.

Kosterlitz, Julie. "Dangerous Diagnosis." *National Journal*, 16 January 1993, pp. 127–30.

Lasswell, Harold D. "The Policy Orientation." In *The Policy Sciences*, edited by Daniel Lerner and Harold D. Lasswell, 3–15. Stanford, Calif.: Stanford University Press, 1951.

Lederman, Leonard A., and Margaret Windus. *Federal Funding and National Priorities: An Analysis of Programs, Expenditures, and Research and Development*. New York: Praeger, 1971.

Lichter, Daniel T. "Marriage as Public Policy." *PPI Policy Report*, 10 September 2001.

Lieberman, Trudy. *Slanting the Story: The Forces That Shape the News*. New York: New Press, 2000.

Lindblom, Charles E. "The Science of Muddling Through." *Public Administration Review* 19 (1959): 79–88.

Lindblom, Charles E., and David Cohen. *Usable Knowledge*. New Haven, Conn.: Yale University Press, 1979.

Lindblom, Charles E., and Edward J. Woodhouse. *The Policy-Making Process, Second Edition.* Englewood Cliffs, N.J.: Prentice-Hall, 1980.

Lipset, Seymour Martin. *Neoconservatism: Myth and Reality.* Berlin: John F. Kennedy–Institut für Nordamerikastudien der Freien Universität Berlin, 1988.

Lowi, Theodore J. *The End of Liberalism.* New York: Norton, 1979.

Lynn, Laurence E., Jr. *Knowledge and Policy: The Uncertain Connection.* Washington, D.C.: National Academy of Sciences, 1978.

Maass, Arthur. *Congress and the Common Good.* New York: Basic Books, 1983.

Magat, Richard. *The Ford Foundation at Work: Philanthropic Choices, Methods, and Styles.* New York: Plenum Press, 1979.

Maggs, John. "Tax Cuts, Big and Small." *National Journal,* 7 August 1999, pp. 2286–9.

Malbin, Michael. *Unelected Representatives: Congressional Staff and the Future of Representative Government.* New York: Basic Books, 1980.

Marmor, Theodore R., and Jerry L. Mashaw. "Cassandra's Law." *The New Republic,* 14 February 1994, p. 20.

Martin, Cathie Jo. "Business and the New Economic Activism: The Growth of Corporate Lobbies in the Sixties." *Polity* 27 (1994): 49–76.

Matlack, Carol. "Marketing Ideas." *National Journal,* 8 July 1995, pp. 1552–5.

Masterson, Karen. "Tax Showdown Looms in D.C." *The Houston Chronicle,* 22 May 2001, p. A1.

Mayhew, David R. *Divided We Govern: Party Control, Lawmaking, and Investigations, 1946–1990.* New Haven, Conn.: Yale University Press, 1991.

Mazmanian, Daniel, and Paul Sabatier. *Implementation and Public Policy.* Lanham, Md.: University Press of America, 1989.

McCaughey, Elizabeth. "Health Plan's Devilish Details." *The Wall Street Journal,* 30 September 1993, p. A18.

"No Exit." *The New Republic,* 7 February 1994.

"She's Baaack!" *The New Republic,* 28 February 1994.

McGann, James G. *The Competition for Dollars, Scholars and Influence in the Public Policy Research Industry.* New York: University Press of America, 1995.

Merriam, Charles E. *New Aspects of Politics.* Chicago: University of Chicago Press, 1970.

Milbank, Dana. "White House Hopes Gas Up a Think Tank." *The Washington Post,* 8 December 2000, p. A39.

Miller, T. Christian, and Maria L. LaGanga. "Voters Unswayed by Candidates' Tax Cut Push." *The Los Angeles Times,* 19 January 2000, p. A14.

Mills, Mike. "The New Kings of Capitol Hill." *The Washington Post,* 23 April 1995, p. H1.

Mitchell, Neil J. *The Generous Corporation.* New Haven, Conn.: Yale University Press, 1989.

Moe, Terry M. *The Organization of Interests.* Chicago: University of Chicago Press, 1980.

Moffit, Robert E. *Congress and the Taxpayers: A Double Standard on Health Care Reform?* Washington, D.C.: Heritage Foundation, 1992.

Morin, Richard, and Claudia Deane. "Dude, Let's Talk Policy." *The Washington Post,* 11 May 1999, p. A19.

"Live from Massachusetts Ave., It's WONK-TV." *The Washington Post,* 25 September 2001, p. A21.

Murray, Charles. *Losing Ground: American Social Policy, 1950–1980.* New York: Basic Books, Inc., 1984.

Neustadt, Richard E. *President Power and the Modern Presidents: The Politics of Leadership from Roosevelt to Reagan.* New York: Free Press, 1990.

Newhouse, Joseph P., and the Insurance Experiment Group. *Free for All? Lessons from the RAND Health Insurance Experiment.* Cambridge, Mass.: Harvard University Press, 1993.

Nitschke, Lori. "Tax-Cut Bipartisanship Down to One Chamber." *Congressional Quarterly Weekly Report,* 10 March 2001, pp. 529–32.

"Scaled-Down Version of Bush Tax Plan Taking Bipartisan Form at Senate Finance." *Congressional Quarterly Weekly Report,* 5 May 2001, p. 1003.

"Tax Cut Deal Reached Quickly as Appetite for Battle Fades." *Congressional Quarterly Weekly Report,* 26 May 2001, pp. 1251–5.

Nitschke, Lori, and Bill Swindell. "Grassley–Baucus Tax Blueprint Heads for Rough and Tumble Markup." *Congressional Quarterly Weekly Report,* 12 May 2001, pp. 1069–70.

Noam, Eli M. "Beyond Telecommunications Liberalization: Past Performance, Present Hype, and Future Direction." In *The New Information Infrastructure: Strategies for U.S. Policy,* edited by William J. Drake. New York: The Twentieth Century Fund Press, 1995.

"Not Enough Regulatory Parity." *Communications Daily,* 10 June 1993, p. 4.

Nownes, Anthony J. "Public Interest Groups and the Road to Survival." *Polity* 27 (1995): 379–404.

Nownes, Anthony J., and Grant Neeley. "Public Interest Group Entrepreneurship and Theories of Group Mobilization." *Political Research Quarterly* 49 (1996): 119–46.

O'Connor, Alice. *Poverty Knowledge: Social Science, Social Policy, and the Poor in Twentieth-Century U.S. History.* Princeton, N.J.: Princeton University Press, 2001.

Oliver, Thomas R. "Health Care Reform in Congress." *Political Science Quarterly* 106 (1991): 453–77.

Olson, Mancur. *The Logic of Collective Action.* Cambridge, Mass.: Harvard University Press, 1965.

"Packwood and McCain Opposed: Senate Commerce Panel Passes Telecommunications Bill." *Communications Daily,* 12 August 1994, p. 1.

Parks, Daniel J. "Bush May Test Capitol Hill Clout Early with Expedited Tax-Cut Proposal." *Congressional Quarterly Weekly Report,* 6 January 2001, p. 41.

Patman, Wright. *Statement before House Committee on Ways and Means.* Washington, D.C.: Government Printing Office, 1969.

Pauly, Mark V. "A Plan for Responsible National Health Insurance." *Health Affairs* (Spring 1991): 5–25.

Pauly, Mark V., et al. *Responsible National Health Insurance.* Washington, D.C.: The AEI Press, 1992.

Peschek, Joseph G. *Policy-Planning Organizations: Elite Agendas and America's Rightward Turn.* Philadelphia: Temple University Press, 1987.

Peterson, Mark A. "Momentum Toward Health Care Reform in the U.S. Senate." *Journal of Health Politics, Policy, and Law* 17 (1992): 553–73.

"The Politics of Health Care Policy: Overreaching in an Age of Polarization." In *The Social Divide: Political Parties and the Future of Activist Government*, edited by Margaret Weir, 181–229 Washington, D.C.: Brookings Institution Press, 1998.

Petracca, Mark P. *The Politics of Interests: Interest Groups Transformed.* Boulder, Colo.: Westview Press, 1992.

Pollack, Ronald, and Phyllis Torda. "The Pragmatic Road Toward National Health Insurance." *The American Prospect* 6 (Summer 1991): 92–100.

Polsby, Nelson. "Tanks but No Tanks." *Public Opinion* 6 (1983): 14–16, 58–9.

Posner, Richard A. *Public Intellectuals: A Study of Decline.* Cambridge, Mass.: Harvard University Press, 2001.

Pressman, Jeffrey, and Aaron Wildavsky. *Implementation*, Third Edition. Berkeley: University of California Press, 1984.

Priest, Dana. "The Federal Page – A Floor at a Time...Room to Room." *The Washington Post*, 13 August 1992, p. A23.

"Congressional Scorer of Health Care Bills Finds Itself at Hub of Frenzied Reform Competition." *The Washington Post*, 16 August 1994, p. A8.

Public Papers of the Presidents of the United States: Lyndon B. Johnson, 1966, Book II. Washington, D.C.: Government Printing Office, 1967.

Rector, Robert. "The Effectiveness of Abstinence Education Programs in Reducing Sexual Activity Among Youth." *Heritage Backgrounder*, 8 April 2002.

"Using Welfare Reform to Strengthen Marriage." *American Experiment Quarterly*, Summer 2001.

Ricci, David M. *The Transformation of American Politics: The New Washington and the Rise of Think Tanks.* New Haven, Conn.: Yale University Press, 1993.

Rich, Andrew. *Think Tanks, Public Policy, and the Politics of Expertise.* Ph.D. Dissertation, Yale University, 1999.

"The Politics of Expertise in Congress and the News Media." *Social Science Quarterly* 82 (2001): 583–601.

Rich, Andrew, and R. Kent Weaver. "Advocates and Analysts: Think Tanks and the Politicization of Expertise." In *Interest Group Politics*, Fifth Edition, edited by Allan J. Cigler and Burdett A. Loomis, 235–54. Washington, D.C.: CQ Press, 1998.

"Think Tanks in the National Media," *Harvard Journal of Press/Politics*, 5 (2000): 81–103.

Rich, Spencer. "The Federal Page: Ideas and Findings – Making Active Shoppers of the Uninsured: Heritage Foundation Plan for Health Coverage Relies on Market." *The Washington Post*, 12 March 1992, p. A25.

"Health Care, Minus U.S. Controls; Nickles Bill Would End Employer-Paid Benefits." *The Washington Post*, 5 December 1993, p. A19.

Rivlin, Alice M. *Systematic Thinking for Social Action.* Washington, D.C.: Brookings Institution Press, 1971.

"Robber Barons of the '90s," *Common Cause Report*, June 1995. Rasell, M. Edith, Dean Baker, and Kainan Tang. "The Impact of the Clinton Health Care Plan on Jobs, Investment, Wages, Productivity, and Exports." In *Economic Policy Institute Briefing Paper*. Washington, D.C.: Economic Policy Institute, 1994.

Robinson, William H. "The Congressional Research Service: Policy Consultant, Think Tank and Information Factory." In *Organizations for Policy Analysis: Helping Government Think*, edited by Carol H. Weiss, 181–200. Beverly Hills, Calif.: Sage Publications, 1992.

Rochefort, David A., and Roger W. Cobb. *The Politics of Problem Definition: Shaping the Policy Agenda*. Lawrence: University Press of Kansas, 1994.

Rosner, Jeremy D. "A Progressive Plan for Affordable, Universal Health Care." In *Mandate for Change*, edited by Will Marshall and Martin Schram, 107–28. New York: Berkley Books, 1993.

Rothwell, C. Easton. "Foreword." In *The Policy Sciences*, edited by Daniel Lerner and Harold D. Lasswell, vii–xi. Stanford, Calif.: Stanford University Press, 1951.

Sabatier, Paul A., and Hank C. Jenkins-Smith. *Policy Change and Learning: An Advocacy Coalition Approach*. Boulder, Colo.: Westview Press, 1993.

Salamon, Lester. *The Nonprofit Sector and the Rise of Third-Party Government*. Washington, D.C.: Urban Institute, 1983.

Salisbury, Robert H. "An Exchange Theory of Interest Groups." *Midwest Journal of Political Science* 13 (1969): 1–32.

——— "Interest Representation: The Dominance of Institutions." *American Political Science Review* 78 (1984): 64–76.

Saloma, John S., III. *Ominous Politics: The New Conservative Labyrinth*. New York: Hill and Wang, 1984.

Sard, Barbara, and Margy Waller. "Housing Strategies to Strengthen Welfare Policy and Support Working Families." *Policy Brief*. The Brookings Institution Center on Urban and Metropolitan Policy and the Center on Budget and Policy Priorities, April 2002.

Sawhill, Isabel. "What Can Be Done to Reduce Teen Pregnancy and Out-of-Wedlock Births?" *Brookings Policy Brief*. October 2001.

Sawhill, Isabel, and Adam Thomas. "A Tax Proposal for Working Families with Children." *Brookings Policy Brief, Welfare Reform and Beyond*. January 2001.

Scheibla, Shirley. "Ivory-Tower Activists," *Barron's*, 13 October 1969, p. 9.

Schlozman, Kay Lehman, and John T. Tierney. *Organized Interests and American Democracy*. New York: Harper & Row, 1986.

Schuck, Peter. "The Politics of Rapid Legal Change: Immigration Policy in the 1980s." In *The New Politics of Public Policy*, edited by Marc K. Landy and Martin A. Levin, 47–87. Baltimore: The Johns Hopkins University Press, 1995.

"Senate Panel Sets Markup on 191-page Telecommunications Bill." *Communications Daily*, 10 August 1994, p. 1.

"Senate Telecommunications Leadership Introduces New Bill." *Communications Daily*, 4 February 1994, p. 1.

Shulock, Nancy. "The Paradox of Policy Analysis: If It Is Not Used, Why Do We Produce So Much of It?" *Journal of Policy Analysis and Management* 18 (1999): 226–44.

Shuman, Michael. "Why Progressive Foundations Give Too Little to Too Many." *The Nation* 12–19, January 1998, pp. 11–16.

Skocpol, Theda. *Boomerang: Clinton's Health Security Effort and the Turn against Government in U.S. Politics.* New York: Norton, 1996.

Skowronek, Stephen. *Building a New American State, The Expansion of National Administrative Capacities, 1877–1920.* New York: Cambridge University Press, 1982.

Smith, Bruce L.R. *The RAND Corporation: Case Study of a Nonprofit Advisory Corporation.* Cambridge, Mass.: Harvard University Press, 1966.

Smith, James A. *Brookings at Seventy-Five.* Washington, D.C.: The Brookings Institution, 1991.

The Idea Brokers: Think Tanks and the Rise of the New Policy Elite. New York: The Free Press, 1991.

Smith, Mark A. *American Business and Political Power.* Chicago: University of Chicago Press, 2000.

Starobin, Paul. "Rethinking Brookings." *National Journal,* 22 July 1995, pp. 1875–9.

Starr, Paul. *The Social Transformation of American Medicine.* New York: Basic Books, 1982.

The Logic of Health Care Reform: Transforming American Medicine for the Better. Knoxville, Tenn.: Whittle Direct Books, 1992.

"State Health Care Reform Initiatives, 1993," Employee Benefit Research Institute, 14 (3), September 1993.

Stefancic, Jean, and Richard Delgado. *No Mercy: How Conservative Think Tanks and Foundations Changed America's Social Agenda.* Philadelphia: Temple University Press, 1996.

Steinfels, Peter. *The Neoconservatives: The Men Who Are Changing America's Politics.* New York: Touchstone Books, 1979.

Stevenson, Richard W. "Bush to Propose Broad Tax Cut in Iowa Speech." *The New York Times,* 1 December 1999, p. A1.

Stone, Deborah. "Causal Stories and the Formation of Policy Agendas." *Political Science Quarterly* 104 (1989): 281–300.

Stone, Diane. *Capturing the Political Imagination: Think Tanks and the Policy Process.* Portland, Ore.: Frank Cass, 1996.

"Tax Credits for Health: Wrong Rx." *The New York Times,* 16 December 1991, p. A18.

The Telecom Revolution: An American Revolution. Washington, D.C.: Progress and Freedom Foundation, 1995.

Teles, Steven M. "The Dialectics of Trust: Ideas, Finance, and Pensions Privatization in the U.S. and U.K." Paper presented at the Conference on the Varieties of Welfare Capitalism in Europe, Cologne, Germany. 11–13 June 1998.

Thierer, Adam D. "A Guide to Telecommunications Deregulation Legislation." *Heritage Issue Bulletin #191,* 3 June 1994.

"Free Markets for Telecom: No Halfway House on Deregulation." *The Wall Street Journal*, 23 June 1994, p. A14.

"How to Solve the CBO's Telecom Tax Problem." *Heritage Foundation Executive Memorandum*, #414, 23 May 1995.

"Senator Dole's Welcome Proposal for Telecommunication Freedom." *Heritage Backgrounder Update* #233. 24 August 1994.

"Treasury Pressed for Closer Check on Foundations." *Congressional Quarterly Weekly Report*, 27 October 1967, p. 2176.

Truman, David B. *The Governmental Process*. New York: Knopf, 1951.

Victor, Kirk. "Road Warriors." *National Journal*, 20 March 1993, p. 681.

"Nope, These Baby Bells Aren't Tykes." *National Journal*, 20 August 1994, p. 1996.

"How Bliley's Bell Was Rung." *National Journal*, 22 July 1995, pp. 1892–3.

"Will the Real Chairman Stand Up." *National Journal*, 18 April 1995, p. 892.

"They're in a League of Their Own." *National Journal*, 27 May 1995, p. 1307.

Vogel, David. *Fluctuating Fortunes: The Political Power of Business in America*. New York: Basic Books, 1989.

Kindred Strangers: The Uneasy Relationship between Politics and Business in America. Princeton, N.J.: Princeton University Press, 1996.

VonDrehle, David. "With Friends in High Places, Democratic Think Tank Bids for Glory." *The Washington Post*, 7 December 1992, p. A17.

Walker, Jack L., Jr. *Mobilizing Interest Groups in America*. Ann Arbor: University of Michigan Press, 1991.

Weaver, R. Kent. "The Changing World of Think Tanks." *P.S. Political Science and Politics*, September 22 (1989): 563–79.

"The Role of Policy Research in Welfare Debates, 1993–1996." Paper presented at Inequality Summer Institute 1999, 24 June 1999.

Ending Welfare as We Know It. Washington, D.C.: The Brookings Institution, 2000.

The WEFA Group. *Economic Impact of Deregulating U.S. Communications Industries*. Burlington, Mass.: The WEFA Group, 1995.

Weir, Margaret, and Theda Skocpol. "State Structures and the Possibilities for 'Keynesian' Responses to the Great Depression in Sweden, Britain, and the United States." In *Bringing the State Back In*, edited by Peter B. Evans, Dietrich Rueschemeyer, and Theda Skocpol. New York: Cambridge University Press, 1985.

Weiss, Carol H. *Using Social Research in Public Policy Making*. Lexington, Mass.: Lexington Books, 1977.

"Research for Policy's Sake: The Enlightenment Function of Social Research." *Policy Analysis* 3 (1977): 531–45.

"Congressional Committees as Users of Analysis." *Journal of Policy Analysis and Management* 8 (1989): 411–31.

Organizations for Policy Analysis: Helping Government Think. Newbury Park, Calif.: Sage, 1992.

Weiss, Carol H., and Eleanor Singer. *Reporting of Social Science in the National Media*. New York: Russell Sage Foundation, 1988.

"We're for a Universal Health Care System." *Business Week*, 7 October 1991, p. 158.

Whiteman, David. *Communication in Congress: Members, Staff, and the Search for Information*. Lawrence: University Press of Kansas, 1995.

Wildavsky, Aaron. *Speaking Truth to Power*. Boston: Little, Brown, 1979.

Wildavsky, Aaron, and Ellen Tenenbaum. *The Politics of Mistrust*. Beverly Hills Calif.: Sage, 1981.

Wilson, James Q. "The Politics of Regulation." In *The Politics of Regulation*, edited by James Q. Wilson. New York: Basic Books, 1980.

Index

Aaron, Henry, 168, 170, 178, 179–80, 215
Allott, Sen. Gordon (R.-Colo.), 53, 54
American Enterprise Institute, 207 (n2), 208 (n4), 216
  changes in publications, 68
  criticism of in 1970s, 54 (n63)
  formation of, 44
  health care reform in 1993–4 and, 174–6, 176 (n52), 180
  perceptions of by congressional staff and journalists, 80, 82, 229
  relationship to formation of Heritage Foundation, 53–4, 152–3
  tax cut in 2001 and, 134
  transportation deregulation and, 214
American Prospect, The, 116
Andrews, Rep. Michael (D.-Tex.), 163
Annie E. Casey Foundation, child tax credit in 2001 and, 198–200
Armacost, Michael, 70 (n101)

Badger, Doug, 119 (n41), 172, 180
Barnet, Richard, 47
Baucus, Sen. Max (D.-Mont.), 137
Baumgartner, Frank R., 143 (n87)
Bell, Daniel, 50
Bennett, William, 208 (n4)
Berkowitz, Herb, 215 (n16)
Berry, Jeffrey, 10, 10 (n25)
Bimber, Bruce, 87, 87 (n16)
Blau, Bob, 148
Bliley, Rep. Thomas (R.-Va.), 128, 129, 185
Bonior, Rep. David (D.-Mich.), 189
Broder, David, 120 (n42)
Brookings Institution, 208 (n4), 215, 216

changes 1960s–1990s, 58, 60, 62, 65–6, 69, 70 (n101, n102)
child tax credit in 2001 and, 146, 198–200, 201, 202, 211–12
formation of, 40, 205
health care reform in 1993–4 and, 168, 168 (n23), 179
Lyndon Johnson tribute, 1
marketing of research, 67–8, 69–70
perceptions of by congressional staff and journalists, 80, 82–3, 229, 231
transportation deregulation and, 214
welfare reform reauthorization, 4
See also Institute for Government Research; Institute of Economics
Brookings, Robert S., 39–40, 229
Brooks, Rep. Jack (D.-Tex.), 125, 125 (n51)
Brown, Gretchen, 115 (n29), 167, 179
Brown, Richard, 115, 115 (n29), 167, 179
Bureau of Municipal Research (N.Y.)
  comment about, 29
  formation of, 34–7
Burke, Sheila, 174, 202 (n104)
Burson-Marsteller Public Relations/Public Affairs, 81, 225
Buse, Mark, 188
Bush, President George H.W., 116–17
Bush, President George W., and the 2001 tax cut, 131–8, 144, 198
business political mobilization, 49–50
Butler, Stuart, 171, 174

Campaign for America's Future, 221
Carnegie, Andrew, 40
Carnegie Endowment for International Peace, 40

Carnegie Foundation (Carnegie
Corporation), 40
Cato Institute
formation of, 55–6
health care reform in 1993–4 and, 157,
174, 176
perceptions of by congressional staff and
journalists, 78, 80, 82, 229
Social Security reform and, 214
Center for Defense Information, 204
Center for Defense of Free Enterprise, 204
Center for Democracy and Technology,
204
Center for Equal Opportunity, 204
Center for Military Readiness, 204
Center for New Black Leadership, 204
Center for Strategic and International
Studies, 204
Center on Budget and Policy Priorities
child tax credit in 2001 and, 146,
198–200, 201
health care reform in 1993–4 and, 157
perceptions of by congressional staff and
journalists, 81, 82
welfare reform reauthorization, 4
Cerisano, John, 180
Chafee, Sen. John (R.-R.I.), 173–4
Chafee, Sen. Lincoln (R.-R.I.), 198
Christian groups, mobilization into
politics, 51–2
Citizens for a Sound Economy
hybrid organizational nature, 219 (n24)
telecommunications reform in 1995–6
and, 181–3, 188, 190, 194–6
Cleveland, Frederick, 37–9
Clinton, President Bill
and 1993–4 health care reform, 114–20,
144, 163–6, 169 (n27), 170, 178,
179
and 1995–6 telecommunications reform,
120–5
and 1996 welfare reform, 104
and proposed tax cuts in 1999, 133–4
Coats, Sen. Dan (R.-Ind.), 173 (n40)
Cobb, Roger W., 108, 111, 214
Collins, Sen. Susan (R.-Me.), 198
Committee for Economic Development,
43–4
Congressional Budget Office, 211
and 1993–4 health care reform, 118,
202 (n104)
and 1995–6 telecommunications reform,
191–2
and 2001 tax cut, 135, 202
conservative politics, growth of, 49–53
Coors, Joseph, 54

Council for Affordable Health Insurance
(CAHI), 173 (n40)
Crandall, Robert, 186
Crane, Ed, 55–6
Critchlow, Donald, 35
Cutting, Fulton, 39

Danforth, Sen. John (R.-Mo.), 125
Darman, Richard, 117 (n33), 175
Defense Department, support of contract
research, 62–3
deJanosi, Peter, 62
Delaware Public Policy Institute, 15
deLeon, Peter, 107 (n7)
Democratic Leadership Council (DLC),
169, 169 (n27)
Demos, 218
Derthick, Martha, 149
Dickson, Paul, 13 (n31), 46–7, 47 (n46)
Dingell, Rep. John (D.-Mich.), 125,
125 (n51), 129
Dodge, Cleveland, 39
Dole, Sen. Bob (R.-Kans.)
health care reform in 1993–4 and, 174
telecommunications reform in 1995–6
and, 127–8, 181, 183–4, 188,
194 (n88)
DuPont, Pierre S., 15

Economic Policy Institute, 211
health care reform in 1993–4 and, 157,
168
Economic Strategy Institute,
telecommunications reform in
1995–6 and, 192–3, 196
Eisenach, Jeff, 185, 186
Ellwood, Paul, 162–3, 163 (n10), 174
Employee Benefit Research Institute,
156 (n2)
Empower America, 208 (n4)
Enthoven, Alain, 115, 115 (n30), 116 (n31),
118, 157–63, 174, 176–7
Etheredge, Lynn, 162–3
Exon, Sen. James (D.-Neb.), 130 (n65)

Falwell, Jerry, 51
Families USA, 116
Family Research Council, 219
Faux, Jeff, 211
Feder, Judy, 116, 166
Feldstein, Martin, 171
Ferguson, Christine, 174, 174 (n42)
Feulner, Edwin, 53–4, 64–5, 152
Fields, Rep. Jack (R.-Tex.), 125, 185
Fisher, Joseph, 60
Fleishman, Joel, 207

Fleming, Scott, 115 (n30)
Folsom, Marion B., 43
Forbes, Steve, 133
Ford Foundation, 205, 213 (n11)
  changes in priorities in 1970s, 61–2
  criticism of in relation to TRA of 1969,
    58, 58 (n72)
  support of Institute for Policy Studies,
    47
Fred C. Koch Foundation, 56 (n68), 64
Fried, Bruce, 116, 166
Friedman, Milton, 52

Gans, Herbert, 89
Garamendi, John, 118, 164–5, 177–8,
  179
Gattuso, James, 181–3, 186, 188, 194–5,
  219
Gawande, Atul, 163
Gephardt, Rep. Richard (D.-Mo.), 135
German Marshall Fund, 222
Gilder, George, 189
Gingrich, Newt, 185, 187
  tribute to Heritage Foundation, 1
Glazer, Nathan, 50
Gleid, Sherry, 113 (n22)
Golden Rule Insurance Company, 173
Goldwater, Barry, 52, 54, 152
Goodman, John, 173, 176, 180, 206
Goodnow, Frank, 37–8
Gordon, Kermit, 60
Gore, Vice President Al, 121–3, 125, 134,
  193 (n87)
Gorham, William, 48, 67, 68
Graber, Doris, 89
Gramm, Sen. Phil (R.-Tex.), 136, 180
Grassley, Sen. Charles (R.-Iowa), 137
Greene, Jerome
  comment on Bureau of Municipal
    Research, 29
  role in formation of think tanks, 38–9
Greenstein, Robert, 199–200, 201

Haass, Richard, 70, 70 (n102)
Hacker, Jacob, 115 (n30), 116 (n31), 162,
  164
Haislmaier, Edmund, 171
Hall, Peter, 8
Harris, Robert, 189
Hastings Center, 156 (n2)
Hausman, Jerry, 189
Hazlett, Tom, 186
health care reform in 1993–4
  agenda-setting moments of, 112–18
  characteristic of entrepreneurial politics,
    109–10

experts and policy research during,
  157–67
think tanks and, 167–76
Health Insurance Association of America,
  144
Hellebust, Lynn, 13–14, 221
Helms, Robert, 174, 175 (n45), 180
Heritage Foundation, 216
  formation of, 53–5, 152–3, 206
  funding of, 64–5
  health care reform in 1993–4 and,
    171–2, 180
  involvement with state think tanks,
    56 (n69)
  marketing of research, 67, 207,
    215 (n16), 219
  Newt Gingrich tribute, 1
  perceptions of by congressional staff and
    journalists, 78, 80, 82–3, 229, 231
  telecommunication reform in 1995–6
    and, 181, 183–4, 189–90, 194–6
  welfare reform reauthorization, 4
Hewlett, William, 15
Hodgson, Godfrey, 51–2, 52 (n60)
Hollings, Sen. Ernest (D.-S.C.), 125, 127–8,
  181
Hoover Institution, 134
Huber, Peter, 185, 186, 189
Hudson Institute, 185, 216 (n17)
  changes in funding, 66
  criticism of in 1968, 46 (n43)
  formation of, 45–7, 47 (n46)

Inouye, Sen. Daniel (D.-Ha.), 125
Institute for Energy Research, 221
Institute for Gay and Lesbian Strategic
  Studies, 221
Institute for Government Research, 38–40.
  See also Brookings Institution
Institute for Policy Studies
  changes during 1990s, 68, 70–1
  formation of, 47–8
  George McGovern on, 71 (n105)
Institute of Economics, 40–1

Jackson Hole Group, 162–4, 169, 170, 177
  (n53), 178
Jacobs, Rep. Andy (D.-Ind.), 173 (n40)
James Madison Institute, 15
Jeffords, Sen. James (R.-Vt.), 198
Jenkins-Smith, Hank, 108
John M. Olin Foundation, 64, 212 (n11)
Johnson, Haynes, 120 (n42)
Johnson, Lyndon B., tribute to Brookings
  Institution, 1
Jones, Bryan D., 143 (n87)

Kahn, Herman, 45–6
Kahn, Jonathan, 36–7
Kendall, David, 163, 178
Kennedy School of Government, Harvard
    University, 189–90
Kerrey, Sen. Bob (D.-Neb.), 114–15,
    115 (n29), 142–3, 166–7, 179
Kerry, Sen. John (D.-Mass.), 200
Keyworth, George, 185
Kingdon, John, 2, 5, 209, 217
Klain, Ronald, 134
Koch, Charles, 55–6
Kotler, Milton, 48
Kristol, Irving, 50

Lasswell, Harold, 2, 6, 209, 210, 220
Lenkowsky, Leslie, 216 (n17)
Lewin-VHI, 118, 118 (n37), 212
Lilly Foundation, 64
Lincoln, Sen. Blanche (D.-Ark.), 200
Lindblom, Charles, 108
Lindsey, Lawrence, 134, 135
Lipset, Seymour Martin, 51
Lipsky, Michael, 213 (n11)
Lott, Sen. Trent (R.-Miss.), 187, 197
Lowi, Theodore, 9 (n19)

MacLaury, Bruce, 69
Magaziner, Ira, 119, 119 (n39), 164–165
    (n41)
Manhattan Institute
    and 1993–4 health care reform, 119, 156
        (n2), 174, 176
    and 1995–6 telecommunications reform,
        190
    and Charles Murray, 104
Mann, Thomas, 208 (n4)
Markey, Rep. Edward (D.-Mass.), 123
Marmor, Theodore R., 119 (n39)
Martin, Cathie Jo, 49 (n52)
Mashaw, Jerry L., 119 (n39)
Mayhew, David R., 112 (n20)
McCain, Sen. John (R.-Ariz.), 127 (n56),
    133, 183, 188
McCaughey, Elizabeth, 119, 119 (n39,
    n41)
McClean, Chris, 127 (n56)
McClellan, Donald, 127, 130 (n64), 185,
    186, 195
McGovern, George, on the Institute for
    Policy Studies, 71 (n105)
McKittrick, Beverly, 183, 188,
    194–5
Merriam, Charles, 2, 5 (n10), 209, 210,
    220
Mihalski, Ed, 174
Miller, Sen. Zell (D.-Ga.), 136

Moffit, Robert, 171–2
Monetarism, appeal of, 52–3
Moon, Marilyn, 168, 170, 207 (n2)
Morgan, J. P., 39
Murray, Charles, 104

Nathan Cummings Foundation, 218
National Bureau for Economic Research
    (NBER), 40, 41
    changes in 1960s, 69 (n100)
National Center for Policy Analysis
    (NCPA), 206
    health care reform in 1993–4 and,
        156 (n2), 173, 176, 180
National Committee for Responsive
    Philanthropy, 64, 64 (n84), 218
neoconservatives, 50–1
New America Foundation, 218, 218
    (n20)
Nickles, Sen. Don (R.-Okla.), 170–2,
    180
Nixon, President Richard, 52
Noam, Eli, 124

O'Connor, Alice, 105 (n3)
Office of Technology Assessment, 86
Olbeter, Erik, 187, 192, 196
Olson, Mancur, 33 (n10)
Ornstein, Norman, 207 (n2)

Packwood, Sen. Bob (R.-Ore.), 127 (n56),
    174
Patman, Rep. Wright (D.-Tex.), 57–8,
    59 (n73, n74)
Pauly, Mark, 175, 176 (n52), 180
Piereson, James, 212 (n11)
Pitsch, Peter, 186
Pollack, Ron, 116, 165–6, 178
Posner, Richard, 207, 208 (n4)
Pressler, Sen. Larry (R.-S.D.), 128–9, 185,
    187–92
Progress and Freedom Foundation, and
    1995–6 telecommunications reform,
        185–7
Progressive Policy Institute
    designation as centrist think tank,
        19 (n40)
    health care reform in 1993–4 and,
        169 (n27), 169–77
    perceptions of by congressional staff and
        journalists, 80, 82
    welfare reform reauthorization, 4
Public Interest, The, 50
Public Policy Institute of California, 15

Quello, James (FCC chairman), 123
Quirk, Paul, 149

RAND Corporation
  changes in 1970s, 63
  changes in funding, 66
  evaluation of health insurance
    deductibles, 114
  formation of, 42, 205
  health care reform in 1993–4 and, 157
  links to Herman Kahn, 45
  perceptions of by congressional staff and
    journalists, 86
Rasell, Edith, 168
Raskin, Marcus, 47
Reagan, President Ronald, 52
Rector, Robert, 104, 104 (n2)
Reed, Bruce, 116, 166, 169 (n27)
Reich, Robert, 164–5
Resources for the Future, 58, 60
Ricci, David, 32
Roberts, Oral, 51
Robertson, Pat, 51
Robinson, Ken, 186
Robinson, Marshall, 61
Rochefort, David, 108, 111, 214
Rockefeller Foundation, 29, 39–40, 41,
  205
Rockefeller, John D., Sr., 36, 39, 40–1
Rockefeller, John D., III, 59 (n73)
Rooney, Pat, 173
Rosner, Jeremy, 169, 170, 178 (n27)
Rothwell, Easton, 5–6
Russell Sage Foundation, formation of,
  34

Sabatier, Paul, 108
Salisbury, Robert, 33 (n10)
Sarah Mellon Scaife Foundation, 64
Sawhill, Isabel, 199–200, 212
Schuck, Peter, (n17), 8 (n18)
Shuman, Michael, 68, 71
Sidak, Greg, 186
Smith, Bruce L.R., 42 (n35)
Smith, James A., 7, (n15), 32, 41–2
Smith Richardson Foundation, 64
Snowe, Sen. Olympia (R.-Me.), 138,
  198–200, 201, 211
Specter, Sen. Arlen (R.-Pa.), 198
Stark, Rep. Pete (D.-Calif.), 120 (n42)
Starr, Paul, 164–5
Stearns, Rep. Cliff (R.-Fla.), 170–2
Steelman, Deborah, 175
Stein, Herbert, 43, 208, 218 (n4)
Steurle, Eugene, (n26)
Stone, Deborah, 142
Stone, Diane, 13 (n31)

Taft Commission, 37–8
Tanner, Michael, 176

tax cut of 2001
  as example of majoritarian politics, 110
  politics of, 131–8
  think tanks and experts and, 196–201
Tax Reform Act of 1969, 57–61
telecommunications reform in 1995–6
  characteristic of interest-group politics,
    110
  politics of, 120–31
  think tanks and experts and, 180–96
Thierer, Adam, 183–4, 186, 187–8, 192,
  194–6
think tanks
  business support of, 36–7
  calculating the number of, 13–14, 15
    (n34)
  conservative proliferation of, 53–6
  defining influence of, 153–5
  definition of, 11–12
  formation of during Progressive Era,
    34–41
  formation of during 1930s and 1940s,
    41–3
  growth in number of, 15 (n35)
  ideologies of, 18–22, 24 (n43)
  lack of scholarly attention to, 6–11 (n25)
  media and congressional visibility,
    87–103
  scope of research mission, 16–18
  size of organizations, 16, (n44) 22–3
    (n45)
  state-level organizations, 15–16, 18,
    20–4
  survey of congressional staff and
    journalists about, 77–86
Thomas, Adam, 199, 212
Thomas, Rep. Bill (R.-Calif.), 173
Truman, David, 33 (n10)
Tsongas, Sen. Paul (D.-Mass.), 114

Urban Institute, 48–49, 207 (n2)
  and 1993–4 health care reform, 118, 168,
    (n37) 169 (n26)
  changes in funding, 63, 67
  marketing research, 68

Victor, Kirk, 122 (n46)
Vogel, David, 50

Walker, Jack, 33 (n10)
Waskow, Arthur, 47
Weaver, R. Kent
  on the Brookings Institution, 7
  on welfare reform in 1996, 104, 105,
    (n3) 106, (n5) 217
WEFA Group, 189
Weiner, Joshua, 168

Weinstein, Michael, 162–3, 177
Weiss, Carol H., 76–7, 100
welfare reform in 1996, 104–5, 147–8
welfare reform reauthorization in 2002,
    3–4
Weyrich, Paul, 53–4, 152
Wharton School, University of
    Pennsylvania, 175
White, Joseph, 168 (n23)

Willoughby, William, 37–9
Wilson, David, 127, 128, 184, 188, 189
Wilson, James Q., 109
Wofford, Sen. Harris (D.-Pa.), 113, 165
Woodhouse, Edward J., 108
Worldwatch Institute, 84, 231

Zelman, Walter, 118, 164–5, 177–8, (n55)
    179 (n60)

.